Microsoft® Works 3.0

for Windows™
Illustrated

Michael Halvorson

Course Technology, Inc. One Main Street, Cambridge, MA 02142

An International Thomson Publishing Company

I(T)P

Microsoft Works 3.0 for Windows Illustrated is published by Course Technology, Inc.

Managing Editor	Marjorie Schlaikjer
Product Managers	David Crocco
	Barbara Clemens
Developmental Editor	Joeth Barlas
Director of Production	Myrna D'Addario
Production Editor	Catherine Griffin
Composition	Gex, Inc.
Copyeditor	Warren Ross
Proofreader	Andrea Goldman
Indexer	Alexandra Nickerson
Product Testing and Support Supervisor	Jeff Goding
Technical Reviewers	Snehal Shah
	Julia Tulchinskaya
Prepress Production	Gex, Inc.
Manufacturing Manager	Elizabeth Martinez
Instructional Designer	Debbie Krivoy
Text Designer	Leslie Hartwell
Cover Designer	John Gamache

Microsoft Works 3.0 for Windows Illustrated © 1995 Michael Halvorson

All rights reserved. This publication is protected by federal copyright law. No part of this publication may be reproduced, stored in a retrieval system, or transmitted in any form or by any means, electronic, mechanical, photocopying, recording, or otherwise, or be used to make any derivative work (such as translation or adaptation), without prior permission in writing from Course Technology, Inc.

Trademarks

Course Technology and the open book logo are registered trademarks of Course Technology, Inc.

I(T)P   The ITP logo is a trademark under license.

Microsoft is a registered trademark and Windows is a trademark of Microsoft Corporation.

Some of the product names used in this book have been used for identification purposes only and may be trademarks or registered trademarks of their respective manufacturers and sellers.

Disclaimer

Course Technology, Inc. reserves the right to revise this publication and make changes from time to time in its content without notice.

ISBN 1-56527-255-2

Printed in the United States of America

10 9 8 7 6 5 4 3

From the Publisher

At Course Technology, Inc., we believe that technology will transform the way that people teach and learn. We are very excited about bringing you, instructors and students, the most practical and affordable technology-related products available.

The Course Technology Development Process

Our development process is unparalleled in the higher education publishing industry. Every product we create goes through an exacting process of design, development, review, and testing.

Reviewers give us direction and insight that shape our manuscripts and bring them up to the latest standards. Every manuscript is quality tested. Students whose background matches the intended audience work through every keystroke, carefully checking for clarity, and pointing out errors in logic and sequence. Together with our technical reviewers, these testers help us ensure that everything that carries our name is error-free and easy to use.

Course Technology Products

We show both *how* and *why* technology is critical to solving problems in college and in whatever field you choose to teach or pursue. Our time-tested, step-by-step instructions provide unparalleled clarity. Examples and applications are chosen and crafted to motivate students.

The Course Technology Team

This book will suit your needs because it was delivered quickly, efficiently, and affordably. In every aspect of business, we rely on a commitment to quality and the use of technology. Every employee contributes to this process. The names of all our employees are listed below: Tim Ashe, David Backer, Stephen M. Bayle, Josh Bernoff, Michelle Brown, Ann Marie Buconjic, Jody Buttafoco, Kerry Cannell, Jim Chrysikos, Barbara Clemens, Susan Collins, John M. Connolly, Kim Crowley, Myrna D'Addario, Lisa D'Alessandro, Howard S. Diamond, Kathryn Dinovo, Joseph B. Dougherty, MaryJane Dwyer, Chris Elkhill, Don Fabricant, Kate Gallagher, Laura Ganson, Jeff Goding, Laurie Gomes, Eileen Gorham, Andrea Greitzer, Catherine Griffin, Tim Hale, Roslyn Hooley, Nicole Jones, Matt Kenslea, Susannah Lean, Suzanne Licht, Laurie Lindgren, Kim Mai, Elizabeth Martinez, Debbie Masi, Don Maynard, Dan Mayo, Kathleen McCann, Jay McNamara, Mac Mendelsohn, Laurie Michelangelo, Kim Munsell, Amy Oliver, Michael Ormsby, Kristine Otto, Debbie Parlee, Kristin Patrick, Charlie Patsios, Jodi Paulus, Darren Perl, Kevin Phaneuf, George J. Pilla, Cathy Prindle, Nancy Ray, Marjorie Schlaikjer, Christine Spillett, Michelle Tucker, David Upton, Mark Valentine, Karen Wadsworth, Anne Marie Walker, Renee Walkup, Donna Whiting, Janet Wilson, Lisa Yameen.

Preface

Course Technology, Inc. is proud to present this new book in its Illustrated Series. *Microsoft Works 3.0 for Windows Illustrated* provides a highly visual, hands-on introduction to Microsoft Works. The book is designed as a learning tool for Works novices but will also be useful as a source for future reference.

Organization and Coverage

Microsoft Works 3.0 for Windows Illustrated contains a Windows overview and thirteen units that cover basic Works skills. In these units students learn how to plan, build, edit, and enhance Works documents, spreadsheets, and databases. The book thoroughly covers Works' word processing, spreadsheet, charting, database, telecommunications, and draw features, as well as its integration capabilities.

Approach

Microsoft Works 3.0 for Windows Illustrated distinguishes itself from other textbooks with its highly visual approach to computer instruction.

Lessons: Information Displays

The basic lesson format of this text is the "information display," a two-page lesson that is sharply focused on a specific task. This sharp focus and the precise beginning and end of a lesson make it easy for students to study specific material. Modular lessons are less overwhelming for students, and they provide instructors with more flexibility in planning classes and assigning specific work. The units are also modular and can be presented in any order.

Each lesson, or "information display," contains the following elements:

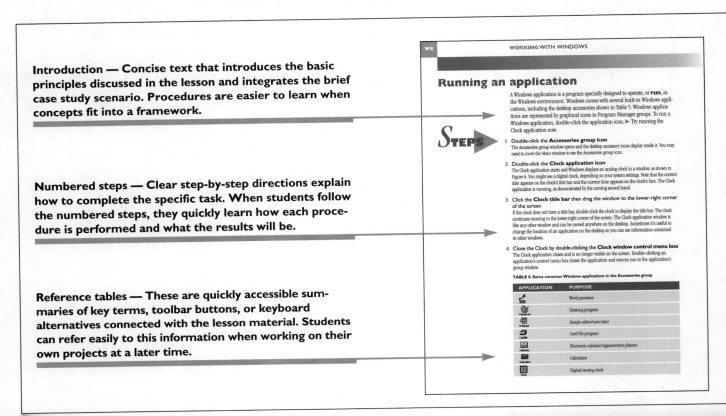

Introduction — Concise text that introduces the basic principles discussed in the lesson and integrates the brief case study scenario. Procedures are easier to learn when concepts fit into a framework.

Numbered steps — Clear step-by-step directions explain how to complete the specific task. When students follow the numbered steps, they quickly learn how each procedure is performed and what the results will be.

Reference tables — These are quickly accessible summaries of key terms, toolbar buttons, or keyboard alternatives connected with the lesson material. Students can refer easily to this information when working on their own projects at a later time.

Features

Microsoft Works 3.0 for Windows Illustrated is an exceptional textbook because it contains the following features:

- "Read This Before You Begin" Pages — These pages, one for the Windows section and one before Unit 1, provide essential information that both students and instructors need to know before they begin working through the units.

- Windows Overview — The "Working with Windows" introduction is provided so students can begin working in the Windows environment right away. This introductory section introduces students to the graphical user interface and helps them learn basic skills they can use in all Windows applications.

- Real-World Case — The case study used throughout the textbook is designed to be "real-world" in nature and representative of the kinds of activities that students will encounter when working with an integrated program. With a real-world case, the process of solving the problem will be more meaningful to students.

- End of Unit Material — Each unit concludes with a meaningful Concepts Review that tests students' understanding of what they learned in the unit. The Concepts Review is followed by an Applications Review, which provides students with additional hands-on practice of the skills they learned in the unit. The Applications Review is followed by one or two Independent Challenges, which pose open-ended problems for students to solve. The Independent Challenges allow students to learn by exploring, and develop critical thinking skills.

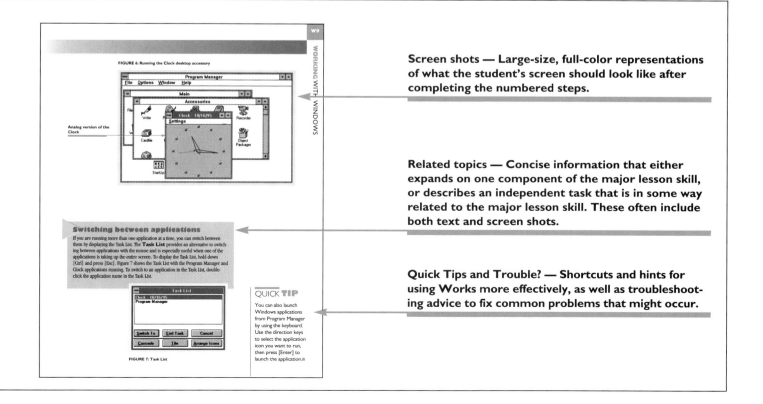

Screen shots — Large-size, full-color representations of what the student's screen should look like after completing the numbered steps.

Related topics — Concise information that either expands on one component of the major lesson skill, or describes an independent task that is in some way related to the major lesson skill. These often include both text and screen shots.

Quick Tips and Trouble? — Shortcuts and hints for using Works more effectively, as well as troubleshooting advice to fix common problems that might occur.

The Student Disk

The Student Disk bundled with the instructor's copy of this book contains all the data files students need to complete the step-by-step lessons.

Adopters of this text are granted the right to post the Student Disk on any standalone computer or network used by students who have purchased this product.

For more information on the Student Disk, see the sections in this book called "Read This Before You Begin," one just before the Windows section, and one before Unit 1, the first Works unit.

The Supplements

Instructor's Manual — The Instructor's Manual is quality assurance tested. It includes:

- Solutions to all lessons, Concept Reviews, Application Reviews, and Independent Challenges
- Extra Independent Challenge Exercises
- A disk containing solutions to all of the lessons, Concept Reviews, Application Reviews, and Independent Challenges
- Unit notes, which contain tips from the author about the instructional progression of each lesson
- Transparency masters of key concepts

Test Bank — The Test Bank contains 50 questions per unit in true/false, multiple choice, and fill-in-the-blank formats, plus two essay questions. Each question has been quality assurance tested by students to achieve clarity and accuracy.

Electronic Test Bank — The Electronic Test Bank allows instructors to edit individual test questions, select questions individually or at random, and print out scrambled versions of the same test to any supported printer.

Acknowledgments

A number of talented professionals have worked hard to bring this book to you. The author would like to thank Marjorie Schlaikjer for her vision and encouragement, David Crocco and Barbara Clemens for shepherding the project and answering dozens of questions, the talented student testers for putting each lesson and exercise through its paces, Anne Marie Buconjic for sending all the faxes and overnight packages, and Kim Halvorson for lending her small business expertise to the project. Extra special thanks go to development editor Joeth Barlas and academic advisor Jasmine Dali for poring over each draft of the manuscript in detail and making hundreds of valuable comments and suggestions. Thanks also to Catherine Griffin for production management and to Warren Ross for copyediting.

Brief Contents

Contents

TABLES

Read This Before You Begin
Working with Windows

To the Student

The Working with Windows section gives you practice using the main features of Windows, the control program that lets you work easily with your computer and many programs you run. You need a copy of the Student Disk to complete this section.

Your instructor might provide you with your own copy of the Student Disk, or might make the Student Disk files available to you over a network in your school's computer lab. See your instructor or your technical support person for further information.

To the Instructor

Student Disk: The instructor's copy of this book is bundled with the Student Disk, which contains all the files your students need to complete the step-by-step lessons in this book. Your students will not need the Student Disk files to complete this Working with Windows section, but they will need the disk itself to create a practice directory called MY_FILES, which they can use later to store the files they modify as they go through the steps of each usnit.

If you choose to make the Student Disk files available to students over a network, then be sure to tell students where you want them to create the MY_FILES directory and save their modified files. For more information on the Student Disk, see Read This Before You Begin Microsoft Works 3.0 for Windows.

Screens: This Working with Windows section assumes students will use the default Windows setup. If you want your students' screen to look like those in the figures, set up the Program Manager window to look like Figure 1, and make sure the Clock accessory is in analog mode with the title bar displayed at the top.

OBJECTIVES

▶ Start Windows

▶ Use the mouse

▶ Use Program Manager groups

▶ Run an application

▶ Resize a window

▶ Use menus and dialog boxes

▶ Save a file

▶ Use File Manager

▶ Arrange windows and icons

▶ Exit Windows

Working WITH WINDOWS

Microsoft Windows 3.1 is the **graphical user interface** (GUI) that works hand in hand with MS-DOS to control the basic operation of your computer and the programs you run on it. Windows is a comprehensive control program that helps you run useful, task-oriented programs known as **applications**. ▶ This introduction will help you to learn basic skills that you can use in all Windows applications. First you'll learn how to start Windows and how to use the mouse in the Windows environment. Next you'll get some hands-on experience with Program Manager, and you'll learn how to work with groups, run an application, resize a window, use menus and dialog boxes, save files, use File Manager, and arrange windows and icons. Then you'll learn how to exit a Windows application and exit Windows itself. ▶

Starting Windows

Windows is started, or **launched**, from MS-DOS with the Win command. Once started, Windows takes over most of the duties of MS-DOS and provides a graphical environment in which you run your applications. Windows has several advantages over MS-DOS. As a graphical interface, it uses meaningful pictures and symbols known as **icons** to replace hard-to-remember commands. Windows lets you run more than one application at a time, so you can run, for example, a word processor and a spreadsheet at the same time and easily share data between them. ▶ Each application is represented in a rectangular space called a **window**. The Windows environment also includes several useful desktop accessories, including Clock and Notepad, which you can use for day-to-day tasks. ▶ Try starting Windows now.

1 Turn on your computer

The computer displays some technical information as it starts up and tests its circuitry. MS-DOS starts automatically, then displays the **command prompt** (usually C:\>). The command prompt gives you access to MS-DOS commands and applications. If your computer is set up so that it automatically runs Windows when it starts, the command prompt will not display. You can then skip Step 2.

2 Type win then press [Enter]

This command starts Windows. The screen momentarily goes blank while the computer starts Windows. An hourglass displays, indicating Windows is busy processing a command. Then the Windows Program Manager displays on your screen, as shown in Figure 1. Your screen might look slightly different depending on which applications are installed on your computer.

TABLE I:
Elements of the Windows desktop

DESKTOP ELEMENT	DESCRIPTION
Program Manager	The main control program of Windows. All Windows applications are started from the Program Manager.
Window	A rectangular space framed by a double border on the screen. The Program Manager is framed in a window.
Application icon	The graphic representation of a Windows application.
Title bar	The area directly below the window's top border that displays the name of a window or application.
Sizing buttons	Buttons in the upper-right corner of a window that you can use to minimize or maximize a window.
Menu bar	The area under the title bar on a window. The menu bar provides access to most of an application's commands.
Control menu box	A box in the upper-left corner of each window; provides a menu used to resize, move, maximize, minimize, or close a window. Double-clicking this box closes a window or an application.
Mouse pointer	An arrow indicating the current location of the mouse on the desktop.

FIGURE 1: Program Manager window

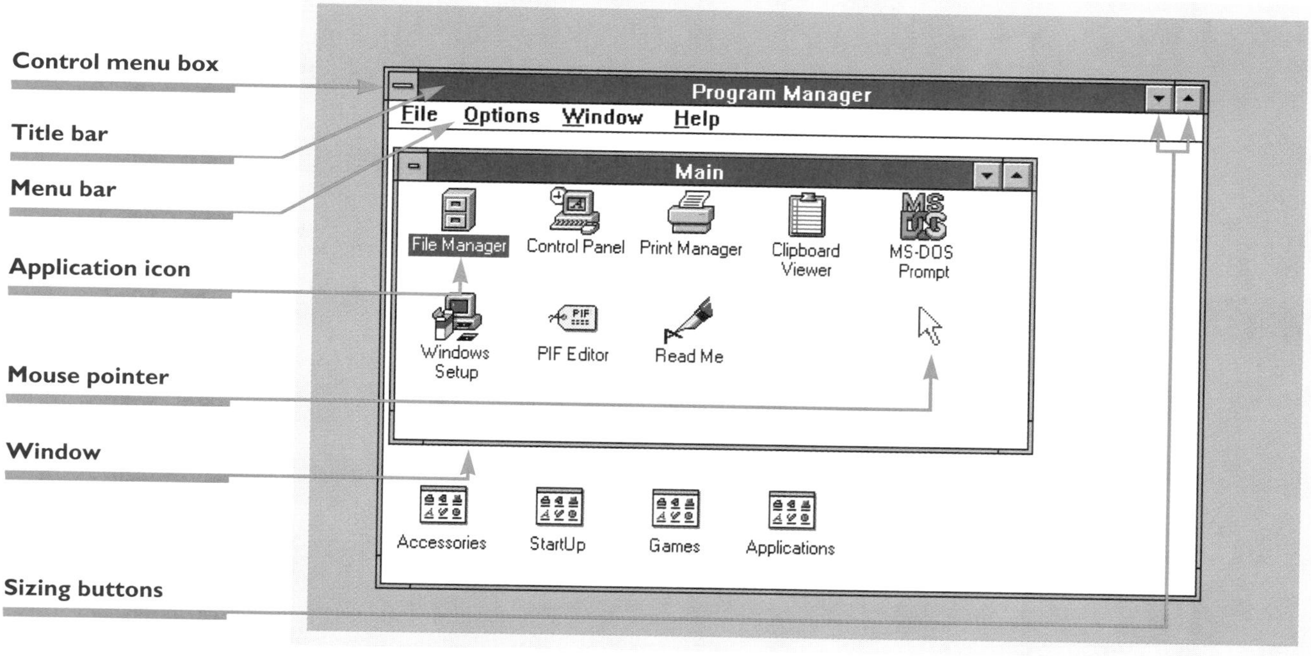

The Windows desktop

The entire screen area on the monitor represents the Windows desktop. The **desktop** is an electronic version of a desk that provides workspace for different computing tasks. Windows allows you to customize the desktop to support the way you like to work and to organize the applications you need to run. Use Table 1 to identify the key elements of the desktop, referring to Figure 1 for their locations. Because the Windows desktop can be customized, your desktop might look slightly different.

Using the mouse

The **mouse** is a handheld input device that you roll on your desk to position the mouse pointer on the Windows desktop. When you move the mouse on your desk, the **mouse pointer** on the screen moves in the same direction. The buttons on the mouse are used to select icons and choose commands, and to indicate the work to be done in applications. Table 2 lists the four basic mouse techniques. Table 3 shows some common mouse pointer shapes. ▶ Try using the mouse now.

1 Locate the mouse pointer ⌖ on the Windows desktop and move the mouse across your desk

Watch how the mouse pointer moves on the Windows desktop in response to your movements. Try moving the mouse pointer in circles, then back and forth in straight lines.

2 Position the mouse pointer over the Control Panel icon in the Main group window

Positioning the mouse pointer over an icon is called **pointing**. The Control Panel icon is a graphical representation of the Control Panel application, a special program that controls the operation of the Windows environment. If the Control Panel icon is not visible in the Main group window, point to any other icon. The Program Manager is customizable so the Control Panel could be hidden from view.

3 Press and release the left mouse button

Pressing and releasing the mouse button is called **clicking**. When you position the mouse pointer on an icon in Program Manager then click, you **select** the icon. When the Control Panel icon is selected, its title is highlighted, as shown in Figure 2. If you clicked an icon that caused a menu to open, click the icon again to close the menu. You'll learn about menus later. Now practice a mouse skill called **dragging**.

4 With the icon selected, press and hold the left mouse button and move the mouse down and to the right

The icon moves with the mouse pointer, as shown in Figure 3. When you release the mouse button, the icon relocates in the group window.

5 Drag the Control Panel icon back to its original position

TABLE 2:
Basic mouse techniques

TECHNIQUE	HOW TO DO IT
Pointing	Move the mouse pointer to position it over an item on the desktop.
Clicking	Press and release the mouse button.
Double-clicking	Press and release the mouse button twice quickly.
Dragging	Point at an item, press and hold the mouse button, move the mouse to a new location, then release the mouse button.

FIGURE 2: Selecting an icon

Selected icon

Main group window

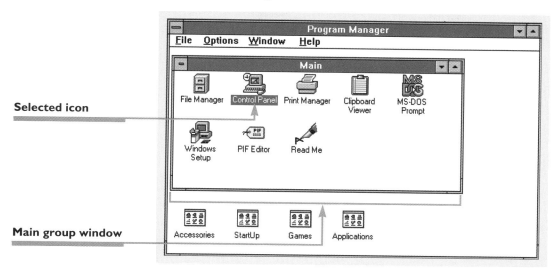

FIGURE 3: Dragging an icon

Mouse pointer on
Control Panel

Outline of the icon as
you drag

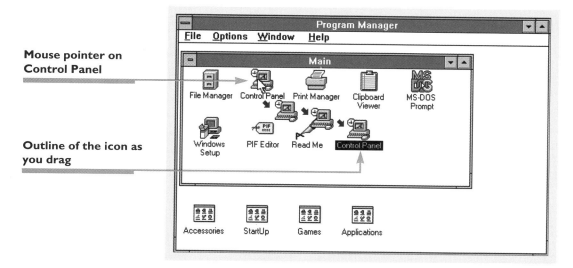

TABLE 3: Common mouse pointer shapes

SHAPE	USED TO
⬧	Select items, choose commands, start applications, and work in applications.
I	Position mouse pointer for editing or inserting text. This icon is called an insertion point.
⧗	Indicate Windows is busy processing a command.
⟷	Change the size of a window. This icon appears when mouse pointer is on the border of a window.

Using Program Manager groups

In Program Manager, you launch applications and organize your applications into windows called groups. A **group** can appear as an open window or as an icon in the Program Manager window. Each group has a name related to its contents, and you can reorganize the groups to suit your needs. The standard Windows groups are described in Table 4. ▶ Try working with groups now.

STEPS

1 If necessary, double-click the **Main group icon** to open the Main group window
The Main group icon is usually located at the bottom of the Program Manager window.

2 Double-click the **Accessories group icon**
When you double-click the Accessories group icon, it expands into the Accessories group window, as shown in Figure 4. Now move the Accessories group window to the right.

3 Click the **Accessories group window title bar** and drag the group window to the right
An outline of the window moves to the right with the mouse. When you release the mouse button, the Accessories group window moves to the location you've indicated. Moving a window lets you see what is beneath it. Any window in the Windows environment can be moved with this technique.

4 Click the **title bar** of the Main group window
The Main group window becomes the **active window**, the one you are currently working in. Other windows, including the Accessories group window, are considered background windows. Note that the active window has a highlighted title bar. Program Manager has a highlighted title bar because it is the **active application**.

5 Activate the **Accessories group window** by clicking anywhere in that window
The Accessories group window moves to the foreground again. Now try closing the Accessories group window to an icon.

6 Double-click the **control menu box** in the Accessories group window
When you double-click this box, the Accessories group window shrinks to an icon and the Main group window becomes the active window. Double-clicking the control menu box is the easiest way to close a window or an application.

TABLE 4:
Standard Windows groups

GROUP NAME	CONTENTS
Main	Applications that control how Windows works; the primary Windows group.
Accessories	Useful desktop accessories for day-to-day tasks.
StartUp	Programs that run automatically when Windows is started.
Games	Game programs for Windows.
Applications	Group of applications found on your hard disk.

FIGURE 4: Accessories group expanded into a window

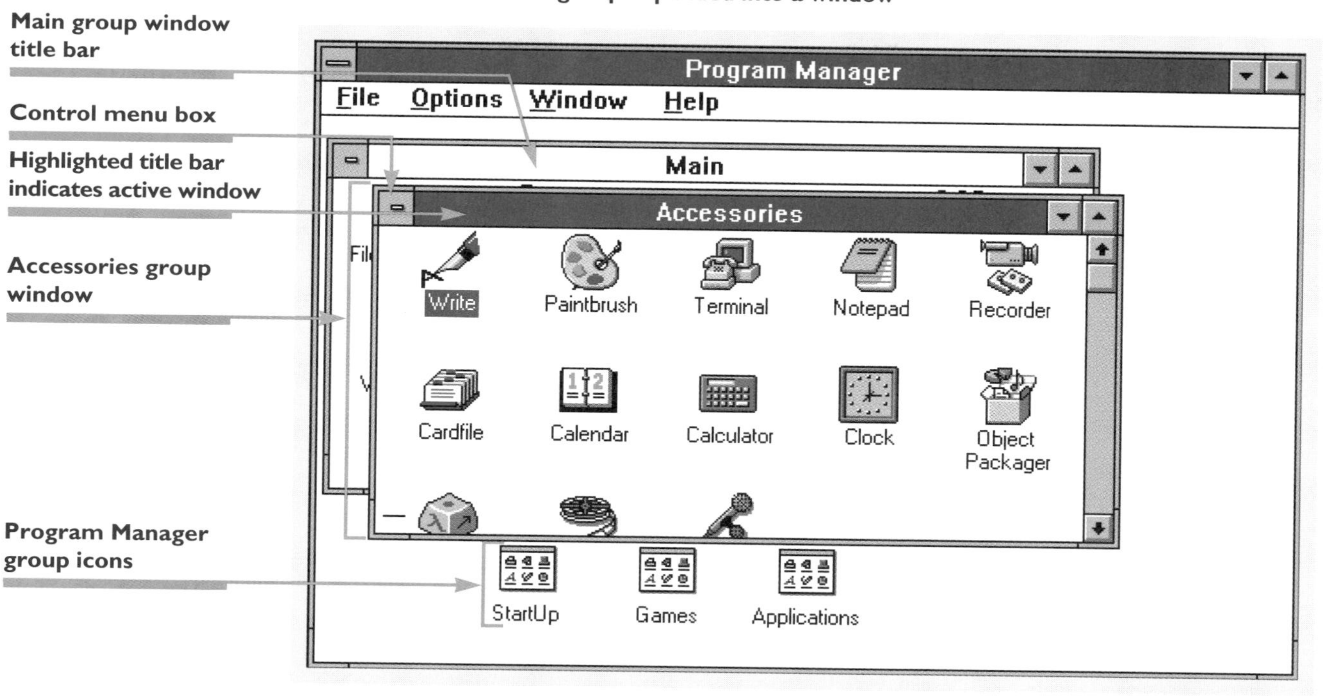

Main group window
title bar

Control menu box

Highlighted title bar
indicates active window

Accessories group
window

Program Manager
group icons

Scroll bars

If a group contains more icons than can be displayed at one time, **scroll bars** appear on the right and/or bottom edges of the window to give you access to the remaining icons, as shown in Figure 5. Vertical or horizontal arrows appear at the ends of the bars. To use scroll bars, click the vertical or horizontal arrows that point in the direction you want the window to scroll or drag the scroll box along the scroll bar. Scroll bars appear whenever there is more information than can fit in a window. You'll see them in many Windows applications.

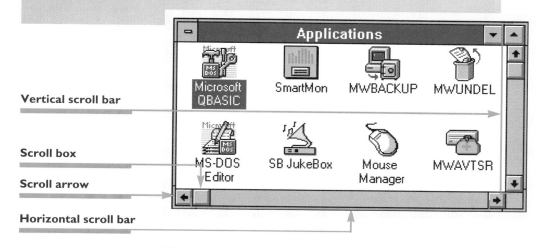

Vertical scroll bar

Scroll box

Scroll arrow

Horizontal scroll bar

FIGURE 5: Vertical and horizontal scroll bars on a window

QUICK **TIP**

You can use the direction keys on the keyboard to scroll the contents of the active window. To scroll vertically, press [↑] or [↓]. To scroll horizontally, press [←] or [→].■

Running an application

A Windows application is a program specially designed to operate, or **run**, in the Windows environment. Windows comes with several built-in Windows applications, including the desktop accessories shown in Table 5. Windows applications are represented by graphical icons in Program Manager groups. To run a Windows application, double-click the application icon. ▶ Try running the Clock application now.

STEPS

1 Double-click the **Accessories group icon**
The Accessories group window opens and the desktop accessory icons display inside it. You may need to move the Main window to see the Accessories group icon.

2 Double-click the **Clock application icon**
The Clock application starts and Windows displays an analog clock in a window, as shown in Figure 6. You might see a digital clock, depending on your system settings. Note that the current date appears on the clock's title bar and the current time appears on the clock's face. The Clock application is running, as demonstrated by the moving second hand.

3 Click the **Clock title bar** then drag the window to the lower-right corner of the screen
If the clock does not have a title bar, double-click the clock to display the title bar. The clock continues running in the lower-right corner of the screen. The Clock application window is like any other window and can be moved anywhere on the desktop. Sometimes it's useful to change the location of an application on the desktop so you can see information contained in other windows.

4 Close the Clock by double-clicking the **Clock window control menu box**
The Clock application closes and is no longer visible on the screen. Double-clicking an application's control menu box closes the application and returns you to the application's group window.

TABLE 5: Some common Windows applications in the Accessories group

APPLICATION	PURPOSE
Write	Word processor
Paintbrush	Drawing program
Notepad	Simple editor/note taker
Cardfile	Card file program
Calendar	Electronic calendar/appointment planner
Calculator	Calculator
Clock	Digital/analog clock

FIGURE 6: Running the Clock desktop accessory

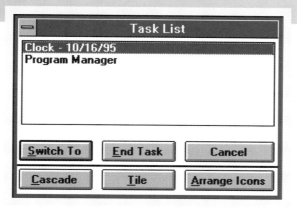

Analog version of the
Clock

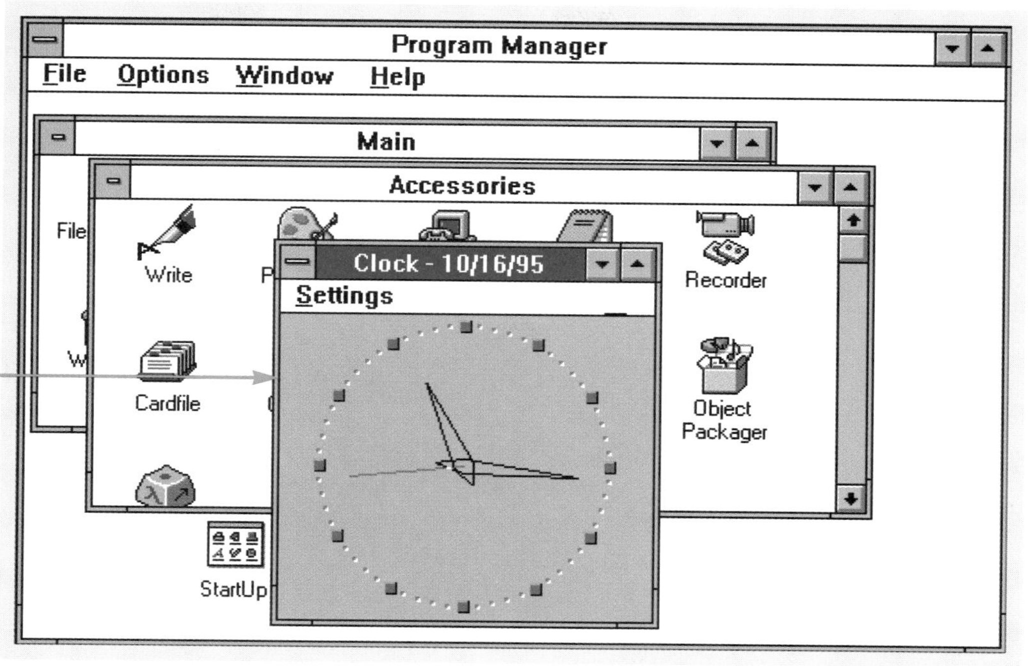

Switching between applications

If you are running more than one application at a time, you can switch between them by displaying the Task List. The **Task List** provides an alternative to switching between applications with the mouse and is especially useful when one of the applications is taking up the entire screen. To display the Task List, hold down [Ctrl] and press [Esc]. Figure 7 shows the Task List with the Program Manager and Clock applications running. To switch to an application in the Task List, double-click the application name in the Task List.

FIGURE 7: Task List

Resizing a window

The Windows desktop can get cluttered with icons and windows if you use lots of applications. Each window is surrounded by a standard border and sizing buttons that allow you to minimize, maximize, and restore windows as needed. The sizing buttons are shown in Table 6. They help you keep the desktop organized. ▶ Try sizing the Clock window now.

1 Double-click the **Clock application icon**
The Clock application restarts.

2 Click the **Minimize button** in the upper-right corner of the Clock window
The Minimize button is the sizing button on the left. When you **minimize** the clock, it shrinks to an icon at the bottom of the screen, as shown in Figure 8. Notice that the Clock icon continues to show the right time, even as an icon. Windows applications continue to run after you minimize them.

3 Double-click the **Clock icon** to restore the Clock window to its original size
The clock is restored to its original size, and the application continues to run.

4 Click the **Maximize button** in the upper-right corner of the Clock window
The Maximize button is the sizing button to the right of the Minimize button. When you **maximize** the clock, it takes up the entire screen, as shown in Figure 9. Although it's unlikely you'll want to maximize this application very often, you'll find the ability to maximize other Windows applications very useful.

5 Click the **Restore button** in the upper-right corner of the Clock window
The Restore button, as shown in Figure 9, is located to the right of the Minimize button *after* an application has been maximized. The Restore button returns an application to its original size.

6 Double-click the **Clock window control menu box** to close the application

TABLE 6:
Buttons for managing windows

BUTTON	PURPOSE
▼	Minimizes an application to an icon on the bottom of the screen.
▲	Maximizes an application to its largest possible size.
▲▼	Restores an application, returning it to its original size.

FIGURE 8:
Minimized Clock
application as an icon

Minimize button

Maximize button

Minimized clock with
current time and date

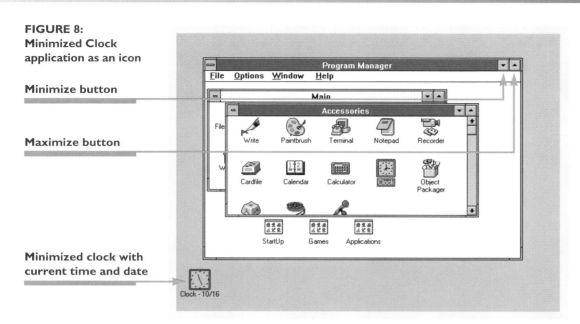

FIGURE 9:
Maximized clock filling
entire screen

Restore button
appears after a window
has been maximized

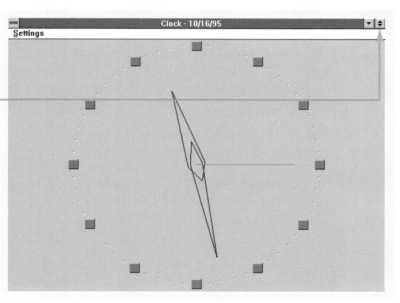

Changing the dimension of a window

The dimension of a window can also be changed, but the window will always be a rectangle. To change the dimension of a window, position the mouse pointer on the window border you want to modify. The mouse pointer changes to ⟨⟶⟩. Drag the border in the direction you want to change. Figure 10 shows the width of the Clock window being increased, which will make the clock face larger.

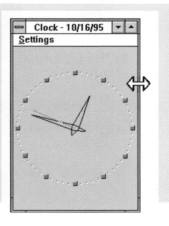

FIGURE 10: Increasing the width of the Clock window

Using menus and dialog boxes

A **menu** is a list of commands that you can use to accomplish certain tasks. Each Windows application has its own set of menus, which are listed on the **menu bar** along the top of the application window. Sometimes when you select a command from a menu, the application needs more information before it can complete the task, in which case a **dialog box** opens, giving you more options. See Table 7 for some of the typical conventions used on menus and dialog boxes. ► Try using the Control Panel which lets you customize your Windows desktop.

1 Click the **Main group window** to make it active, then double-click the **Control Panel icon**
   Drag other windows out of the way, if necessary. The Control Panel window opens.

2 Click **Settings** on the menu bar
   A menu displays listing all the commands that let you adjust different aspects of your desktop. See Table 7.

3 Click **Desktop** to display the Desktop dialog box
   This dialog box provides options to customize your desktop. See Figure 11. Next, locate the Screen Saver section of the dialog box. A **screen saver** is a moving pattern that fills your screen after your computer has not been used for a specified amount of time.

4 Click the **Name list arrow** in the Screen Saver section
   A list of available screen saver patterns displays.

5 Click the screen saver pattern of your choice, then click **Test**
   The Test button is a **command button**. The two most common command buttons are OK and Cancel which you'll see in almost every dialog box. The screen saver pattern you chose displays. It will remain on the screen until you move the mouse or press a key.

6 Move the mouse to exit the screen saver
   Next, you'll adjust the cursor blink rate in the Cursor Blink Rate section. The **cursor** is the vertical line that shows you where you are on the screen. See Figure 11.

7 Drag the scroll box all the way to the right of the scroll bar, then click the **left arrow** in the scroll bar a few times
   By moving the scroll box between Slow and Fast on the scroll bar, you can adjust the cursor blink rate to suit your needs.

8 Click **OK** to save your changes and close the dialog box
   Clicking OK accepts your changes; clicking Cancel rejects your changes. Now you can exit the Control Panel.

9 Double-click the **Control Panel control menu box** to close this window

FIGURE 11:
Desktop dialog box

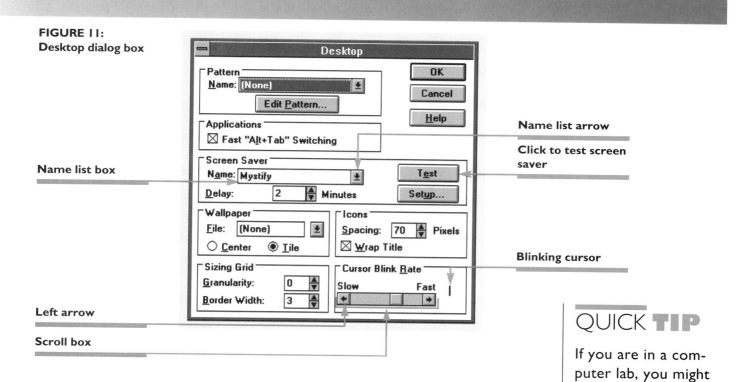

Name list arrow

Click to test screen saver

Name list box

Blinking cursor

Left arrow

Scroll box

QUICK TIP

If you are in a computer lab, you might want to return the desktop settings you changed to their original state.■

TABLE 7: Typical items on menus and dialog boxes

ITEM	MEANING	EXAMPLE
Dimmed command	A menu command that is not currently available.	Undo
Ellipsis	Choosing this menu command opens a dialog box that asks for further information.	Paste Special...
Triangle	Clicking this button opens a cascading menu containing an additional list of menu commands.	Axis ▶
Keyboard shortcut	A keyboard alternative for executing a menu command.	Cut Ctrl+X
Underlined letter	Pressing the underlined letter executes this menu command.	Copy Right
Check box	Clicking this square box turns a dialog box option on or off.	⊠ Wrap Title
Text box	A box in which you type text.	tours.wk4
Radio button	Clicking this small circle selects a single dialog box option.	◉ Tile
Command button	Clicking this button executes this dialog box command.	OK
List box	A box containing a list of items. To choose an item, click the list arrow, then click the desired item.	c: ms-dos_5

Saving a file

The documents you create using a computer are stored in the computer's random access memory (RAM). **RAM** is temporary storage space that is erased when the computer is turned off. To store a document permanently, you need to save it to a disk. You can either save your work to a 3.5-inch or a 5.25-inch disk that you insert into the disk drive of your computer (i.e., drive A or B), or a hard disk, which is a disk built into the computer (usually drive C). Your instructor has provided you with a Student Disk to use as you proceed through the lessons in this book. This book assumes that you will save all of your files to your Student Disk. Refer to the Read This Before You Begin page immediately preceding this section for more information on your Student Disk. ▶ In this lesson, you'll create a simple document using Notepad, then you will save the document to your Student Disk. **Notepad** is a simple text editor that lets you create memos, record notes, or edit text files. A **text file** is a document containing words, letters, or numbers, but no special computer instructions, such as formatting.

1 Insert your Student Disk into drive A or drive B
   Check with your instructor if you aren't sure which drive you should use.

2 Click the **Accessories group window** to activate it

3 Double-click the **Notepad application icon** to start Notepad
   The Notepad application starts, and the Notepad window displays. Now, enter some text.

4 Type **Today I started working with Notepad.** then press **[Enter]**
   Your screen should look like Figure 12.

5 Click **File** on the Notepad menu bar, then click **Save**
   The Save As dialog box displays, as shown in Figure 13. In this dialog box you enter a name for your file and specify where you want to save it.

6 Type **MYNOTES** in the File Name text box
   Your entry replaces the highlighted (selected) *.txt. Notepad will automatically add the extension when you click OK. Now you need to specify the drive where your Student Disk is located.

7 Click the **Drives list arrow** to display the drives on your computer, then click **a:** or **b:**, depending on which drive contains your Student Disk
   Notice that the list of files that are on your Student Disk displays below the File Name text box.

8 Click **OK**
   The Save As dialog box closes and MYNOTES is now saved on your Student Disk.

9 Click **File** on the Notepad menu bar, then click **Exit** to close Notepad

FIGURE 12: Notepad window with text entered

Menu bar

Cursor

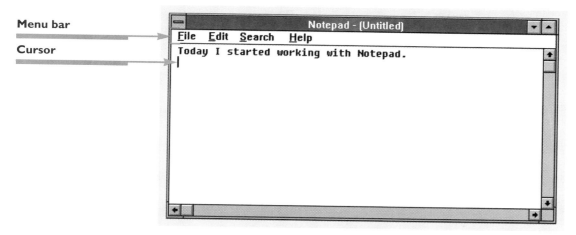

FIGURE 13: Save As dialog box

Highlighted File Name
text box

Your list of directories
might be different

Drives list arrow

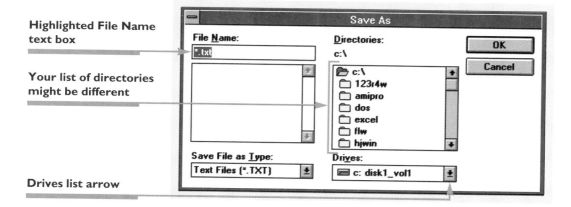

QUICK **TIP**

Save your work
often, at least every
15 minutes and
before printing.■

Using File Manager

File Manager is an application included with Windows that can help you organize files and directories. A **directory** is like a file folder—it is a part of a disk where you can store a group of related files. For example, you might want to create a directory called PROJECT1 and store all of the files relating to a particular project in that directory. You can use File Manager to create the directory, then move the related files into it.
▶ Use File Manager to create a directory called MY_FILES on your Student Disk and then move the Notepad file you created and saved in the previous lesson into that directory. Make sure your Student Disk is in drive A or drive B before beginning the steps.

1   Double-click the **Main program group icon**, or if it is already open, click the **Main group window** to activate it

2   Double-click the **File Manager application icon** in the Main group window
    File Manager opens to display the directory window, as shown in Figure 14. Your File Manager will contain different files and directories. The directory window is divided by the split bar. The left side of the window displays the structure of the current drive, or the directory tree. The right side of the window displays a list of files in the selected directory. See Table 8 for a description of the various icons used in the directory window. The status bar displays the information about the current drive and directory and other information to help you with file management tasks.

3   Click the **drive icon** that corresponds to the drive containing your Student Disk
    The contents of your Student Disk displays. Now create a directory on this disk.

4   Click **File** on the menu bar, then click **Create Directory**
    The Create Directory dialog box displays listing the current directory, which in this case is the top level directory indicated by the backslash (\). You will type a new directory name in the text box provided. Directory names can have up to 11 characters but cannot include spaces, commas, or backslashes.

5   Type **MY_FILES** in the Name text box, then click **OK**
    You can type in the directory name in either uppercase or lowercase letters. The new directory appears in both sides of the directory window.

6   Press and hold the mouse button to select MYNOTES.TXT, then drag the file into the MY_FILES directory on the left side of the window
    The mouse pointer changes as you drag the file, as shown in Figure 15. Don't worry if you move a file to the wrong place; simply drag it again to the correct location. (You can drag it to the MY_FILES directory in either the left or right side of the window.)

7   Click **Yes** in the Confirm Mouse Operation dialog box
    Notice that the file no longer appears in the list of files. Now check that the file is in the newly created directory.

8   Double-click the **MY_FILES icon**
    The file appears in the list of files. If you want, you can use this directory throughout this book to store the files that you save. Now that you have created a directory and moved a file into it, you can exit File Manager.

9   Double-click the **control menu box** to exit File Manager

FIGURE 14: File Manager

Menu bar

Drive icons

Directory tree

Selected directory

Status bar

Split bar

List of files

Directory window

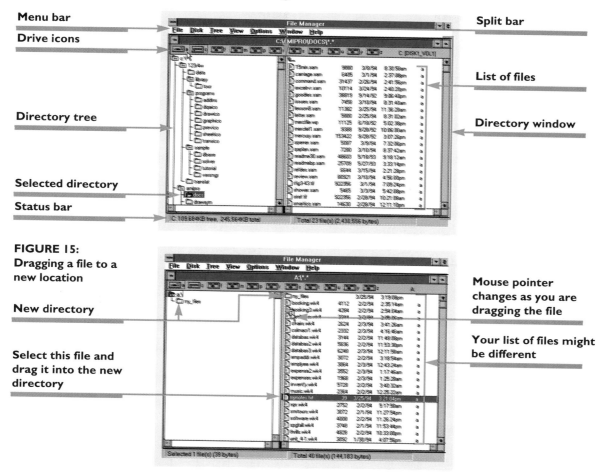

FIGURE 15: Dragging a file to a new location

New directory

Select this file and drag it into the new directory

Mouse pointer changes as you are dragging the file

Your list of files might be different

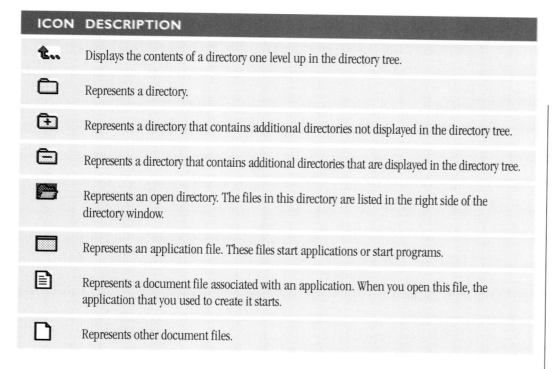

TABLE 8: Directory window icons

ICON	DESCRIPTION
🔼	Displays the contents of a directory one level up in the directory tree.
🗀	Represents a directory.
⊞	Represents a directory that contains additional directories not displayed in the directory tree.
⊟	Represents a directory that contains additional directories that are displayed in the directory tree.
📂	Represents an open directory. The files in this directory are listed in the right side of the directory window.
▭	Represents an application file. These files start applications or start programs.
🖹	Represents a document file associated with an application. When you open this file, the application that you used to create it starts.
▯	Represents other document files.

QUICK **TIP**

To select a group of files, click the first file, then press [Shift] and click the last file. To select noncontiguous files (files not next to each other in the file list), click the first file, then press [Ctrl] and click each additional file.■

Arranging windows and icons

If your desktop contains many groups that you open regularly, you might find that the open windows clutter your desktop. The Tile and Cascade commands on the Window menu let you view all your open group windows at once in an organized arrangement. You can also use the Window menu to open all the program groups installed on your computer. ▶ Once you are comfortable working with Windows, you might decide to reorganize your group windows. You can easily move an icon from one group window to another by dragging it with the mouse. In the following steps, you'll drag the Clock icon from the Accessories group window to the StartUp group window. The StartUp group window contains programs that automatically start running when you launch Windows.

1 Click the **Program Manager Maximize button** to maximize this window, then click **Window** on the menu bar

The Window menu opens, as shown in Figure 16, displaying the commands Cascade, Tile, and Arrange Icons, followed by a numbered list of the program groups installed on your computer. You might see a check mark next to one of the items, indicating that this program group is the active one. Locate StartUp on the numbered list. If you don't see StartUp, click More Windows at the bottom of the list, then double-click StartUp in the dialog box that displays. If you still can't find StartUp, see your instructor or technical support person for assistance.

2 Click **StartUp**

The StartUp group window opens. Depending on how your computer is set up, you might see some program icons already in this window. At this point, your screen is getting cluttered with three program group windows open (Main, Accessories, and StartUp). Use the Cascade command to arrange them in an orderly way.

3 Click **Window** on the menu bar, then click **Cascade**

The windows display in a layered arrangement, with the title bars of each showing. This formation is neatly organized and shows all your open group windows, but it doesn't allow you to easily drag the Clock icon from the Accessories group window to the StartUp group window. The Tile command arranges the windows so that the contents of all the open windows are visible.

4 Click **Window** on the menu bar, then click **Tile**

The windows are now positioned in an ideal way to copy an icon from one window to another. Before continuing to step 5, locate the Clock icon in the Accessories group window. If you don't see the icon, use the scroll bar to bring it into view.

5 Drag the Clock application icon from the Accessories group window to the StartUp group window

Your screen now looks like Figure 17. The Clock application will automatically start the next time Windows is launched. If you are working on your own computer and want to leave the Clock in the StartUp group, skip Step 6 and continue to the next lesson, "Exiting Windows." If you are working in a computer lab, move the Clock icon back to its original location in the Accessories group window.

6 Drag the Clock application icon from the StartUp group window to the Accessories group window

The Clock icon is now back in the Accessories group.

FIGURE 16:
Window menu

Check mark
indicates the active
program group

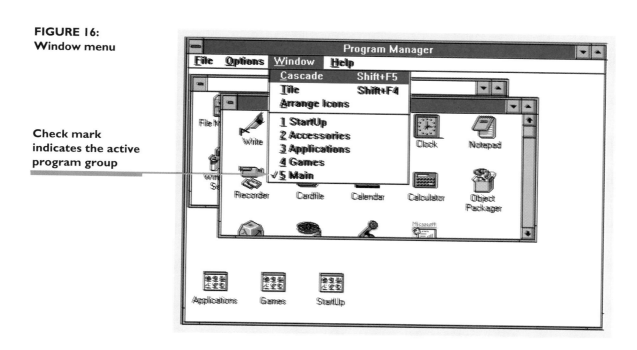

FIGURE 17:
Tiled group windows

StartUp group window
with Clock icon

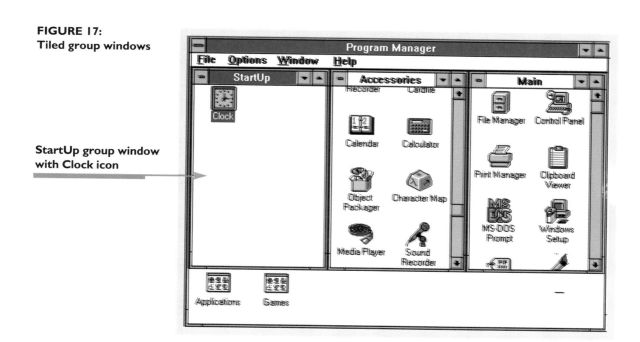

QUICK **TIP**

To move a copy of an
icon from one group
window to another,
hold down [Ctrl] as
you drag the icon.■

Exiting Windows

When you are finished working with Windows, close all the applications you are running and exit Windows. Do not turn off the computer while Windows is running; you could lose important data if you turn off your computer too soon. ▶ Now try closing all your active applications and exiting Windows.

1 **Close any active applications or group windows by double-clicking the control menu boxes of the open windows, one at a time**
   The windows close. If you have any unsaved changes in your application, a dialog box displays, asking if you want to save them.

2 **Click File on the Program Manager menu bar**
   The File menu displays, as shown in Figure 18.

3 **Click Exit Windows**
   Program Manager displays the Exit Windows dialog box, as shown in Figure 19. You have two options at this point: Click OK to exit Windows, or click Cancel to abort the Exit Windows command and return to the Program Manager.

4 **Click OK to exit Windows**
   Windows finishes its work and the MS-DOS command prompt appears. You can now safely turn off the computer.

FIGURE 18: Exiting Windows using the File menu

Menu bar

Exit Windows command

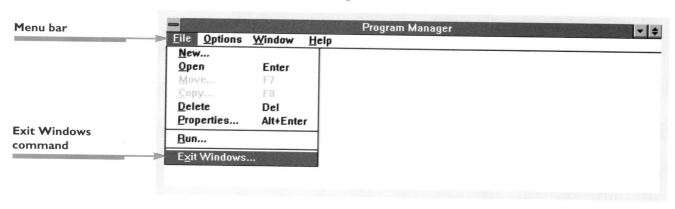

FIGURE 19: Exit Windows dialog box

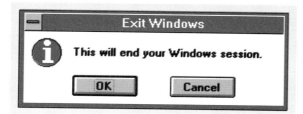

Exiting Windows with the Program Manager control menu box

You can also exit Windows by double-clicking the control menu box in the upper-left corner of the Program Manager window, as shown in Figure 20. After you double-click the control menu box, you see the Exit Windows dialog box. Click OK to exit Windows.

Double-click the control menu box

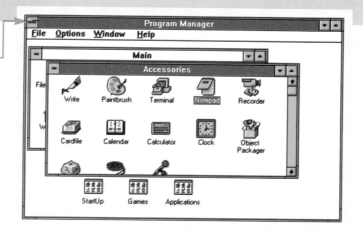

FIGURE 20: Exiting Windows with the Program Manager control menu box

TROUBLE?

If you do not exit from Windows before turning off the computer, you might lose data from the applications you used while you were running Windows. Always close your applications and exit from Windows before turning off your computer. Do not turn off the computer if you are in a computer lab.

CONCEPTSREVIEW

**Label each of the elements
of the Windows screen
shown in Figure 21.**

1 _____

2 _____

3 _____

4 _____

5 _____

6 _____

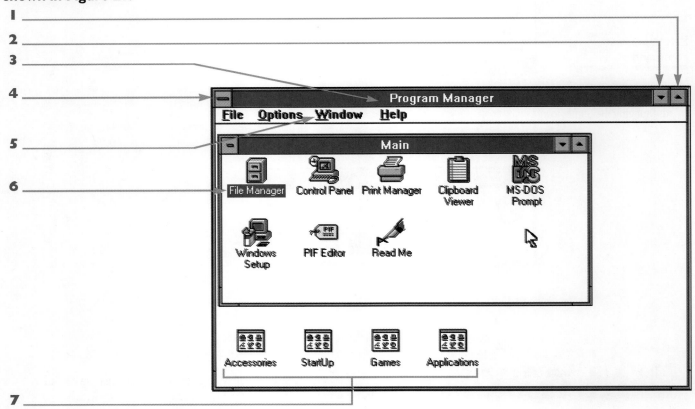

7 _____

FIGURE 21

**Match each of the statements with the term
it describes.**

8 Shrinks an application
window to an icon

9 Displays the name of the
window or application

10 Serves as a launching pad
for all applications

11 Requests more information
that you supply before execut-
ing command

12 Lets the user point at screen
menus and icons

a. Program Manager

b. Dialog box

c. Mouse

d. Title bar

e. Minimize button

Select the best answer from the list of choices.

13 The acronym GUI means:

a. Grayed user information

b. Group user icons

c. Graphical user interface

d. Group user interconnect

14 The term for starting Windows is:

a. Prompting

b. Launching

c. Applying

d. Processing

15 The small pictures that represent items such as applications are:

a. Icons

b. Windows

c. Buttons

d. Pointers

16 All of the following are examples of using a mouse, EXCEPT:

a. Clicking the Maximize button

b. Pressing [Enter]

c. Pointing at the control menu box

d. Dragging the Games icon

17 When Windows is busy performing a task, the mouse pointer changes to a(n):

a. Hand

b. Arrow

c Clock

d. Hourglass

18 The term for moving an item to a new location on the desktop is:

a. Pointing

b. Clicking

c. Dragging

d. Restoring

19 The Clock, Notepad, and Calendar applications in Windows are known as:

a. Menu commands

b. Control panels

c. Sizing buttons

d. Desktop accessories

20 The Maximize button is used to:

a. Return a window to its original size

b. Expand a window to fill the computer screen

c. Scroll slowly through a window

d. Run programs from the main menu

21 What appears if a window contains more information than can be displayed in the window?

a. Program icon

b. Cascading menu

c. Scroll bars

d. Check box

22 A window is active when its title bar is:

a. Highlighted

b. Dimmed

c. Checked

d. Underlined

23 What is the term for changing the dimensions of a window?

a. Selecting

b. Resizing

c. Navigating

d. Scrolling

24 The menu bar provides access to an application's functions through:

a. Icons

b. Scroll bars

c. Commands

d. Control menu box

25 File Manager is a Windows application that lets you:

a. Select a different desktop wallpaper

b. Move a file from one location to another

c. Type entries into a text file

d. Determine what programs begin automatically when you start Windows

26 When your desktop is too cluttered, you can organize it by all the following methods, EXCEPT:

a. Double-clicking the control menu box to close unneeded windows

b. Using the Tile command to view all open group windows

c. Using the Cascade command to open group window title bars

d. Clicking File, clicking Exit Windows, then clicking OK

27 You can exit Windows by double-clicking the:

a. Accessories group icon

b. Program Manager control menu box

c. Main window menu bar

d. Control Panel application

APPLICATIONS
REVIEW

1 Start Windows and identify items on the screen.

a. Turn on the computer, if necessary.

b. At the command prompt, type "WIN," then press [Enter]. After Windows loads, the Program Manager displays.

c. Try to identify as many items on the desktop as you can, without referring to the lesson material. Then compare your results with Figure 1.

2 Minimize and restore the Program Manager window.

a. Click the Minimize button. Notice that the Program Manager window reduces to an icon at the bottom of the screen. Now try restoring the window.

b. Double-click the minimized Program Manager icon. The Program Manager window opens.

c. Practice minimizing and restoring other windows on the desktop.

3 Resize and move the Program Manager window.

a. Click anywhere inside the Program Manager window to activate the window.

b. Move the mouse pointer over the lower-right corner of the Program Manager window. Notice that the mouse pointer changes to a double-ended arrow.

c. Press and hold the mouse button and drag the corner of the window up and to the right until the Program Manager takes up the top third of your screen.

d. Drag the Program Manager title bar to reposition the window at the bottom of the screen.

4 Practice working with menus and dialog boxes.

a. Click Window on the Program Manager menu bar, then click Accessories (if you can't find it in the menu, click More Windows, then double-click it from the list that appears, scrolling if necessary).

b. Double-click the Calculator icon to open the Calculator application.

c. Click numbers and operators as you would on a handheld calculator to perform some simple arithmetic operations, like 22 multiplied by 3.99, to see how much it would cost to take a bus of 22 employees on the way back from a conference to a fast-food place for a quick lunch. (Multiplication is indicated by an asterisk *.)

d. Double-click the Calculator control menu box when you are finished.

5 Practice working with files:

a. Open File Manager from the Main group window.

b. Be sure your Student Disk is in drive A or drive B, then double-click the drive icon containing your Student Disk.

c. Double-click the drive C icon, then choose Tile from the Window menu. The open drive windows display, one above the other. If you have more windows open, double-click their control menu boxes to close them, then choose Tile again.

d. Double-click the c:\ folder icon on the left side of the drive C window, then scroll down the left side of the drive C window using the vertical scroll bar to see the available directories. When you see the Windows folder icon, double-click it to see the directories and files available in the Windows folder.

e. Scroll down the right side of the drive C window using the vertical scroll bar to see the files contained in the Windows folder. If you needed to copy a file from the Windows folder to your Student Disk, you could drag it from the list of files in the drive C window to the drive A window, but don't do so now.

6 Exit Windows.

a. Close any open application by double-clicking the application's control menu box.

b. Double-click the control menu box in the upper-left corner of the Program Manager window. The Exit Windows dialog box displays.

c. Click OK. Windows closes and the DOS command prompt displays.

INDEPENDENT
CHALLENGE

Windows 3.1 provides an on-line tutorial which can help you master essential Windows controls and concepts. The tutorial features interactive lessons that teach you how to use Windows elements such as the mouse, Program Manager, menus, and icons. The tutorial also covers how to use Help.

The tutorial material you should use depends on your level of experience with Windows. Some users might want to review the basics of the Windows work area. Others might want to explore additional Windows topics, such as managing files and customizing windows.

Ask your instructor or technical support person about how to use the Windows tutorial.

Microsoft® Works 3.0
for Windows™

Read This Before You Begin
Microsoft Works 3.0 for Windows

To the Student

The exercises and examples in these units feature several ready-made Works document files which are contained on the Student Disk provided to your instructor. To complete the step-by-step exercises in this book, you must have a Student Disk. Your instructor will either provide you with your own copy of the Student Disk or will make the Student Disk files available to you over a network in your school's computer lab. See your instructor or technical support person for further information.

Using Your Own Computer

If you are going to work through this book using your own computer, you need a computer system running Microsoft Windows 3.1, Microsoft Works 3.0 for Windows, and a Student Disk. *You will not be able to complete the step-by-step lessons and exercises in this book using your own computer until you have your own Student Disk.* This book assumes the default settings under a standard installation of Microsoft Works 3.0 for Windows.

To the Instructor

Bundled with the instructor's copy of this book is the Student Disk, which contains all the files your students need to complete the step-by-step exercises in this book. Adopters of this text are granted the right to distribute the files on the Student Disk to any student who has purchased a copy of the text. You are free to post all these files to a network or standalone workstations, or simply provide copies of the disk to your students. The instructions in this book assume that the students know which drive and directory contain the Student Disk files, so it's important that you provide disk location information before the students start working through the units. You also need to provide instructions about where students should save their modified files. We assume that students will save all files to their Student Disks in the MY_FILES directory they create in the Working with Windows section.

Using the Student Disk files

To keep the original files on the Student Disk intact, the instructions in this book for opening files require two important steps: (1) Open the existing file and (2) Save it as a new file with a new name. This procedure ensures that the original file will remain unmodified in case the student wants to redo the exercise. For more information about opening a file and saving it with a new name, please refer to the lesson "Opening a File" in Unit 2.

UNIT I

Getting STARTED WITH MICROSOFT WORKS 3.0 FOR WINDOWS

ow that you have learned the basics of Windows, you will begin working with Microsoft Works for Windows version 3.0, a multipurpose or **integrated software package** that includes word processor, spreadsheet, database, and communications applications, as well as several supporting **accessories**. ▶ This unit will introduce you to Works and help you learn basic skills you can use in each Works application. First you'll learn how to start Works and how to start a Works application. Next you'll learn how to work with Works menus, dialog boxes, toolbars, and the Help system. Finally, you'll learn how to create a company letterhead with a WorksWizard, save the completed letterhead to disk, and exit the Works application. You'll also get to know Outdoor Designs, a company that makes kits and patterns for recreational equipment such as backpacks or tents. Outdoor Designs uses Works to write memos and reports, manage inventory and sales data, track customers, and publish instructions for its products. ▶

Starting Works

You start Works from the Windows Program Manager by double-clicking the Microsoft Works icon in the Microsoft Works for Windows group window. Once started, Works displays the Works Startup dialog box, where you can open Works applications, templates, and WorksWizards. ▶ Imagine that you have just been hired as a summer intern for the Outdoor Designs company. They want you to use Works for Windows in several different projects. You'll begin to build your skills by starting Works now.

1   From the Program Manager, double-click the **Microsoft Works for Windows group icon**
The Microsoft Works for Windows program group opens and its contents display in a window, as shown in Figure 1-1. The group window contains the Microsoft Works program icon, the Works Troubleshooting icon, and the Microsoft Works Setup icon.

2   Double-click the **Microsoft Works program icon** to start the Works program
The Works Startup dialog box displays, as shown in Figure 1-2. If this is the first time the Works software has been used, you may see the Welcome to Microsoft Works dialog box instead. In that case, read the contents of the Welcome dialog box, then click **Start Works Now** to start Works and display the Works Startup dialog box.

The Works Startup dialog box is your pathway to the four Works applications, the automated WorksWizards and templates, and any Works documents used recently. Use Figure 1-2 to identify the key elements of the Works Startup dialog box. Table 1-1 lists the four Works applications and a few of the useful documents you can create with them.

TABLE 1-1:
Documents that can be created with Works

APPLICATION	DOCUMENTS
Word Processor	Memo, letter, multi-column newsletter, term paper, letterhead with art
Spreadsheet	General ledger, expense report, sales figures, 3D pie charts
Database	Customer database, music collection, commission reports, form letters
Communications	Electronic mail, stock quotes, on-line research, document distribution

FIGURE 1-1: The Microsoft Works for Windows group in Program Manager

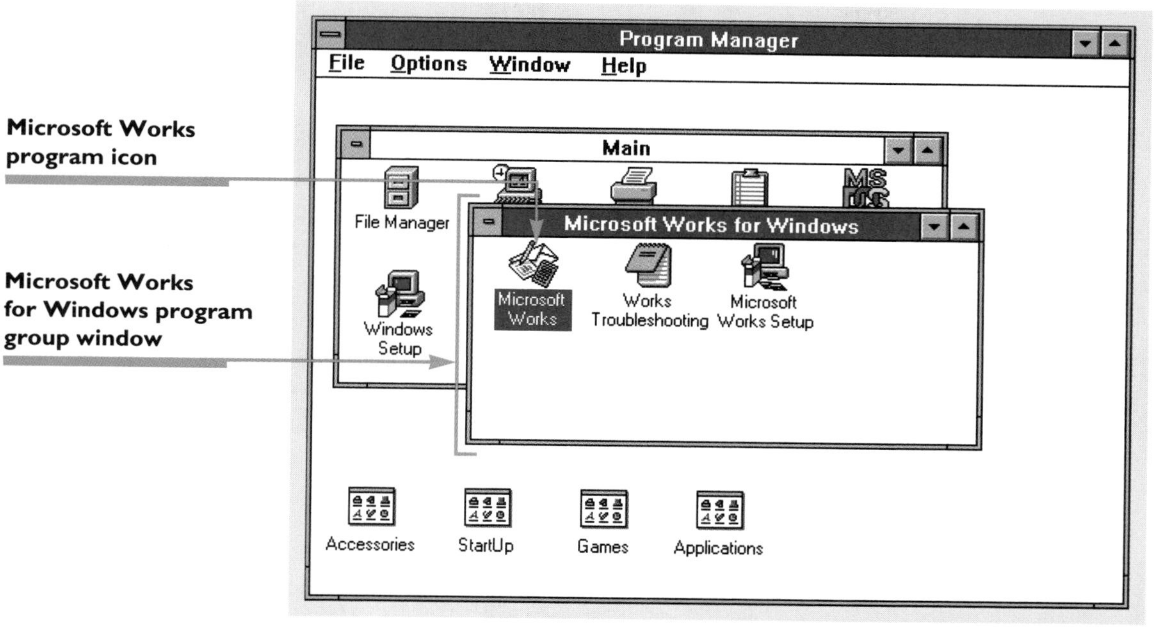

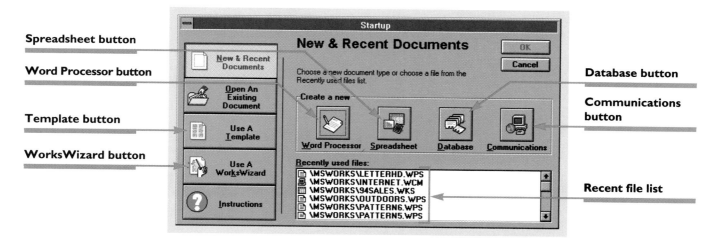

Microsoft Works
program icon

Microsoft Works
for Windows program
group window

FIGURE 1-2: The Works Startup dialog box

Spreadsheet button

Word Processor button

Template button

WorksWizard button

Database button

Communications
button

Recent file list

TROUBLE?

If you have trouble
starting the Works
software or don't see
the Works Startup dia-
log box, the program
may not have been
properly installed on
your computer.■

Starting a Works application

From the Works Startup dialog box, you can start the Works Word Processor, Spreadsheet, Database, or Communications applications. Each of the Works applications has been designed with a similar **graphical interface**. Once you learn how to use the buttons, menus, and toolbars in one Works application, you'll know how to use the interface elements in all of them. Table 1-2 lists some of the interface elements common to all Works applications. ▶ You'll start the Works Word Processor now to practice the techniques you'll use throughout the book.

I   Click the **Word Processor button** to start the Works Word Processor

The Works Startup dialog box disappears and the Works Word Processor opens in a window, as shown in Figure 1-3. The Works Word Processor manipulates text-based documents, such as memos, newsletters, and term papers. The Works Word Processor is the electronic equivalent of paper, typewriter, eraser, dictionary, and thesaurus.

Use Figure 1-3 to identify the elements of the Word Processor. Refer to Table 1-2 to identify the interface elements.

TABLE 1-2:
Interface elements common
to all Works applications

ELEMENT	DESCRIPTION
Menu bar	The area under the title bar containing the menu names. Each menu opens to provide access to a group of Word Processor commands
Toolbar	The row of drop-down list boxes and command buttons beneath the menu bar
Document window	A window containing the application's workspace
Scroll bars	Horizontal and vertical bars at the bottom and right edge of the window, used to view parts of a document not currently displayed in the window
Toggle indicators	Indicators for the Num-lock, Caps-lock, and Insert toggle keys
Sizing buttons	Minimize, Maximize, and Restore buttons for the Works program window and each document window
Control menu boxes	Control menu boxes for the Works program and each document window

FIGURE 1-3: The Works Word Processor

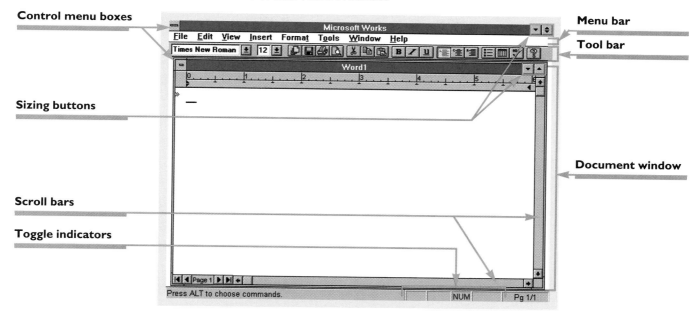

Control menu boxes

Sizing buttons

Scroll bars

Toggle indicators

Menu bar

Tool bar

Document window

Switching back to Windows

As you learned in the Working with Windows section, you can run more than one Windows program at once and switch between them using the **Task List**. This feature is available in Works too: it lets you switch back to Windows while you're working with Works. To bring up the Task List in Works, hold down **[Ctrl]** and press **[Esc]**. To switch to Program Manager in the Task List, double-click **Program Manager**. To return to Works from Program Manager, hold down **[Ctrl]** and press **[Esc]** again to display the Task List, then double-click **Microsoft Works** in the Task List.

QUICK **TIP**

If you want to exit the Word Processor and quit Works, double-click the Works control menu box or hold down **[Alt]** and press **[F4]**.∎

Using dialog boxes

To make things happen in Works you choose commands from menus. If more information is needed to carry out a command, Works displays a **dialog box** to present the available options. You can use check boxes, option buttons, list boxes, drop-down list boxes, text boxes, and command buttons to specify options. A dialog box can sometimes contain **tabs**, which organize the information into logical groups. Figure 1-4 illustrates the dialog box options. Figure 1-5 shows a dialog box with tabs. You'll work with dialog boxes now.

I Click **Format** on the Word Processor menu bar
The contents of the Format menu display. The Format menu includes commands that are useful in changing the style and presentation of text in the Word Processor.

2 Click **Font and Style** on the Format menu
The Font and Style dialog box displays, as shown in Figure 1-4. The dialog box lets you choose the font, style, size, color, and position of the text in the Word Processor. The Sample rectangle shows you a sample of what the text in the Word Processor will look like when you click the OK button. Take a moment to identify the dialog box options shown in Figure 1-4.

3 Press and hold the **up scroll arrow** in the Font list box to scroll to the top of the box
The font names in the Font list box scroll vertically and the Arial font displays at the top of the list. (Your list of fonts may be different from the list shown in Figure 1-4.)

4 Click **Arial** in the Font list box
The Arial font is highlighted in the Font list box and displays in the Font text box above the Font list box. The font of the text in the Sample rectangle changes to Arial.

5 Click the **Bold** and **Italic check boxes** under Style, and click **16** in the Size list box
An x displays in each check box and the text in the Sample rectangle changes to bold and italic. A 16 displays in the Size text box and the size of the text in the Sample rectangle changes to 16 points. (A point is $\frac{1}{72}$ of an inch.) If 16 is not displayed in your Size list box, use the list box scroll bars to scroll to 16, then click 16.

6 Click the **Color drop-down list box** to display the list of available text colors, then click **Blue**
After the first click, the Color drop-down list box displays the available colors. When you choose Blue, the color of the text in the Sample rectangle changes to blue. Text colors help emphasize special words on the screen and are printed in color by color printers.

7 Click **Superscript** under Position
The Position indicator changes from Normal to Superscript. Only one option button in a group can be chosen. In the Word Processor, Superscript position places text above the line; however, the Sample rectangle does not show this change.

You're done with the options in this dialog box. Now discard your font and style selections.

8 Click **Cancel**
The Font and Style dialog box closes without saving your new selections.

Drop-down list box

Text boxes

FIGURE 1-4: Dialog box options in the Font and Style dialog box

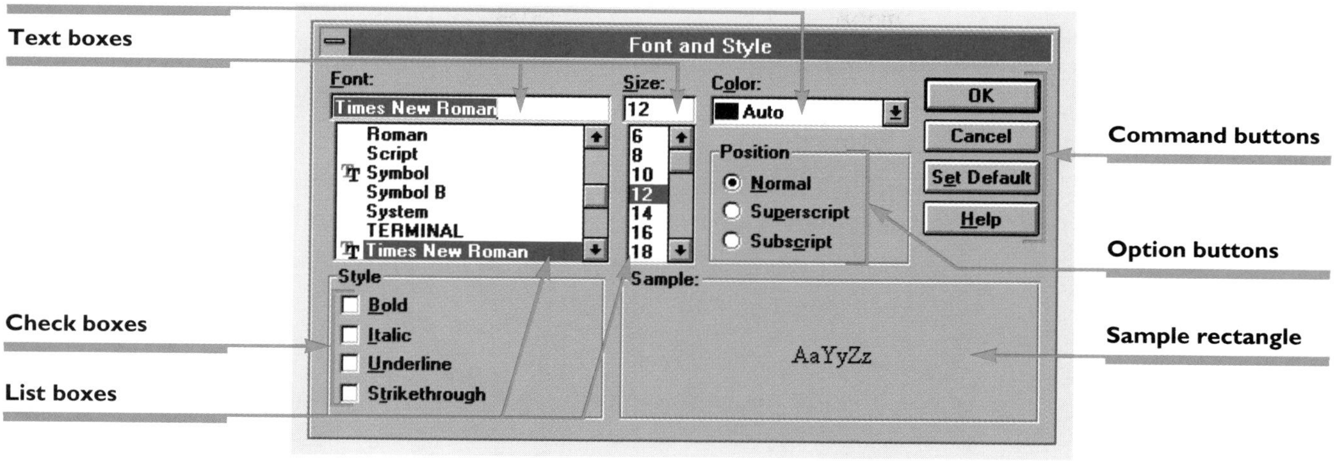

Command buttons

Option buttons

Check boxes

Sample rectangle

List boxes

Dialog box tabs

A dialog box with tabs contains multiple screens

If a dialog box has more than one screen of options, the dialog box contains tabs, as shown in Figure 1-5. To view the different dialog box screens, click the different tabs. The dialog box options within each screen work as described in this lesson.

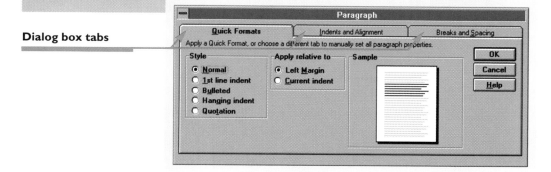

FIGURE 1-5: A dialog box with tabs

QUICK **TIP**

To move a dialog box, click its title bar, hold down the mouse button, and drag the box to the desired location.

Using toolbars

A **toolbar** is a customizable set of buttons and drop-down list boxes, located below the menu bar of a Works application. Toolbars provide rapid access to the most common Works commands. The buttons on Works toolbars are often easier to remember than menu and keyboard commands, because they contain graphic representations of the tasks they accomplish. The toolbar buttons found in most Works applications are listed in Table 1-3. You'll practice working with the Word Processor toolbar buttons now.

1 Type **Mississippi** in the Word Processor
The word Mississippi displays in the document window. As you type, the blinking cursor or **insertion point** moves to the right.

2 Double-click the word **Mississippi**
Now the word Mississippi is highlighted or **selected**, as shown in Figure 1-6. To work with text in a Works application, you need to select it first. You'll learn more about selecting text in Unit 2.

3 Click the **Bold button** **B** on the toolbar
The Bold button is pushed in and the style of the selected text changes to bold. The Bold button has the same effect as changing the text style to bold with the Font and Style command on the Format menu, but it is much quicker.

4 Click **B** again
The Bold button pops out and the style of the selected text returns to normal.

5 Click the **Center-align button** on the toolbar
The Center-align button is pushed in and the selected text is aligned to the center of the document. Notice that the alignment buttons function like option buttons; when the Center-align button is pushed in, the Left-align button pops out.

6 Click the **Right-align button** on the toolbar
The Right-align button is pushed in and the selected text is aligned to the right margin of the document.

7 Click the **Cut button** to delete the selected text
The word Mississippi is removed from the document. The Cut button is an easy way to remove selected text from a document. You'll learn more about text editing in Unit 2.

FIGURE I-6: The Bold button changes the selected text to bold

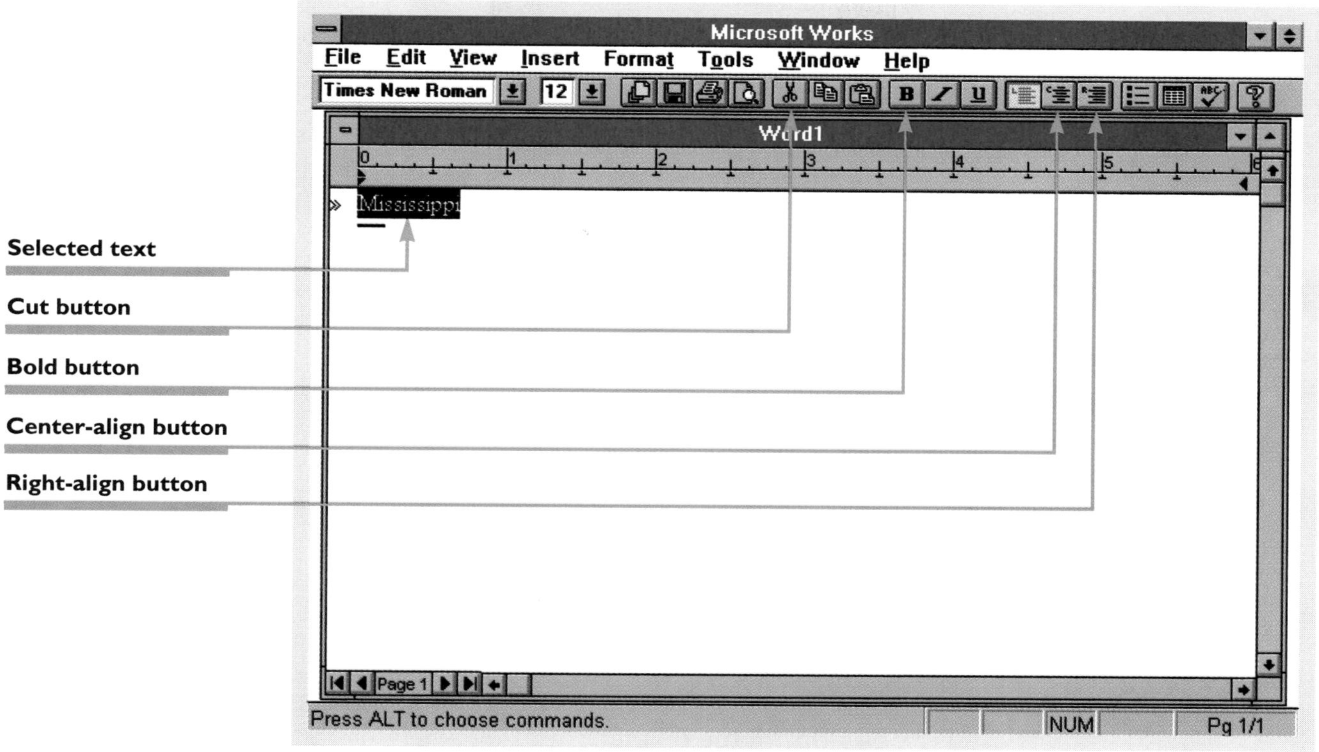

Selected text

Cut button

Bold button

Center-align button

Right-align button

TABLE I-3: Useful toolbar buttons and their functions

TOOLBAR BUTTON	FUNCTION
	Display Startup dialog box
	Save current document to disk
	Print current document
	Display current document as it will be printed
	Cut selected text
	Copy selected text
	Paste selected text
B	Change style of selected text to bold
	Change style of selected text to italic
U	Change style of selected text to underline
	Display Learning Works dialog box

QUICK **TIP**

Position the mouse pointer on a button or list box on the toolbar. After a moment, the tool's name displays in a yellow pop-up box.■

Using the Help system

If you have a question about a feature or procedure in Works, you can use the **Help system** to get more information. The Help system explains the current application and lets you search for help on a specific topic, review basic skills, run the Works online tutorial, and start **Cue Cards**, a helpful on-screen adviser.

▶ As an eager summer intern, you pride yourself on learning about Works on your own. You'll use the Help system now to review the toolbar and the elements of a Works application window.

1   Click **Help** on the Word Processor menu bar

The contents of the Help menu display. You'll want to use the commands on the Help menu regularly when you have a question about how to do something in Works. The Word Processor overview, Basic Skills, and Tutorial commands are especially useful if you want extra practice with Works fundamentals.

2   Click the **Search for Help on command**

The Search dialog box appears. The Search dialog box is your pathway to the Works Help system. It contains a text box where you can enter the Help topic you're interested in, as well as a list box to refine your search.

3   Type **toolbar** in the text box

As you type, notice the Help topics that display in the list box. The words in the text box gradually adjust to match the spelling of the word *toolbar* as you type it.

4   Click **Show Topics** in the Search dialog box

A list of Help topics related to the toolbar displays in the Topic list box, as shown in Figure 1-7.

5   Double-click **The parts of the Works window** in the Topic list box

The Search dialog box disappears and a Help window containing the topic *The parts of the Works window* opens. Read the Help topic, using the scroll bars to view the related words at the end of the article. If you don't know the meaning of a word with a dotted green underline, click the word; its definition appears in a box on the screen. (After you've read the definition, click the definition box to make it disappear.) Words with a solid underline are **related topics**. To view a related topic in the Help system, click a word or phrase with a solid green underline.

6   Click **File** on the Help menu bar

The contents of the File menu display. The File menu includes commands that let you open other Help files, print the current Help topic, or exit the Help system.

7   Click **Exit** on the File menu

The Help window closes and you return to the Word Processor.

FIGURE 1-7: The Search dialog box with a list of toolbar topics

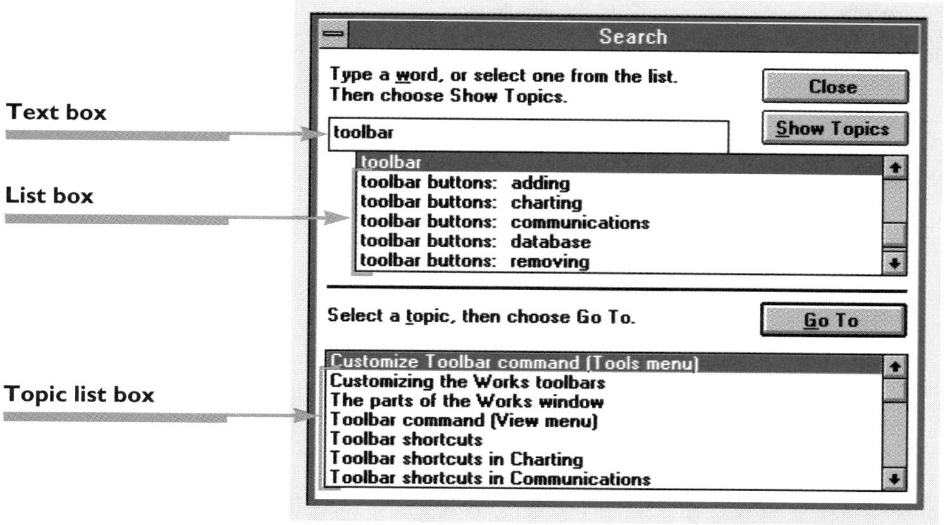

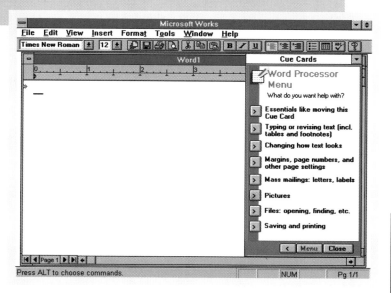

Text box

List box

Topic list box

Using Cue Cards

You can get helpful on-screen advice from Cue Cards as you work on your document. To start Cue Cards, click the Cue Cards command on the Help menu and follow the directions. Figure 1-8 shows the Cue Cards included with the Word Processor.

FIGURE 1-8: Cue Cards offers helpful on-screen advice

QUICK **TIP**

Click the Question mark button ⍰ on the toolbar to display the Learning Works dialog box with information about Cue Cards, the Help Library, the on-line Tutorial, and WorksWizards.■

Using a WorksWizard

A **WorksWizard** is an automated tool that creates the structure and formatting of a document for you. Works offers twelve built-in WorksWizards that give you a head start with managing addresses, tracking inventory, mailing form letters, designing company letterhead, entering footnotes, and other common tasks. You'll use a WorksWizard now to create a company letterhead for Outdoor Designs.

I Click **File** in the menu bar, then click **WorksWizards**
The Startup dialog box appears with twelve WorksWizards shown in the list box.

2 Click **Letterhead** in the list box, then click **OK**
A window opens to explain what the Letterhead WorksWizard does. At the bottom of the window are four navigation buttons that help you run the WorksWizard. See Figure 1-9.

3 Click **Next** to start the Letterhead WorksWizard
The Letterhead WorksWizard starts and asks if you want to personalize your letterhead with your company name, address, and other information.

4 Click **Next** to answer Yes and to move on to the next question
The WorksWizard asks if you want to emphasize your business name or another name.

5 Click **Next** to accept your business name and move on to the next question
The WorksWizard now displays eight text boxes where you can enter the text of Outdoor Design's letterhead. Type the text shown in Figure 1-9, pressing **[Tab]** to move to the next text box and [backspace] if you type the wrong character. Press **[Shift][Tab]** to back up if you accidentally skip a box. When you've entered all the information, click **Next**.

6 Click **Cosmopolitan** to select the Cosmopolitan letterhead style
A preview of your letterhead displays with the Cosmopolitan letterhead style.

7 Click **Next** twice
The WorksWizard moves to the next question, retains the triangle line design, and asks you if you would like to add a decorative border or picture.

8 Click **Picture** and **Next** to add a picture, then click **Next** again to place the picture at the upper left
The Letterhead WorksWizard makes room for a picture, then asks you to choose your clip art.

9 Click **Next** to accept the sun clip art, then click **Create**
The WorksWizard opens a new document window and starts creating the Outdoor Designs letterhead. When finished, the WorksWizard displays a checkered flag and prompts you to continue.

IO Click **OK** to close the WorksWizard and return to the Word Processor
The Outdoor Designs letterhead is now ready for use, as shown in Figure 1-10. Proceed to the next lesson now, to learn how to save the letterhead document to disk.

FIGURE 1-9:
The text for the
Outdoor Designs
letterhead

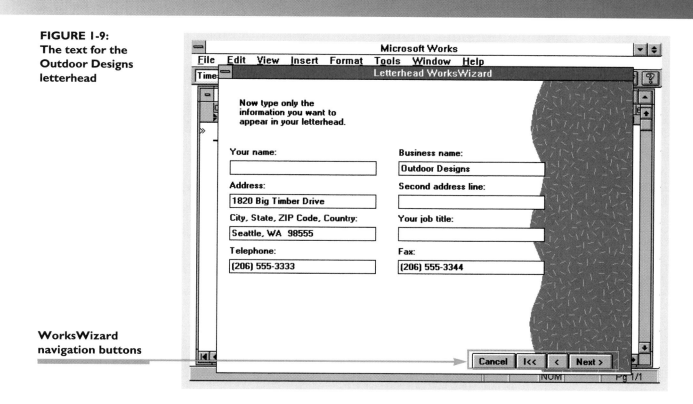

WorksWizard
navigation buttons

FIGURE 1-10: The completed Outdoor Designs letterhead

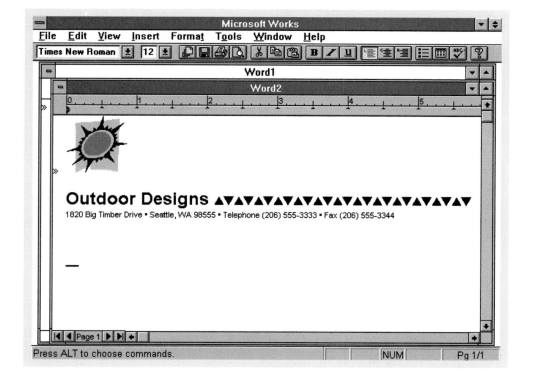

QUICK **TIP**

Press **[Esc]** or
Cancel to cancel
WorksWizard and
return to your
document. If the
WorksWizard created
a new document,
close the document
window by pressing
[Ctrl][F4], then
click **No** to discard
your changes.■

Saving a file

In the last lesson you used the Letterhead WorksWizard to create Outdoor Design's letterhead in the Word Processor. To keep a permanent copy of the letterhead you must **save** the letterhead to disk with the Save or Save As command on the File menu. (Works does not save your edits automatically; you must ask Works to do it specifically.) When you save a document to disk you must also assign it a unique **filename** so you can identify it later. Before you name a document, Works assigns it a temporary filename beginning with the letters Word. Up to now, the two documents you have used in this unit have been named Word1 and Word2.
▶ You'll save the Outdoor Design's letterhead to your Student Disk now.

1 **Make sure your Student Disk is in drive A or B**
In this lesson and throughout the rest of this book we assume it is in drive A.

2 **Click File on the menu bar, then click Save As**
The Save As dialog box displays, as shown in Figure 1-11. The Save As dialog box includes a File Name text box where you can enter a descriptive filename of eight characters or less, a Directories list box where you can choose the destination directory for the file, a Drives drop-down list box where you can choose which disk to store the file on, a Save File as Type drop-down list box where you can identify the type of the file you are saving, and four command buttons. Several of the dialog box elements contain **default** values (which will automatically apply unless you select other values) to help you save your file. Take a moment now to identify the elements of the Save As dialog box. See Figure 1-11 for their locations.

3 **Type letterhd**
The filename letterhd displays in the File Name text box. Now you need to indicate the drive where you want Works to save your letterhd file. You want to save the file to your Student Disk.

4 **Click the Drives drop-down list box, then click a: to select drive A
(or click b: if your Student disk is in drive B)**
A list of your Student Disk files displays in the File Name list box, and the MY_FILES directory that you created in the Working with Windows section displays in the Directories list box. To keep your Student Disk organized, it's a good idea to save your new files in the MY_FILES directory.

5 **Double click the MY_FILES directory icon in the Directories list box**
The folder icon next to MY_FILES changes to a picture of an open folder, indicating that your file will be saved to this directory.

6 **Click OK to save the file**
The Save As dialog box closes. Note that the title bar of the letterhead document now includes LETTERHD.WPS, the filename of your document. Works has added the three-character extension .WPS to your filename to identify the file as a Works Word Processor file. Table 1-4 lists the different three-character extensions in Works and gives some examples of valid filenames.

FIGURE I-11: Save As dialog box

File Name text box

Directories list box

Drives drop-down
list box

Save File as Type
drop-down list box

Command buttons

Save As

File **N**ame:
word2

unit_03.wps
unit_04.wps
unit_05.wps

Di**r**ectories:
a:\my_files

a:\
my_files

Driv**es:**
a:

Save File as Type:
Works WP

OK

Cancel

Help

Make
backup copy
of old file

Template...

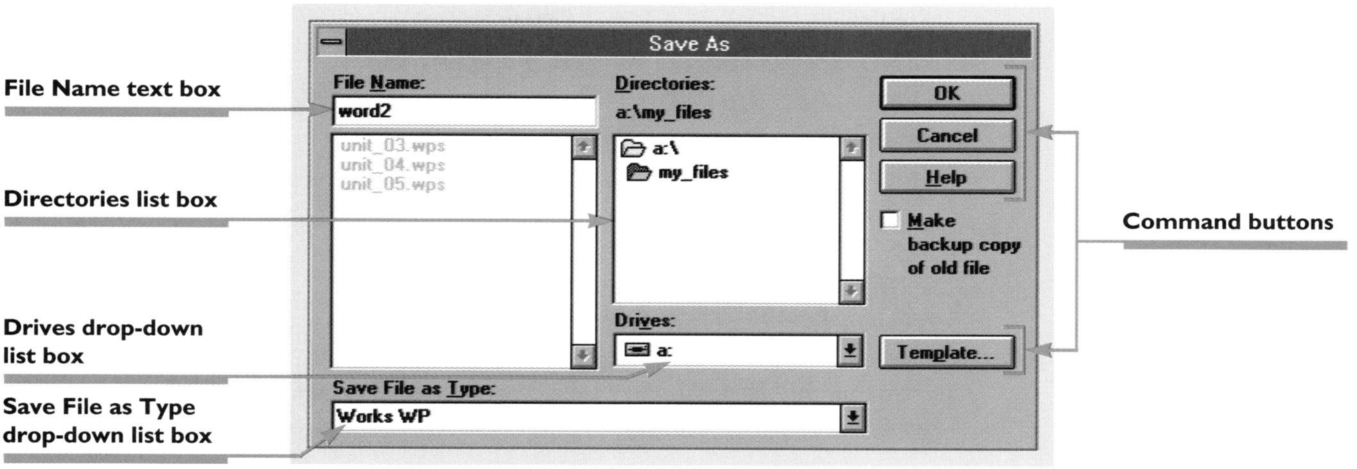

More about filenames

A valid filename in Works contains a descriptive name up to eight characters long,
a period, and a three-character extension supplied by Works. This naming conven-
tion comes from the MS-DOS operating system, the control program that ultimately
manages your files. MS-DOS also reserves the characters ? . " / \ [ ] * : | > < = + , ;
for its own use. When you are naming your files, avoid using the reserved characters
and try to use mnemonic names that you'll remember later.

TABLE I-4: Document extensions in Works

EXTENSION	APPLICATION	SAMPLE FILENAME
.WPS	Works Word Processor	LETTERHD.WPS
.WKS	Works Spreadsheet	94BUDGET.WKS
.WDB	Works Database	NEW_CUST.WDB
.WCM	Works Communications	INTERNET.WCM

TROUBLE?

For more informa-
tion about your
Student Disk, refer
to the section called
"Read This Before
You Begin Microsoft
Works 3.0."

Closing a file and exiting Works

After you save a document, you can safely close it and exit Works. To close a file, use the Close command on the File menu as shown in Figure 1-12. When you have completed all the work you want to get done in a given session, you'll want to quit or **exit** Works. ▶ In the following steps you'll close the LETTERHD.WPS document and then exit Works.

1   Click **File** on the menu bar, then click **Close**
See Figure 1-12. The LETTERHD.WPS document window closes. Use the Close command when you are finished working with a document. Be sure to save your file before you use the Close command, or you will lose the work you have done in the document. (After you have saved a file for the first time, you can also use the Save command to save changes, which saves work in a file named earlier.)

Now you'll exit the Works program.

2   Click **File** on the menu bar, then click **Exit Works**
A Save changes dialog box displays, as shown in Figure 1-13, asking if you would like to save the changes you have made to the Word1 document. You only used the Word1 document to practice using the toolbar, so you don't need to save these edits.

3   Click **No** to discard the contents of the Word1 document and exit Works
The Word1 document closes and the Windows Program Manager displays with the Microsoft Works for Windows group highlighted.

FIGURE 1-12: Closing a document using the Close command

Click here to close a
document

Click here to Exit
Works

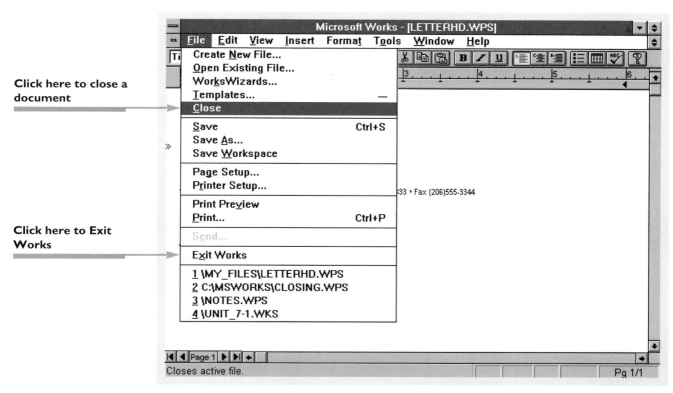

FIGURE 1-13: The Save Changes dialog box

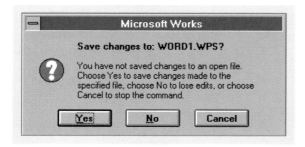

TROUBLE?

Be sure not to turn off
your computer with-
out exiting Works and
Windows first. If you
do, Works and
Windows will not
delete the temporary
files they have created
and your hard disk will
get cluttered.■

CONCEPTSREVIEW

Label each of the elements of the Works Startup dialog box as shown in Figure 1-14.

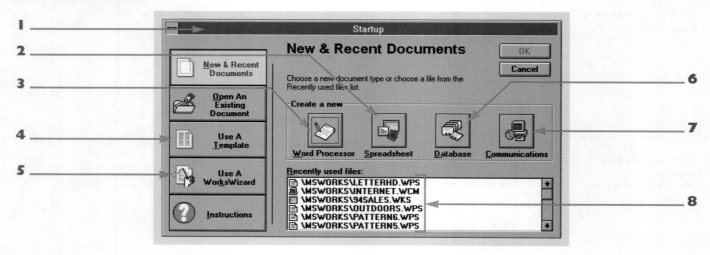

FIGURE 1-14

Match each document with the Works application that creates it.

9 Electronic mail

10 Pie chart

11 Term paper

12 Music collection

a. Word Processor

b. Spreadsheet

c. Database

d. Communications

Select the best answer from the list of choices.

13 The phrase "Works is an integrated software package" means that

a. Works can perform complex mathematical calculations

b. Works contains several useful applications that have been designed to be used together

c. Offices that use Works are politically correct

d. Works contains a communications application

14 You start Works from

a. The Program Manager

b. The MS-DOS prompt

c. The Task List

d. The Internet

15 You start the four Works applications from

a. The Works Help system

b. The Control Panel

c. The Startup dialog box

d. The Microsoft Works for Windows group icon

16 The Word Processor is used to

a. Write memos, letters, and newspapers

b. Track expenses and create pie charts

c. Download files and request stock quotes

d. All of the above

17 Each Works application contains

a. A menu bar

b. Scroll bars

c. A toolbar

d. All of the above

18 The sizing buttons on the Works program and document windows let you

a. Control the size of your hard disk

b. Control the size and shape of the mouse pointer

c. Minimize, maximize, and restore the window

d. Change the color and background pattern of the window

19 To temporarily switch back to the Windows Program Manager from Works you

a. Hold down [Ctrl] and press [Esc]

b. Double-click the control menu box

c. Hold down [Alt] and press [F1]

d. Click the right mouse button

20 Which of the following is not a Works dialog box element?

a. Check box

b. Command button

c. Menu bar

d. Drop-down list box

21 If a dialog box contains multiple sections of dialog box options it contains

a. Function keys

b. Tabs

c. A control menu box

d. Sizing buttons

22 The Word Processor toolbar contains all of the following buttons *except*

a. Italic button

b. Center-align button

c. Cut button

d. Thesaurus button

23 The Works Help system contains which of the following learning resources?

a. The Cue Cards adviser

b. An on-line tutorial

c. A Search dialog box

d. All of the above

24 Identify the true statement(s) about WorksWizards.

a. They are run from the Word Processor Help menu

b. They automate common computer tasks

c. They require no input from the user

d. All of the above

25 All of the following methods save a file *except*

a. Clicking the Save button on the toolbar

b. Clicking the Question mark button on the toolbar

c. Choosing the Save As command from the File menu

d. Choosing the Save command from the File menu

APPLICATIONS
REVIEW

1 Start Works and identify the elements of the Startup dialog box.

a. Start Windows if necessary.

b. Double-click the Microsoft Works for Windows group icon.

c. Double-click the Microsoft Works program icon.

d. Try to identify as many items in the Works Startup dialog box as you can, without referring to the lesson material. Then compare your results with Figure 1-2.

2 Start the Works Word Processor and identify the elements of the Word Processor screen.

a. Click on the Word Processor button in the Startup dialog box.

b. Try to identify as many items of the Word Processor screen as you can, without referring to the lesson material. Then compare your results with Figure 1-3 and Table 1-2.

3 Practice working with a Works dialog box, then click the Cancel button to discard the changes.

a. Click Format on the menu bar.

b. Click the Font and Style command on the Format menu.

c. To practice setting the dialog box elements, set the Font to Times New Roman, the Style to Italic, the Size to 20, the Color to Red, and the Position to Subscript. If you have trouble working with an element, refer to the lesson "Using dialog boxes" for help.

4 Enter text in the Word Processor, select it with the mouse, then use the toolbar to change the text style and the text alignment.

a. Type **Colombia** in the Word Processor.

b. Double-click Colombia to select it.

c. Click the Italic and Right-aligned buttons on the toolbar.

d. Click the Cut button on the toolbar to delete the text.

5 Use the Help Search dialog box to find the Help System article on Cue Cards, the Works on-screen adviser.

a. Click Help on the menu bar.

b. Click the Search for Help on command on the Help menu.

c. Type **Cue Cards** in the text box and click Show Topics.

d. Double-click Getting instructions from Cue Cards as you work and read the Help topic. Exit Help when you finish reading.

6 Use the Letterhead WorksWizard to create an Outdoor Designs letterhead as you did in the lesson "Using WorksWizards." This time, add your own name and job title to the letterhead.

  a. Choose the WorksWizards command from the File menu to run the WorksWizard.

  b. Click the Letterhead WorksWizard and click the OK button. Because you've used this WorksWizard before, it remembers your last answers. You can click the Next button until you get to the eight text boxes that request the names and addresses for the business.

  c. Type your own name in the Your Name text box and the title **Summer Intern** in the Your Job Title text box. Retain the rest of the business information and press the Next button for the remainder of the questions.

  d. Click Create to create the letterhead.

7 Save the letterhead to disk and exit Works.

  a. Click File on the menu bar.

  b. Click the Save As command on the File menu.

  c. Type **MYLETTER** and press [Enter].

  d. Choose the Exit Works command from the File menu. If you have any open documents, Works displays a dialog box which asks you if you want to save them. Click No to discard your edits.

INDEPENDENT
CHALLENGE

All Works applications contain a toolbar that provides quick access to Works commands through intuitive buttons and drop-down list boxes. The toolbar is also customizable, meaning you can add, subtract, or rearrange buttons and drop-down list boxes, based on your work habits and the types of documents you are creating. To customize the toolbar, choose the Customize Toolbar command from the Tools menu and follow the instructions in the Customize Works Toolbar dialog box. Each Works application features a different toolbar, which can be customized based on your needs and computer experience.

To complete this Independent Challenge:

1 Use The Customize Toolbar command on the Tools menu to explore the available buttons and add different functions to the Word Processor toolbar.

2 Open the Customize Works Toolbar dialog box. Click each of the buttons in the set shown under the File category. Read the description that displays as you click each button.

3 Practice adding and removing toolbar buttons. To do this, you'll probably have to remove some existing buttons first. Notice that Works automatically stores each button you remove under the appropriate category.

4 To make more room on the toolbar, try removing the Font Name and Point Size boxes from the toolbar.

5 When you have finished exploring the toolbar buttons, click the Reset button to return to Works' default toolbar settings.

UNIT 2

OBJECTIVES

▶ Open a file

▶ Type a memo

▶ Edit a document

▶ Use the toolbar

▶ View your document

▶ Use the Spelling Checker and Thesaurus

▶ Print your document

Creating
A MEMO WITH THE WORD PROCESSOR

In the last unit you learned fundamental skills in Works and used a WorksWizard to create the Outdoor Designs letterhead. In this unit you will continue to work with the Works Word Processor, the Works application used to create professional-looking memos, reports, research papers, and other text-based documents. ▶ You'll use the Word Processor to create a memo for the company's sales representatives, your first assignment as the new summer intern. Creating the sales memo involves starting the Word Processor, opening the Outdoor Designs letterhead file, typing the text of the memo, saving it to disk, editing it, formatting it with the toolbar, viewing it in Page Layout, checking the spelling, and, finally, printing it. As you work on the memo you'll learn fundamental word processing skills that will help you each time you use the Works Word Processor. ▶

Opening a file

Loading an existing file into a Works application is called **opening** a file. There are two ways to open a file in Works: you can choose the Open Existing File command from the File menu, or you can double-click the file name in the Recently used file list box in the Works Startup dialog box. As your first assignment at Outdoor Designs, you will send a memo to all the Outdoor Designs sales representatives, reminding them that their monthly sales reports are due and asking that they send them directly to you for processing. To create the memo, you'll open UNIT_02.WPS on your Student Disk (a copy of the letterhead file you created in the last unit), and add a suitable reminder. Start Works and open the UNIT_02.WPS file now.

1 Start Works from the Program Manager
The Startup dialog box appears.

2 Put your Student Disk in Drive A or Drive B

3 Click the **Open an Existing Document** button
The Open dialog box appears. See Figure 2-1. It contains a File Name text box and list box, a Directories list box, a Drives drop-down list box, and a List Files of Type drop-down list box. These elements allow you to specify the name, location, and type of the file you want to open. The Find File button starts the File Organizer WorksWizard, which helps you search for a file.

4 Click the **Drives drop-down list box**, then click **a:** to select Drive A (or click **b:** if your Student Disk is in Drive B)
The Works files on your Student Disk display in the File Name list box, as shown in Figure 2-1. UNIT_02.WPS appears in the list.

5 Double-click **UNIT_02.WPS** to open the file in the Word Processor
After a moment the letterhead document opens in a window in the Word Processor, as shown in Figure 2-2. The document window contains several visual elements and controls designed to help you with your word processing. Take a moment to identify the elements, referring to Table 2-1 for a description of the elements. Next you'll save the file with a different name on your Student Disk to protect the original.

6 Click the **File menu**, then click **Save As**
The Save As dialog box displays.

7 Type **repmemo1** in the File Name text box, then double-click the **my_files directory** in the directories list box and press **[Enter]**
A dialog box displays asking if you want to save the file to a different disk.

8 Click **No**
Works saves the new file, REPMEMO1.WPS, on your Student Disk in the MY_FILES directory. The title bar changes to reflect the new name.

FIGURE 2-1: The Open dialog box

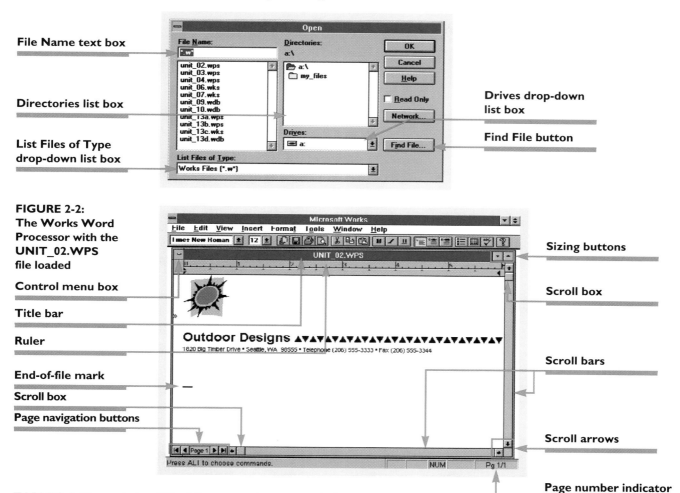

File Name text box

Directories list box

List Files of Type drop-down list box

Drives drop-down list box

Find File button

FIGURE 2-2:
The Works Word Processor with the **UNIT_02.WPS** file loaded

Control menu box

Title bar

Ruler

End-of-file mark

Scroll box

Page navigation buttons

Sizing buttons

Scroll box

Scroll bars

Scroll arrows

Page number indicator

TABLE 2-1: Elements in a Word Processor document window

ELEMENT	DESCRIPTION
Title bar	Bar at the top of the window containing the document file name
Sizing buttons	Minimize, Maximize, and Restore buttons for the window
Control menu box	Control menu box for the window
Ruler	A ruler measuring the body of the document in inches
End-of-file mark	A horizontal bar (like an underline) marking the end of the document
Scroll bars	Horizontal and vertical bars used to access other parts of the document
Scroll box	Box in scroll bar showing approximate position in the document
Page number indicator	Numbers indicating the current page and the total pages in the document
Page navigation buttons	Buttons used to move through the document one or more pages at a time

QUICK **TIP**

To maximize the Word Processor document window, click the Maximize button in the upper-right corner of the document window.

Typing a memo

Now that you've opened the letterhead document and have saved it with a different name, you're ready to type in the contents of the sales rep memo. Type in the memo now, pressing **[↓]** and [Enter] as indicated. Table 2-2 lists keys that will help you move around your document in the future.

1 Press the **down arrow key [↓]** six times
The Word Processor **cursor**, a blinking vertical bar indicating the insertion point, moves to the bottom of the document, indicated by the horizontal **End-of-file mark ——**. The **[↓]** key is one of several keyboard keys that you can use to move the cursor around the document. See Table 2-2. You can also move the cursor around the document by clicking with the mouse.

2 Type the contents of the memo, as shown in **bold** below
Note that when you press **[Enter]**, the cursor moves down one line and to the left margin, just like the carriage does on a typewriter when you press the Return key. Longer lines in the main paragraph **wrap** (continue on the next line) automatically when the cursor reaches the right margin, and the document window scrolls vertically when the cursor reaches the bottom of the window. When you've finished typing, your screen should look like Figure 2-3.
June 27, 1994 [Enter]
[Enter]
[Enter]
Dear Outdoor Designs Sales Representatives, [Enter]
[Enter]
Greetings from Seattle! The end of June is rapidly approaching, and I have been asked by our Sales Manager, Sue Ellen, to remind you that your monthly sales reports are due next week and that you should send these directly to me at the address above. I have just been hired as the Summer Intern for the Outdoor Designs Sales and Marketing group, and will be recording your sales data and processing your commission checks. [Enter]
[Enter]
I look forward to working with you throughout the summer!
[Enter]
[Enter]
Sincerely, [Enter]
[Enter]
[Enter]
[Enter]
Melissa Cavanaugh [Enter]

3 Click the **Save button** 🖫 on the toolbar
Works saves the contents of your memo to disk. You should always save your work after you have typed a paragraph or so, to make sure you have an up-to-date copy on disk at all times.

FIGURE 2-3:
The screen after the
sales rep memo has
been entered

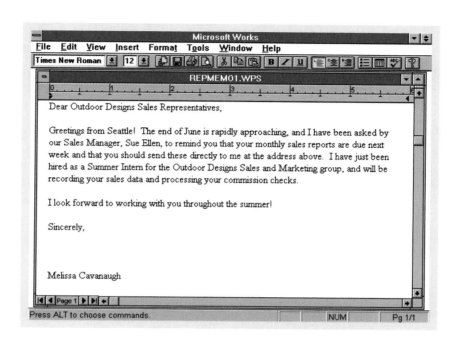

TABLE 2-2: Useful keys for moving the cursor around a document

KEYBOARD KEY	MOVES CURSOR
[→]	One space to the right
[←]	One space to the left
[↑]	Up one line
[↓]	Down one line
[PAGE UP]	Up one page
[PAGE DOWN]	Down one page
[HOME]	To beginning of line
[END]	To end of line
[Ctrl][HOME]	To beginning of document
[Ctrl][END]	To end of document

TROUBLE?

The line wraps on
your screen might
not match Figure 2-3
exactly. Line wraps
will vary depending
on the printer driver
your particular
machine uses.■

QUICK TIP

To see visual repre-
sentations of the Space
and Enter characters,
you would choose **All
Characters** from the
View menu.■

Editing a document

After you have entered text in the Word Processor, you can modify or **edit** the text in several ways. You can delete simple mistakes by moving the cursor to the end of the incorrect word and pressing **[Backspace]** to delete individual letters. You can delete larger blocks of unwanted text by **selecting** the unwanted text, then pressing **[Del]**. Finally, you can move sections of text from one place to another with the Cut and Paste commands on the File menu or a mouse procedure known as **drag-and-drop**. You'll practice using these editing techniques now.

1 **Click after the word *these* in the third line of the main paragraph**
The cursor moves from the bottom of the document window to the space after the word *these*. Notice that when you move the mouse pointer into the document window, the pointer shape changes to the **insertion pointer** I, to help you place the cursor exactly where you want it in the text. Now you'll change the word *these* to *them*.

2 **Press [Backspace] two times, then type m**
The word *these* changes to *them*. Now try selecting some unneeded words and deleting them from the document.

3 **Press [↓] once, then [←] once**
The cursor moves to the left of the letter *O* in *Outdoor Designs*.

4 **Hold down [Shift] and press [→] until the words *Outdoor Designs* and the following blank space are selected, then release both keys**
Outdoor Designs is selected, as shown in Figure 2-4. Selecting text with the keyboard is a fundamental skill used in all Works applications.

5 **Press [Del] to delete the selected text**
The words *Outdoor Designs* are removed from the document. Because you also selected the blank space after the word *Designs*, the spacing is correct between the words *the* and *Sales*. Now try moving some text in the document.

6 **Drag the insertion pointer across the name *Sue Ellen* (including the comma and the space after) in the second line of the main paragraph**
Sue Ellen (including the comma and the space after) is selected. Holding down the mouse button and moving the insertion pointer, or dragging, selects text in a document with the mouse. When you drag horizontally, you select characters. When you drag vertically, you select lines.

7 **Click Edit, then click Cut**
The selected text is removed from the document window and placed in the **Windows clipboard**, a temporary data holding place in the system's memory.

8 **Click in front of the word *our* in the second line of the main paragraph**
The cursor moves directly before the word *our*.

9 **Click Edit, then click Paste**
The text *Sue Ellen* is copied from the Windows clipboard and placed between the words *by* and *our* in the second line of the main paragraph.

10 **Click 🖫 to save your edits**

FIGURE 2-4: Selected text

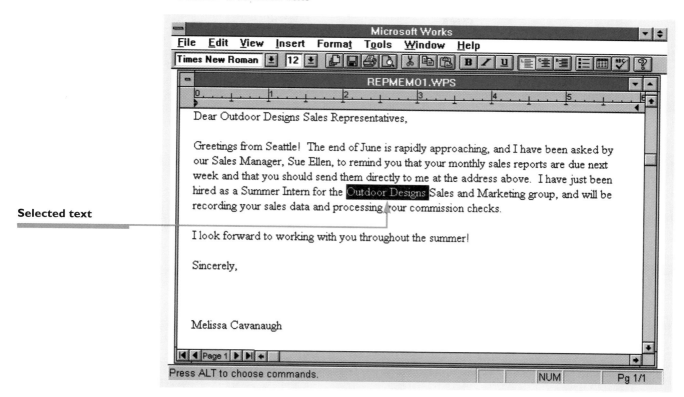

Selected text

Moving text with drag-and-drop

In steps 6 to 9 you learned how to move text from one location to another with the Edit menu and the Windows clipboard. You can also use a faster technique, called **drag-and-drop**, to move text with the mouse. To drag and drop text, you select the text you want to move, then click the selected text and drag it to its new location, using the drag-and-drop insertion pointer to place the text. This technique takes a bit of practice, but is extremely useful once you get the hang of it.

QUICK **TIP**

To undo your latest edit, such as a deletion you didn't want to make, choose Undo Editing from the Edit menu or press **[Ctrl][Z]**.

Using the toolbar

The Word Processor **toolbar** provides quick access to the most common Works commands and procedures. You've already used several of the Word Processor toolbar buttons. In this lesson, you will practice using the Cut, Copy, and Paste buttons to continue refining the Outdoor Designs sales rep memo. Table 2-3 lists the buttons that are unique to the Word Processor application: these buttons will be described in detail in Unit 3. You'll edit the memo with the Word Processor toolbar now.

1   **Move the mouse pointer to the left of the salutation** *Dear Outdoor Designs Sales Representatives*
When the mouse pointer enters the left margin of the document, it changes to the **line pointer** 🖱. The line pointer allows you to select one or more lines at a time.

2   **Click in the left margin to select the entire line**
The line *Dear Outdoor Designs Sales Representatives* is selected.

3   **Click the Cut button ✂ on the toolbar**
The line is removed from the document and placed in the Windows clipboard. The Cut button performs the same function as the Cut command on the Edit menu.

4   **Click the Paste button 📋 on the toolbar**
The line is pasted back into the document from the Windows clipboard. The Paste button works like the Paste command on the Edit menu. In the future, you can use either the Cut and Paste commands, the toolbar buttons, or any combination of them. Both produce identical results.

5   **Select the name** *Sue Ellen* **with the mouse and click the Copy button 📑 on the toolbar**
A copy of the selected text is placed in the Windows clipboard. You'll use the Copy button to place a copy of Sue Ellen's name at the bottom of the memo with cc: in front of it, indicating she'll be receiving a courtesy copy of the letter.

6   **Press [Ctrl][End] to move the cursor to the bottom of the document**
The cursor moves to the line below *Melissa Cavanaugh* at the bottom of the document.

7   **Press [Enter] twice, then type cc: and press [Spacebar]**
cc: appears at the bottom of the document. Now you're ready to paste in Sue Ellen's name.

8   **Click the Paste button 📋 on the toolbar, then click 💾 to save your edits**
The name *Sue Ellen* is pasted into the document from the Windows clipboard, as shown in Figure 2-5. You've finished editing the memo.

TABLE 2-3:
Buttons found only on the Word Processor toolbar

BUTTON	FUNCTION
📋	Add a bulleted list to the document
📊	Insert a spreadsheet table in the document
✅	Check the spelling of the document

FIGURE 2-5: Text pasted into the document

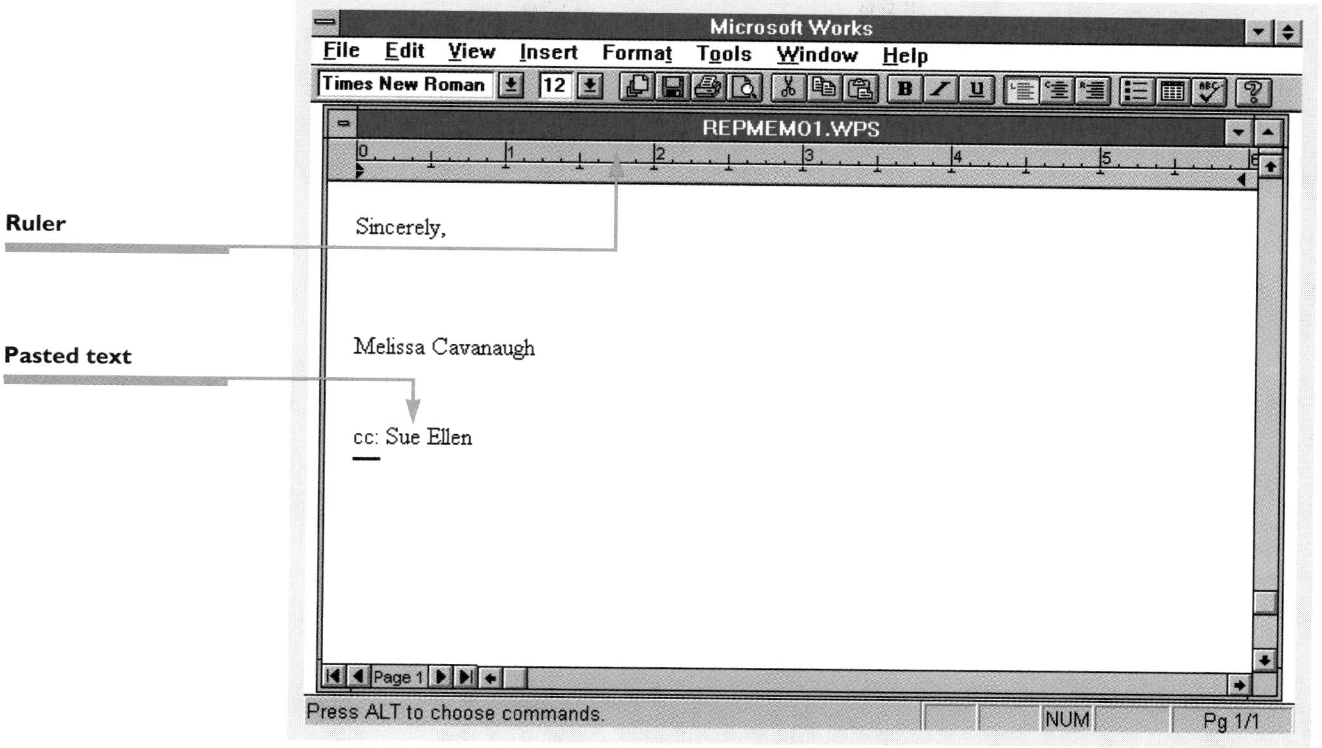

Ruler

Pasted text

```
─                          Microsoft Works                        ▼ ◆
 File  Edit  View  Insert  Format  Tools  Window  Help
Times New Roman  ▼  12  ▼  [icons]  B  I  U  [icons]
─                         REPMEMO1.WPS                            ▼ ▲
 [ruler 0...1...2...3...4...5...6]

     Sincerely,



     Melissa Cavanaugh


     cc: Sue Ellen




 ◄ ◄ Page 1 ► ►► ◄
Press ALT to choose commands.              NUM      Pg 1/1
```

Using the ruler

Below the title bar in the document window is a measuring tool called the **ruler**. The default ruler is marked with measurements in inches, and contains symbols for the left and right margins and the tab stops in the document. The ruler gives you an idea of where your text will appear on the printed page and how big it will be. The ruler in Figure 2-5 indicates the body of the text is 6 inches wide and contains tab stops every ½ inch. To remove the ruler and make more room for your document, choose the **Ruler** command from the View menu.

QUICK **TIP**

To cut selected text with the keyboard, press **[Ctrl][X]**. To paste text with the keyboard, press **[Ctrl][V]**.■

Viewing your document

You can view the different parts of your document with the scroll bars or the keyboard direction keys. When you've finished working and are ready to print, you'll find it useful to examine the document up close with the Print Preview command and the **zoom pointer**, to see what your text will look like when it is printed. While you are creating the document you can also use different **document views**, such as Normal, Page Layout, and Draft View. Now you'll practice using the scroll bars and the Print Preview command to view the sales rep memo.

1 Click the **up arrow** on the vertical scroll bar several times
   The sales rep document scrolls up one line each time you click the up scroll arrow. The **scroll box**, the little square in the middle of the scroll bar, also moves up the scroll bar as you click the arrow. The scroll box indicates your relative position in the document.

2 Drag the **scroll box** to the top of the scroll bar
   The sales rep document scrolls to the top of the document. Use the scroll box when you want to move quickly from one place in the document to another. Now use the Print Preview command to see how the document will look when it prints.

3 Click **File,** then click **Print Preview**
   The Print Preview window opens and the sales rep document displays as it will appear on the printed page. See Figure 2-6. Although you were able to see how the body of the memo looked in the Word Processor, you couldn't see how the text fit on the page. Print Preview lets you see how it will look before you actually print.

4 Move the mouse pointer onto the document page
   The pointer changes to the zoom pointer, a magnifying glass with the word *zoom* beneath it. The zoom pointer lets you closely examine parts of the document in Print Preview.

5 Click the **top half** of the memo with the zoom pointer
   The top part of the document enlarges to half-size in the Print Preview window.

6 Click the **Outdoor Designs letterhead** with the zoom pointer
   The letterhead enlarges to full-size (the size it will print) in the Print Preview window. (You know you are in full-size view when the Zoom In button dims.)

7 Click the **Zoom Out button** twice
   The Print Preview window returns to half-size view, then standard (whole-page) view.

8 Click the **Cancel button**
   The Print Preview window closes and the sales rep document displays.

FIGURE 2-6:
The sales rep document
in Print Preview

Print Preview
command buttons

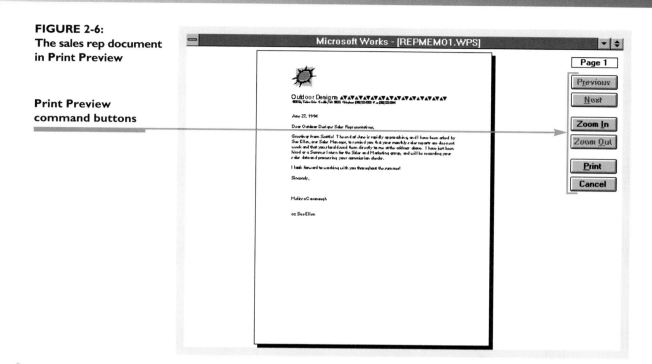

Document view commands on the View menu

In addition to Print Preview, you can use the **Normal**, **Page Layout**, and **Draft View** commands on the View menu to change the way your document displays in the Word Processor. Normal view is the default way a document displays; when you typed the sales rep memo, the Word Processor was in Normal view. Page Layout view is similar to Print Preview, showing you the actual page you're working on, including the margins, headers, footers, and columns. This view is especially useful when you are doing desktop publishing with Works. Draft view displays the entire document in one font; it is useful when you are outlining your thoughts and don't care how they look on the page. Figure 2-7 shows how the sales rep memo looks in Page Layout view. You'll learn more about this view in Unit 4.

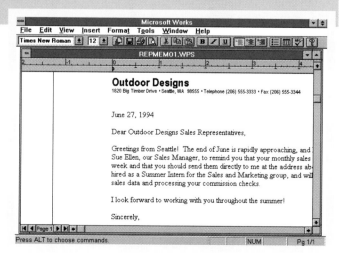

FIGURE 2-7:
The sales rep document
in Page Layout view

QUICK **TIP**

You can also preview your document by clicking the Print Preview button 🔍 on the toolbar.∎

Using the Spelling Checker and Thesaurus

Ever have trouble spelling a word or finding just the right word to use? If so, you'll enjoy the Spelling and Thesaurus commands in the Word Processor. The Spelling command checks your entire document for words that are misspelled, incorrectly hyphenated, or incorrectly capitalized, and lets you make corrections in a dialog box. The Thesaurus command lists one or more **synonyms** (words that have a similar meaning) for the word you have selected. Try working with both commands now.

1   Press **[Ctrl][Home]** to move the cursor to the top of the memo
The cursor appears to the left of the sun in the Outdoor Designs letterhead.

2   Click **Tools**, then click **Spelling**
The Spelling command starts to check the spelling of words in the document, beginning at the cursor and moving down. No deliberate spelling errors were introduced into the memo; if you typed it correctly, the first word the spelling checker should highlight is *Cavanaugh*. (If the Spelling Checker finds another word, that's OK.) When the Spelling Checker finds a word that is not in its dictionary file, the word appears in the Spelling dialog box, as shown in Figure 2-8.

3   Click the **Always Suggest check box**
An x appears in the check box. From now on (until you click the check box again), the spelling checker will suggest corrections for words when it doesn't find them in the dictionary.

4   Click the **Add button** to add *Cavanaugh* to your personal dictionary
The name *Cavanaugh* is added to your **personal dictionary**, a special file on your hard disk used by Works and other programs to verify spelling. When you use the Spelling command in the future, it will recognize the spelling of the word Cavanaugh. After you click the Add button, a dialog box notifies you that the spelling check has finished.

5   Click **OK** to close the dialog box

6   On the line above the date in the memo, type **have sum baloons** and select the line
Type the words exactly as written, typos and all. To select the line, click next to it in the left margin.

7   Click the **Spelling button** 📝 on the toolbar
Clicking the Spelling button is the same as choosing the Spelling command on the Tools menu. Because you have selected a passage of text before running the Spelling Checker, Works will only check the selected text. The Spelling dialog box displays, indicating the word *baloons* has not been found in the dictionary and suggesting that the spelling be changed to *balloons*.

8   Click **Change** to change the spelling, then click **OK**
The spelling changes and the spelling check ends. Note that the Spelling Checker did not flag the word *sum* as incorrect. Although in this context the word should probably be *some*, the Spelling Checker had no way of determining the context of the phrase. This example demonstrates that although the Spelling Checker is useful, it doesn't replace proofreading.

9   Press **[Del]** to delete the selected line, press **[Enter]** to add a blank line, then click 💾 to save your changes

Misspelled word found in check

FIGURE 2-8: The Spelling dialog box

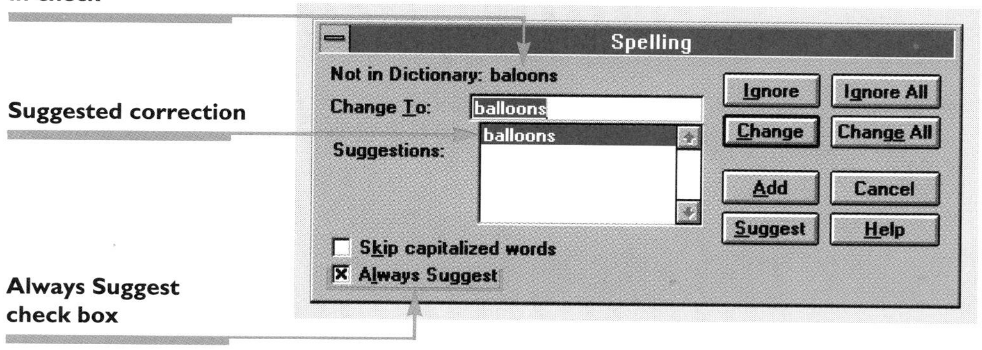

Suggested correction

Always Suggest check box

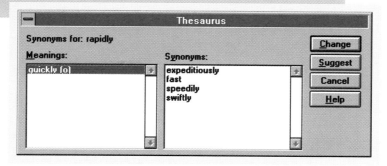

Using the Thesaurus

The Thesaurus is an electronic writing tool that provides vocabulary alternatives, as a printed thesaurus does. To use the Thesaurus, select a word for which you would like to see a list of synonyms, then click **Thesaurus** on the Tools menu. The Thesaurus dialog box shown in Figure 2-9 displays. It provides a one- or two-word definition for the selected word, then lists as many synonyms as it can find in the Synonyms list box. If you would like to use one of the synonyms listed in the box, click the synonym, then click the **Change** button. The Thesaurus replaces the selected word with the synonym and closes the dialog box.

FIGURE 2-9: The Works Thesaurus

QUICK **TIP**

The Works Spelling Checker uses a Houghton-Mifflin dictionary that contains about 110,000 words. You can also use it in the Spreadsheet and Database applications.■

Printing your document

After you have previewed your document with Print Preview, you can print it with the Print command. Each computer can support one or more printers through special connectors called **ports** on the back of the computer. To choose among the different printers attached to your computer, use the Printer Setup command. Ask your instructor or lab manager for specific instructions on how to print from your classroom printer. After you have printed the sales rep memo, use the Exit Works command to close the Word Processor.

1 Click **File**, then click **Printer Setup**
The Printer Setup dialog box displays. See Figure 2-10. The Printer Setup dialog box shows the printers and printer ports active on your system. The highlighted printer is the current or default printer. In Figure 2-10 the default printer is an HP LaserJet III, and it is connected to the LPT1: printer port. The default printer on your system will probably be different. To configure the settings in the default printer, you would click the Setup button and change the settings in the Setup dialog box (your instructor may ask you to do this later).

2 Click **OK** to accept the default printer and printer settings
The Printer Setup dialog box closes.

3 Click **File**, then click **Print**
The Print dialog box displays. See Figure 2-11. The Print dialog box lets you specify the number of copies of the document you want to print, the printing page range if you don't want to print the entire document, the type of document you are printing, whether you're using an advanced feature called **print merge**, and whether the printing should be best quality (the default) or draft quality.

Take a moment now to verify that your printer is on-line and properly connected to your computer.

4 Click **OK** to print the sales rep memo on your printer
The Print dialog box closes and after a few moments the completed sales rep memo emerges from your printer. Congratulations! You've completed your first word processing session and your first assignment at Outdoor Designs. Now save your changes and exit Works.

5 Click 🖫 to save your changes

6 Click **File**, then click **Exit Works**
The REPMEMO1.WPS document closes and the Works program exits. The Windows Program Manager displays, with the Microsoft Works for Windows group highlighted.

FIGURE 2-10: The Printer Setup dialog box

Default printer

Setup button

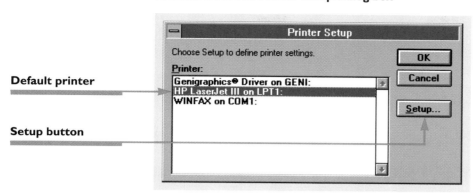

FIGURE 2-11: The Print dialog box

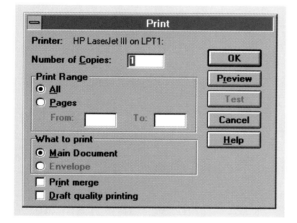

QUICK **TIP**

The Print button on the toolbar is the fastest way to print the entire document in Works. However, it doesn't let you choose the number of copies, print range, or other special conditions.

CONCEPTSREVIEW

**Label each of the elements of the
Works Word Processor application,
as shown in Figure 2-12.**

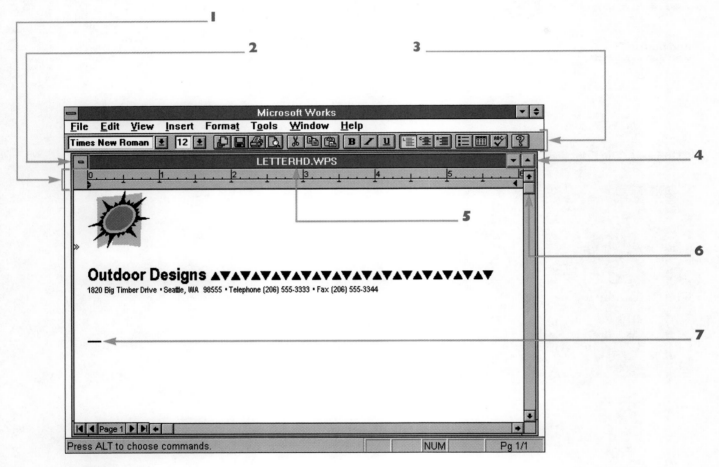

FIGURE 2-12

**Match each button from the Word Processor
toolbar with its function.**

8 ✂

9 ✐

10 ▤

11 💾

12 🔍

a. Save the current document
to disk

b. View the document in Print
Preview

c. Copy the selected text to the
Windows clipboard

d. Cut the selected text and
place it in the Windows
clipboard

e. Change the style of the
selected text to italic

Select the best answer from the list of choices.

13 Loading a file from disk into the Word Processor is called:

a. Closing the file

b. Exiting Works

c. Opening the file

d. Printing the file

14 Which of the following techniques will *not* open a file listed in
the Recently used file list box of the Works Startup dialog box?

a. Double-click the filename

b. Click the filename and click OK

c. Click the filename and press [Enter]

d. Click the filename with the right mouse button

15 The extension .WPS in the UNIT_02.WPS filename means that the file was created with which Works application?

a. Word Processor

b. Spreadsheet

c. Database

d. Communications

16 After you open a file in the Word Processor, the document window title bar contains what information?

a. The name of the directory the file is stored in

b. The filename associated with the document

c. The number of characters in the file

d. All of the above

17 What is the purpose of the Word Processor end-of-file mark?

a. To help you select text in the document

b. To list instructions for the highlighted command on the menu bar

c. To visually mark the last line of the document in the document window

d. To list page numbers for the document

18 Which keyboard key moves the cursor to the end of the current line in a document?

a. [Page Up]

b. [Page Down]

c. [Home]

d. [End]

19 Which technique *cannot* be used to select text in the Word Processor?

a. Double-click on a word

b. Double-click the end-of-file mark

c. Hold down [Shift] and press a direction key

d. Hold down the mouse button and drag the mouse pointer

20 Which of the following techniques *cannot* be used to move text from one location to another in the Word Processor?

a. The [Del] and [Ins] keyboard keys

b. Cut and Paste commands on the Edit menu

c. The drag-and-drop procedure

d. The [✄] and [📋] buttons on the toolbar

21 When does the insertion pointer change to the line pointer?

a. When you move the mouse pointer into the left margin of the document

b. When you place the mouse pointer over a button on the toolbar

c. When you use the scroll box on one of the scroll bars

d. When you drag and drop text

22 Which of the following document view commands is *not* listed on the Word Processor View menu?

a. Normal

b. Page Layout

c. Draft view

d. Print Preview

23 What is the purpose of the zoom pointer in Print Preview?

a. Adds page numbers to the document

b. Prints the document

c. Magnifies the page

d. Speeds up the editing process

24 What is the purpose of the Add button in the Spelling dialog box?

a. Adds a corrected word to the document

b. Adds a word to your personal dictionary

c. Adds a synonym to the Thesaurus

d. Activates the Always Suggest check box

25 Which of the following can you *not* do with the Printer Setup command?

a. Determine the default printer on your system

b. Determine the port the default printer is connected to

c. Change the settings of one or more printers

d. View how your document will be printed by different printers

APPLICATIONSREVIEW

1 Start Works, open the REPMEMO1.WPS file, and save the file as REPMEMO2.WPS.

a. Double-click the Microsoft Works program icon.

b. In the Startup dialog box, click the Open an Existing Document button.

c. In the Open dialog box, click a: in the Drives list box (or b: if your Student Disk is in drive B), make sure the MY_FILES directory is open, and double-click repmemol.wps in the File Name list box.

d. Click File, then click Save As, type **repmemo2** in the File Name text box, and click **OK**.

e. When the dialog box asks if you will be saving to a different floppy disk, click No.

f. Identify the elements of the document window, referring to Table 2-1 for a description of the elements.

2 Add a paragraph to the document and save your changes when you have finished.

   a. Move the cursor to the blank line after the first paragraph, then press [Enter].

   b. Type the following text. Don't press [Enter] until you have typed the last line.

     When you send along your reports, be sure to include a listing of the stores you have visited this past month, how many square feet each store has devoted to merchandise, and a few words about any new businesses that have opened up in your territory. [Enter]

   c. Click the Save button on the toolbar to save the revised memo to disk.

3 Practice editing your document by using the cursor keys and [Backspace] to fix any mistakes you made while typing. Then use the cut-and-paste technique to switch the order of the second and third sentences of the first paragraph.

   a. Use the cursor keys to place the cursor behind any misspelled words, then press [Backspace] to delete the mistake. Type in the correction.

   b. Select the third sentence of the first paragraph with the mouse (the paragraph beginning with *I have just been hired*).

   c. Click the Cut button on the toolbar.

   d. Click the insertion pointer in the space between the first and second sentences of the first paragraph.

   e. Click the Paste button on the toolbar. The third sentence is pasted in between the first and second sentences. Adjust the spacing around the sentence if necessary and click the Save button.

4 Use the Copy and Paste buttons on the toolbar to place a copy of the words *Sales and Marketing group* (from the first paragraph) on the cc: line at the bottom of the memo.

   a. Select the words *Sales and Marketing group* with the mouse and click the Copy button.

   b. Press [Ctrl][End] to move the cursor to the bottom of the document, then press [←] to place the cursor after the name *Sue Ellen* in the cc: line.

   c. Type a comma and a space, then click the Paste button on the toolbar.

   d. Click the Save button on the toolbar to save your edits.

5 Practice viewing your document with Print Preview, using the zoom pointer to magnify the text on the page.

   a. Click File, then click Print Preview.

   b. With the zoom pointer, click the paragraph you just added to the memo. The paragraph enlarges to half-size.

   c. Click the paragraph again with the zoom pointer. The paragraph enlarges to full-size.

   d. Click the Cancel button to return the document to Normal view.

6 Select the paragraph you just added to the memo using the line pointer, then run the spelling checker to verify the spelling of the words in your insert. Use the Thesaurus to examine synonyms for the word *listing* in the new paragraph.

   a. Use the scroll bars to bring the new paragraph into view, then move the mouse pointer to the left margin to change the insertion pointer to the line pointer.

   b. Drag the line pointer vertically in the left margin to select the three lines in the new paragraph.

   c. Click Spelling on the Tools menu to check the spelling of the selected paragraph. Correct any spelling mistakes identified by the Spelling checker.

   d. Double-click on the word *listing* in the paragraph, then click Thesaurus on the tools menu. Double-click on the word *record* in the synonym list to replace *listing* with *record* in the paragraph.

7 Print the revised memo with the Print command on the File menu.

   a. Click the File menu, then click Print.

   b. Verify that your printer is on-line and properly connected to your computer. If you have any questions, ask your instructor or lab manager for help.

   c. Click OK to print the sales rep memo. After a few moments, the revised memo emerges from your printer.

   d. Save any changes you have made and exit Works.

INDEPENDENT CHALLENGE

The Zoom command on the View menu lets you reduce or enlarge the view of your document in the Word Processor, Spreadsheet, and Database applications. The Zoom command includes five preset levels of magnification: 50, 75, 100, 200, and 400 percent, and a custom magnification that can be any percentage between 25 and 1000 percent. 100 percent is the default setting; smaller percentages reduce the size of the document, and larger percentages enlarge the size of the document. Zooming in and out only affects how the document is displayed on the screen, not how it prints.

Practice using the Zoom command on the View menu to view the sales rep document with different magnifications.

UNIT 3

OBJECTIVES

▶ Change the font

▶ Change alignment

▶ Change the margins

▶ Change paragraph style

▶ Insert page breaks

▶ Insert headers and footers

Enhancing
THE LOOK OF YOUR DOCUMENTS

In the last unit, you learned the fundamental document preparation skills in the Word Processor: how to open an existing file, type the body of the document, make changes, save the document, and print it. ▶ In this unit you will use the Word Processor to spruce up a document given to you by Frasier, Outdoor Designs' marketing manager. The document you will **format** is a product information sheet for Outdoor Designs' newest product, the Cascade Ski Sack. The sales reps and public relations specialist use the product information sheet to spread the word about the product and start the sales effort. You will learn to format the document with menu commands and the toolbar. You will learn how to change fonts and font style, change the text alignment, change the margins, use tabs and bullets, insert page breaks, and add a footer. ▶

Changing the font

As you learned in Unit 1, you can use the **Font and Style** command on the Format menu to change the font type, style, size, color, and position in the Word Processor. The Word Processor toolbar contains many of these commands, including drop-down list boxes for font type and font size, and buttons for bold, italic, and underline styles. Table 3-1 shows formatting samples. Open the Outdoor Designs product information sheet now and format it with the buttons on the toolbar.

1 Start **Works** from the Program Manager, then click the **Open an Existing Document button**

2 Open the document **UNIT_03.WPS** from your Student Disk, then save it as **SKISACK2.WPS** in the MY_FILES directory

3 Select the **first two lines** of the SKISACK2.WPS document with the mouse
The first two lines highlight. You must always select text in a document before you format it.

4 Click the **Bold** ☐B and **Italic** ☐ **buttons** on the toolbar
The Bold and Italic buttons are pushed in and the selected text is formatted for bold and italic.

5 Click the **Font Name drop-down list box** on the toolbar, scroll to the top of the list, and click the **Arial** font
The Arial font displays as the active font in the drop-down list box. The selected text is formatted for Arial.

6 Click the **Font Size drop-down list box** on the toolbar, scroll down until 18 appears, then click **18**
18 displays as the active point size in the drop-down list box (1 point is equal to ¹⁄₇₂ of an inch). The selected text is formatted for bold, italic, Arial, and 18 point, as shown in Figure 3-1.

7 Format the **heading** at the beginning of each paragraph with **bold**
The five headings are About the Product, Shipping Info, Description, Competitive Products, and Kit Promotions. To format a heading, select it, then click ☐B on the toolbar.

8 Under the heading Kit Promotions, format the magazine names **Profitable Craft Merchandising** and **Outside Magazine** with italic

9 Click ☐ on the toolbar
Your font and style changes are saved to disk.

TABLE 3-1:
Font and style formatting samples

FONT FORMATS	SAMPLES
Type	Arial, Courier, Times New Roman
Size	Six point, ten point, fourteen point
Style	**Bold**, *italic*, underline

FIGURE 3-1: Selected text formatted with bold, Arial, and 18 points

Font Name drop-down list box

Font Size drop-down list box

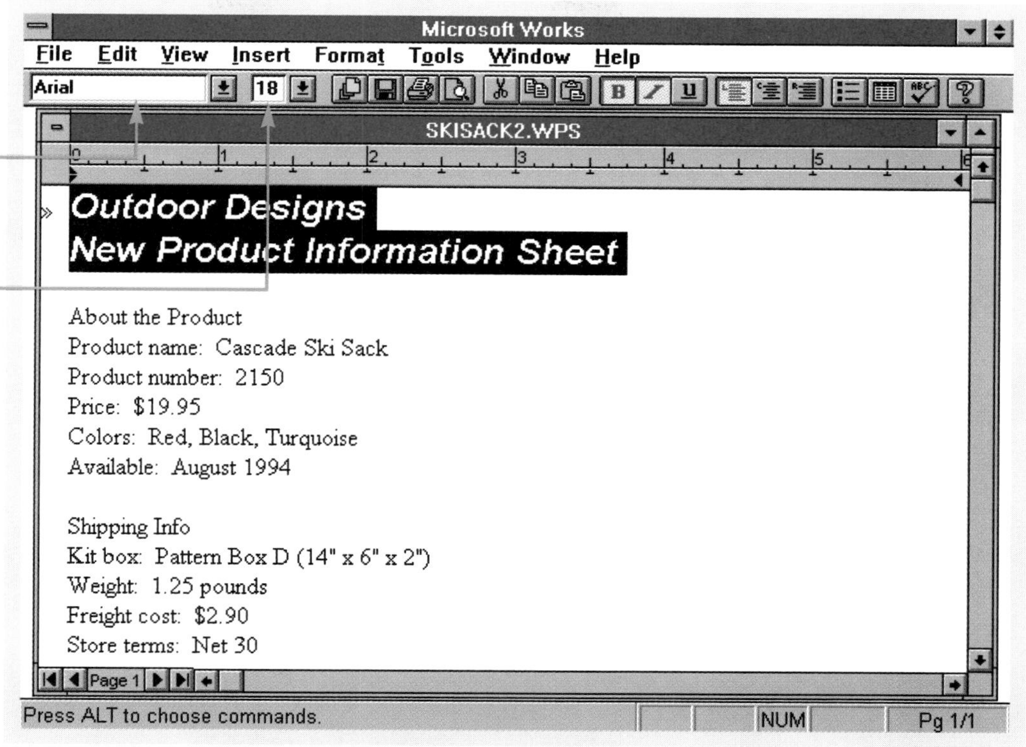

Where do fonts come from?

Font creation or **fontography** is an old business. In ancient times, scribes concerned with the uniformity of letters and symbols wrote in standardized forms so they could easily be understood by the generations to come. In the Middle Ages, several unique writing styles, such as Carolingian miniscule, were developed in Europe to allow texts to be clearly and compactly copied into handwritten books. After the introduction of the printing press in the 15th century, Gothic, Roman, Palatino, and other fonts were created to adapt the earlier handwritten styles to printing technology. The fonts we use today are the descendants of these earlier type styles, as well as other styles developed in modern times.

Before fonts can be used on a computer, they must be **installed**. The Windows operating environment comes with several TrueType fonts, such as Arial and Times New Roman, pre-installed on the system. **TrueType fonts** have the advantage of appearing on the screen in your application as they do when they are printed. TrueType fonts can be identified by the **T** symbol that appears next to them in the Font name list box. Your system may include other useful fonts supplied by the manufacturer of your printer or another company. Ask your instructor or lab manager for an overview of the fonts on your system.

QUICK **TIP**

[Ctrl][B] and **[Ctrl][I]** are the keyboard shortcuts for formatting the selected text in boldface and italic, respectively.

Changing alignment

You can change the alignment of text in a document with the Left, Center, and Right alignment buttons on the toolbar. You can also **justify** text (align it to both right and left margins) with the Paragraph command on the Format menu. You'll use Center and Justified alignment to emphasize a few lines in the product information sheet now.

1 Use the **scroll bars** to scroll to the top of the document
The window scrolls vertically until the top of the document is in view.

2 Select the first two lines of the document
The first two lines (formatted with Arial bold and italic) highlight.

3 Click the **Center-Align button** 📄 on the toolbar
Works centers the first two lines in the document window. Now format the paragraph under the heading Description for justified alignment.

4 Use the scroll bars to scroll down until the paragraph under Description is visible, then select the paragraph with the mouse
The paragraph under Description highlights.

5 Click **Format**, then click **Paragraph**
The Paragraph dialog box displays. The Paragraph dialog box contains three sections or **tabs** of formatting options.

6 Click the **Indents and Alignment tab** if it is not already in front
The Indents and Alignment tab displays in the dialog box, as shown in Figure 3-2. The Indents and Alignment tab presents three indent options (Left, Right, and First Line), and four alignment options (Left, Center, Right, and Justified). All of the alignment options except Justified are available as buttons on the toolbar, as shown in Table 3-2. However, you must use the Paragraph dialog box to choose Justified alignment.

7 Click **Justified**, then click **OK**
The Paragraph dialog box closes and the Description paragraph is formatted for Justified alignment. Notice that the words along both sides of the paragraph are aligned to the margins. When you select Justified alignment, the Word Processor spaces the words in each line so that they align with both the right and left margins. The spacing between words within the paragraph varies, however.

TABLE 3-2:
The Alignment icons on the toolbar

8 Click 💾 to save your formatting changes to disk

ICON	DESCRIPTION
📄	Aligns text to the left margin
📄	Aligns text to the center of the page
📄	Aligns text to the right margin

FIGURE 3-2:
The Paragraph
dialog box

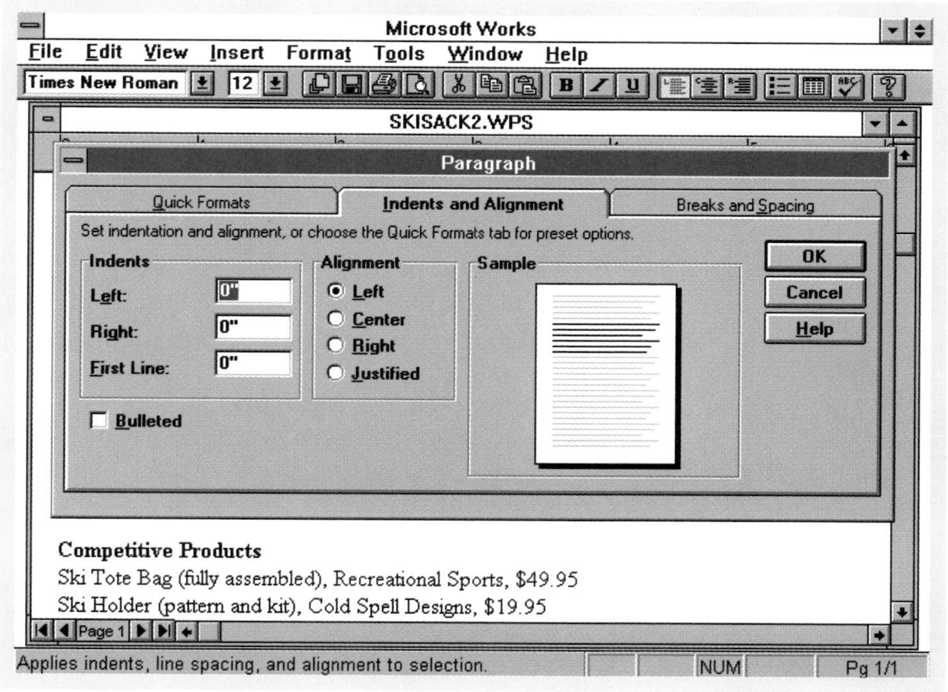

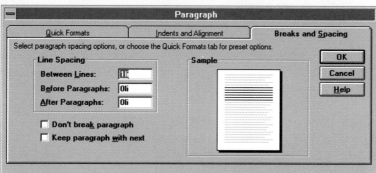

Changing the spacing

The default spacing between lines in the Word Processor is one line (single spacing). You can adjust this in a paragraph or the entire document with the **Breaks and Spacing tab** in the Paragraph dialog box, shown in Figure 3-3. The Breaks and Spacing tab includes options for setting the spacing between lines and the spacing before and after paragraphs. To format a group of lines for double spacing, you would select the lines, choose the **Paragraph command** from the Format menu, click the **Breaks and Spacing tab**, type **2** in the Between Lines text box, and click **OK**. You can also protect paragraphs from breaking across pages by choosing the **Don't break paragraph** or **Keep with next paragraph options**.

FIGURE 3-3: Adjust line spacing with the Breaks and Spacing tab

QUICK **TIP**

To select the entire document in the Word Processor, hold down **[Ctrl]** and click in the left margin.■

Changing the margins

The default page margins in the Word Processor are 1 inch on the top and bottom margins, and 1.25 inches on the left and right margins. You can change margins with the Page Setup command on the File menu. When you change margins, the Word Processor repaginates your document and adjusts line wrapping automatically. When you are evaluating which margin sizes to use, you may want to switch to Page Layout view to look at the actual margins on the page. Try changing the left and right margins in the product information sheet to 1 inch now.

1 Click **File**, then click **Page Setup**
The Page Setup dialog box displays. It contains three tabs: Margins; Source, Size, and Orientation; and Other Options.

2 Click the **Margins tab** if it is not already in front
The Margins tab, shown in Figure 3-4, contains six margin text boxes (one for each margin on the page), a sample window, three command buttons, and a Reset button (to restore the default settings). The first text box, Top margin, is currently selected.

3 Press **[Tab]** twice to select the Left margin text box
The Left margin text box is selected.

4 Type **1"** in the Left margin text box, then press **[Tab]**
1" displays in the Left margin text box. When you press the Tab key, the Right margin text box is selected and the change to the left margin is reflected in the sample window.

5 Type **1"** in the Right margin text box, then click **OK**
The Page Setup dialog box closes and the left and right margins in the product information sheet changes to 1 inch.

6 Click **View**, then click **Page Layout**
The document displays in Page Layout view. In Page Layout view, the document margins are visible, and if you scroll to the edge of the page with the scroll bar, you can also use the ruler to verify the measurement of the left and right margins.

7 Click the **left scroll arrow** to scroll to the left edge of the page
The edge of the page appears. Use the ruler to verify that the left margin is 1 inch. When you are satisfied with the size of the left margin, use the scroll bars and the ruler to check the size of the right margin.

8 Click **View**, then click **Normal**
The document view switches back to Normal view.

9 Click 🖫 to save your new margins

FIGURE 3-4:
The Margins tab in the
Page Setup dialog box

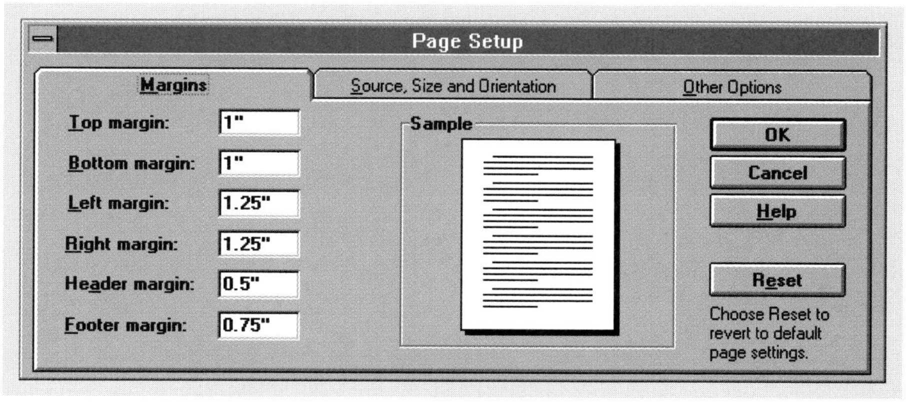

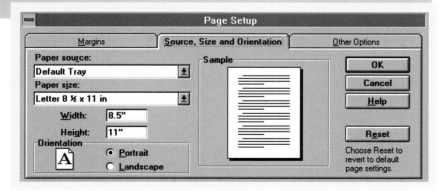

Changing the paper source, size, and orientation

In the Word Processor, the default paper settings are for an 8.5" × 11" sheet, oriented vertically like a portrait painting, and stored in the printer's main paper tray. You can change these settings with the **Source, Size, and Orientation tab** in the Page Setup dialog box, shown in Figure 3-5. The Paper Source drop-down list box in the tab presents one or more paper source options, including manual feed and envelope, depending on the type of printer you have. The Paper Size drop-down list box displays the paper types supported by Works. If you change the paper size in this list box, the page size in your document will be changed automatically and the document will be repaginated. Finally, the Orientation option buttons let you change the document from portrait (vertical) to landscape (horizontal) orientation, useful when a table or other information is too wide for the page you're using.

FIGURE 3-5: The Source, Size, and Orientation tab in the
Page Setup dialog box

QUICK **TIP**

For mechanical reasons, most laser printers require at least a ¼-inch margin around the page.■

Changing paragraph style

In the last lesson you learned how to change the margins of the entire document with the Page Setup command. You can also change the margins of individual paragraphs within the document, creating different **paragraph styles**. In the Word Processor you can format paragraphs with first line indents, hanging indents, bulleted lists, or quotations. You can also modify the alignment of text within paragraphs by using **tab stops**. You'll practice changing the paragraph style in the product information sheet now.

1   Select the paragraph describing the Cascade Ski Sack under the Description heading
    Use the scroll bars to bring the paragraph into view if necessary. The paragraph highlights when selected.

2   Click **Format**, then click **Paragraph**
    The Paragraph dialog box displays with three tabs visible.

3   Click the **Quick Formats tab**
    The Quick Formats tab displays, as shown in Figure 3-6. The Quick Formats tab lets you format the selected paragraph with five indenting styles. It applies your selection to the left margin or, if you have pressed the Tab key, to the current indent. The Quick Formats tab also contains a Sample window so you can see how your paragraph formatting will look in the document.

4   Click each of the five **paragraph style option buttons** one by one, looking in the Sample window to see what style each produces
    Each style has a different indenting scheme, giving the selected paragraph a different emphasis.

5   Click the **1st Line Indent option button**, then click **OK**
    The Paragraph dialog box closes and the Description paragraph is formatted for first line indent. Note that the left margin indicator on the ruler has split in half, and the top part has moved to the right ½ inch, indicating the paragraph is formatted for first line indent. (To change the size of the indent, you would drag the indicator left or right.)

    Now format the Competitive Products paragraph as a bulleted list.

6   Select the two lines under the Competitive Products heading and click the **Bullets button** 📇 on the toolbar
    The lines in the Competitive Products paragraph are formatted as a bulleted list. The Bullets button is the toolbar shortcut for choosing the Bulleted option button in the Quick Formats tab.

7   Click 💾 to save your paragraph formatting

FIGURE 3-6: The Quick Formats tab in the Paragraph dialog box

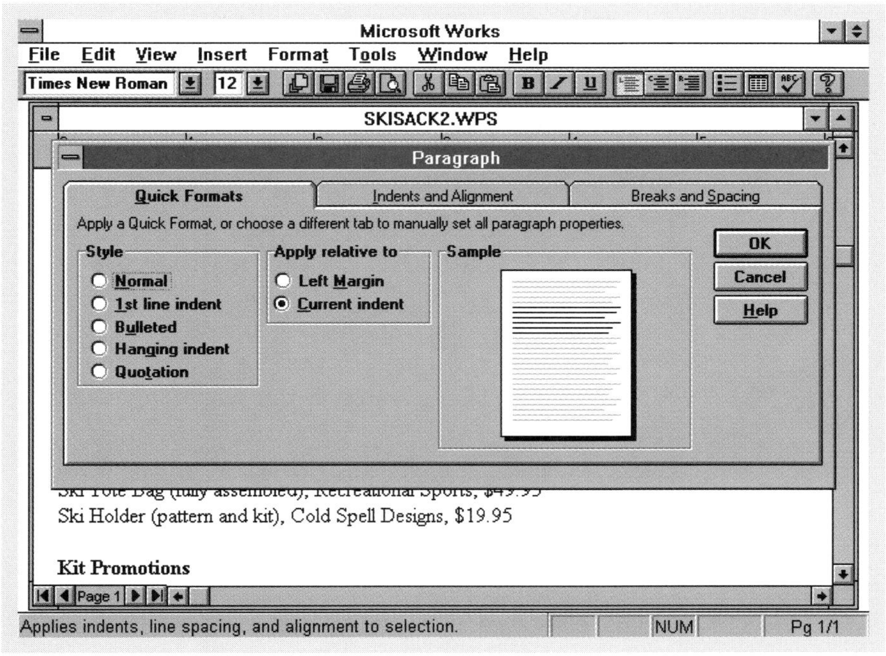

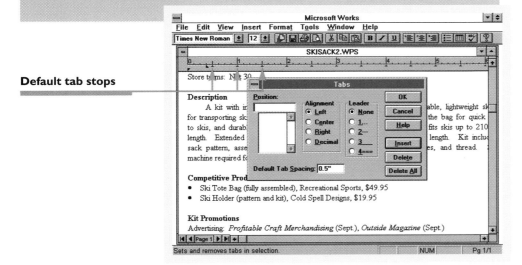

Changing tab stops

Each time you press the tab key in a paragraph, the insertion point moves one **tab stop** to the right. The default setting for tab stops in the Word Processor is every ½ inch. (Tab stops are indicated by little upside down T's on the ruler.) To change the frequency or spacing of the tab stops, choose the **Tabs** from the Format menu to display the Tabs dialog box. The Tabs dialog box, shown in Figure 3-7, can be used to place a tab stop at a specific position in the document, change the alignment of the text around a tab stop, place a leader line between tab stops, or delete tab stops you don't want. To customize more than one paragraph with the same tab stops you must select the paragraphs as a group before you choose the Tabs command.

Default tab stops

FIGURE 3-7: The Tabs dialog box

QUICK **TIP**

You can also double-click the ruler to bring up the Tabs dialog box.■

Inserting page breaks

The Word Processor automatically wraps text in a document to the next page when the last line of the current page is full. You can also manually enter a **page break** in a document with the Page Break command on the Insert menu. The **Page Break command** inserts a page break right after the cursor, and indicates the break with a dotted line across the page. Before you print a document that spans several pages you should preview the page breaks with the Print Preview command. Now you'll practice entering a page break in the product information sheet.

I Click the insertion pointer at the beginning of the line containing the Description header
The cursor blinks at the left margin, right before the word Description.

2 Click the **Insert menu,** then click **Page Break**
A page break is inserted into the document before the Description header, as shown in Figure 3-8.

A dotted line extends across the page, indicating a manual page break, and a double arrow displays on the left margin at the break point. (The double arrow displays at all page breaks; the dotted line displays only when the page break has been inserted manually.) The page number indicator in the lower-right corner of the screen shows that the cursor is resting on the second of two pages (Pg 2/2).

3 Click the **Print Preview button** 🔍 on the toolbar
The first page of the document displays in Print Preview, as shown in Figure 3-9. Notice that only the first two paragraphs of the product information sheet display on the page. The rest of the document displays on the next page, indicated by the darkened type in the Next button.

4 Click the **Next button** to view the second page of the document
The second page of the document displays in Print Preview. The second page is the last page of the document, so the type in the Next button is now dimmed. The previous page is still available, however, so the text of that button appears in a darkened type.

5 Click the **Cancel button** to return the document to Normal view
The product information sheet displays in the document window in Normal view. Now you'll delete the page break from the document.

6 Select the dotted line that indicates the page break by clicking in the left margin next to the line
The dotted line highlights.

7 Press **[Del]** to delete the page break
The dotted line and double arrow are removed from the document and the page number indicator shows that the cursor is in the first page of a one-page document (Pg 1/1).

8 Click 💾 to save your formatting changes

FIGURE 3-8: The Page Break command inserts a page break into the document

Page break dotted line

Break point double arrow

Page number indicator

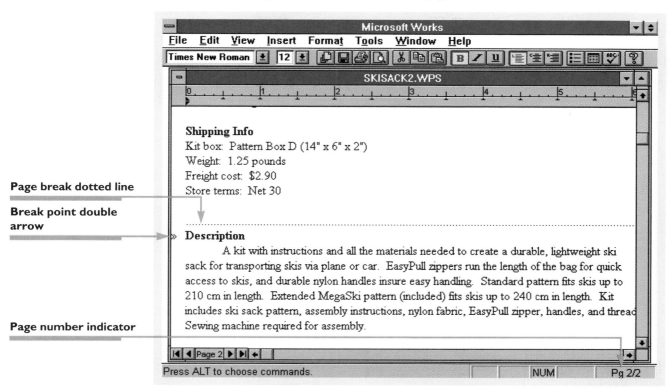

FIGURE 3-9: Viewing page breaks in Page Preview

Previous button

Next button

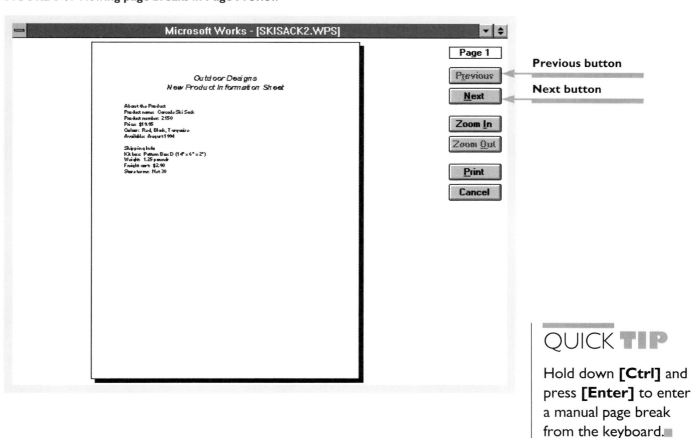

QUICK **TIP**

Hold down **[Ctrl]** and press **[Enter]** to enter a manual page break from the keyboard.■

Inserting headers and footers

When you print your document, you may want to add page numbers, the current date, or some other text to the top or the bottom of each page. You can add this information to your document with the Headers and Footers command on the View menu. A standard header or footer in Works is one line long and can contain one or several **header and footer codes**. Headers and footers don't appear in your document in Normal view, but can be examined in Print Preview or Page Layout view. You'll add a header and a footer to the product information sheet now.

1 Click **View**, then click **Headers and Footers**

The Headers and Footers dialog box appears, as shown in Figure 3-10. The Headers and Footers dialog box lets you enter a one-line header and a one-line footer that will appear on the top and bottom of every page in the document when it is printed. If a header or footer text box is left blank, a line will not be printed. You can also include special header and footer codes in your header and footer. These codes begin with an **ampersand (&)**, as listed in Table 3-3.

2 Type **&cOutdoor Designs Confidential** in the Header text box and press **[Tab]**

This header will center align the text Outdoor Designs Confidential at the top of each page in the document when it prints.

3 Type **&lPrinted on &d &rPage - &p** in the Footer text box

The first part of this footer will print the text *Printed on* and the current date at the left margin of the footer. The second part will print the text *Page -* and the page number at the right margin of the footer.

4 Click **OK** to add the header and footer to the document

The Headers and Footers dialog box closes. Notice that the header and footer do not display when the document is in Normal view. They display only in Print Preview and Page Layout view.

5 Click the **Print Preview button** 🖾 on the toolbar

The document displays in Page Preview, and the header and footer appear on the page in the location you indicated in the Headers and Footers dialog box.

6 Click the header with the zoom pointer

The header displays in larger type so it is easier to check.

7 Click the vertical scroll bar to display the footer

Now you can check the footer text, as shown in Figure 3-11. The Cascade Ski Sack product information sheet is now complete. If necessary, turn on your printer and verify that it is ready to print.

8 Click 🖫 to save your changes and click the **Print button** at the right side of the Print Preview window

The printer prints the product information sheet. Now save your changes and exit Works.

9 Click **File**, then click **Exit Works**

The SKISACK2.WPS document closes and the Works program exits. The Program Manager displays, with the Microsoft Works for Windows group highlighted.

WORKS 3 UNIT 3 ENHANCING THE LOOK OF YOUR DOCUMENTS

FIGURE 3-10:
The Headers and
Footers dialog box

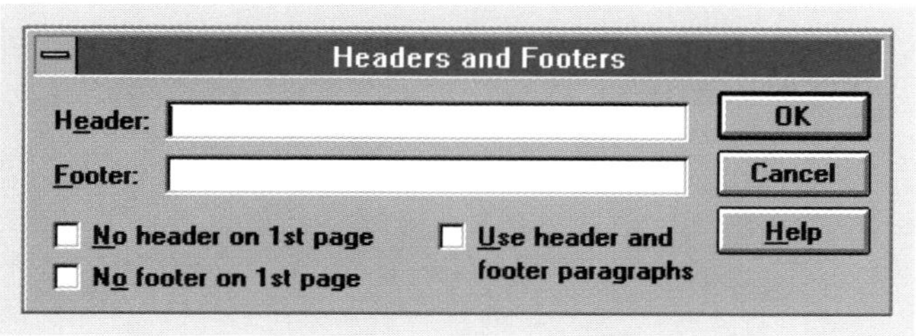

FIGURE 3-11:
The product informa-
tion sheet footer in
Print Preview

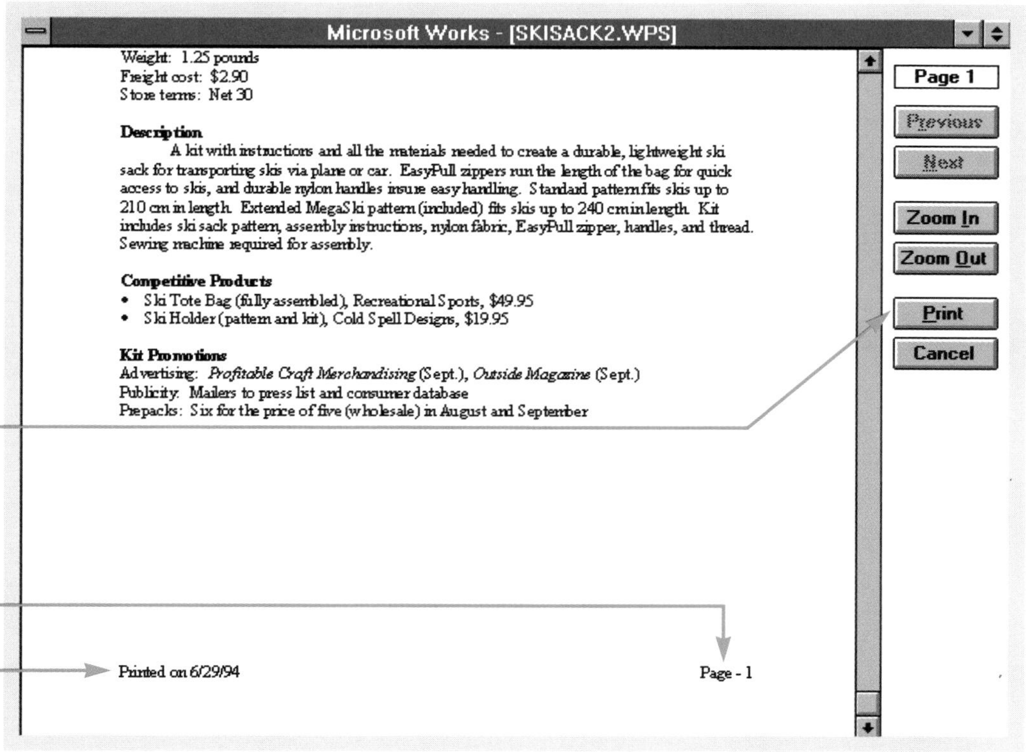

Print button

Page number in footer

Date in footer

TABLE 3-3: Useful header and footer codes

CODE	DESCRIPTION
&c	Aligns the characters that follow to the center of the page
&l	Aligns the characters that follow to the left margin
&r	Aligns the characters that follow to the right margin
&p	Prints the page number
&d	Prints the date when the file is printed
&t	Prints the time when the file is printed
&f	Prints the document file name
&&	Prints a single ampersand character

QUICK **TIP**

To start numbering pages with a number other than 1, choose the Page Setup command from the File menu, click the Other Options tab, then enter the number you want to start with in the 1st page number text box.∎

CONCEPTSREVIEW

The document shown in Figure 3-12 has been formatted with several Word Processor formatting commands. Match the commands from the Format list to the numbered elements in the document.

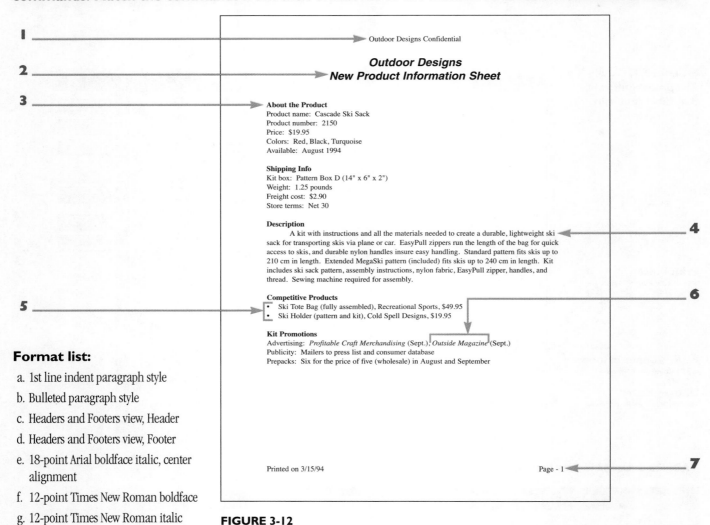

FIGURE 3-12

Format list:

a. 1st line indent paragraph style

b. Bulleted paragraph style

c. Headers and Footers view, Header

d. Headers and Footers view, Footer

e. 18-point Arial boldface italic, center alignment

f. 12-point Times New Roman boldface

g. 12-point Times New Roman italic

Match each header and footer code with the effect it creates.

8 &l

9 &p

10 &d

11 &c

12 &r

a. Prints the page number

b. Prints the date when the file is printed

c. Aligns the characters that follow to the right of the page

d. Aligns the characters that follow to the left of the page

e. Aligns the characters that follow to the center of the page

Select the best answer from the list of choices.

13 Which of the following is *not* an element in the Open dialog box?

    a. File Name text box

    b. Recently used file list box

    c. Find File button

    d. Drives drop-down list box

14 Which of the following is *not* a method for changing the style of selected text to boldface?

    a. Clicking the Bold button on the toolbar

    b. Holding down [Ctrl] and pressing [B]

    c. Changing the color of the text to blue

    d. Clicking the Bold checkbox in the Font and Style dialog box

15 What does the **T** symbol mean when it is listed next to a font in the Font Name list box?

   a. The font is a TrueType font

   b. The font can only be displayed in Works

   c. The font was designed by Technology Typeworks

   d. The font only works with dot-matrix printers

16 One "point" is equivalent to which of the following measurements?

   a. 1 VGA screen pixel

   b. ½ of an inch

   c. 210 centimeters

   d. 1 ounce

17 If the alignment of text in a paragraph is justified, what is true about the text?

   a. It is aligned to the right margin

   b. It is aligned to the left margin

   c. It is aligned to the center of the page

   d. It is aligned to both the right and left margins

18 Which of the tabs in the Paragraph dialog box would you use to change the spacing of a paragraph from single spacing to double spacing?

   a. The Double Spacing tab

   b. The Indents and Alignments tab

   c. The Breaks and Spacing tab

   d. The Quick Formats tab

19 What are the default page margins in the Word Processor?

   a. ½ inch all around the document

   b. 1 inch all around the document

   c. 1.5 inches on the top and bottom margins, 2 inches on the left and right margins

   d. 1 inch on the top and bottom margins, 1.25 inches on the left and right margins

20 Which of the following is *not* a paragraph style option in the Quick Formats tab of the Paragraph dialog box?

   a. 1st line indent

   b. Footnote

   c. Bulleted

   d. Hanging indent

21 The default tab stops in the Word Processor are:

   a. Every ½ inch

   b. Every inch

   c. Every 1.5 inches

   d. There are no default tab stops

22 How do you enter a manual page break in a document?

   a. Choose the Page Break command from the Insert menu

   b. Click Format on the main menu bar, then click New Page

   c. Hold down [Ctrl] and press [Shift]

   d. Double-click in the left margin

23 How do you delete a manual page break?

   a. Double-click the page break

   b. Click the left mouse button

   c. Select the page break and press [Del]

   d. Select the page break and press [PageDown]

24 After you have entered headers and footers with the Headers and Footers command, they appear in which document view?

   a. Normal view

   b. Page Layout view

   c. Draft view

   d. They never appear in the document

25 Which of the following footers will print the centered text *Page 1* at the bottom of the first page?

   a. && Page 1 &&

   b. &l* Page &p *

   c. &c*&p Page *

   d. &c* Page &p *

APPLICATIONSREVIEW

1 Start Works and open the file UNIT_03.WPS located on your Student Disk in drive A, and save the file as SKISACK3.WPS.

   a. Double-click the Microsoft Works program icon.

   b. In the Startup dialog box, click the Open An Existing Document button.

   c. In the Open dialog box, click a: in the Drives list box (or b: if your Student Disk is in drive B), and double-click a:\ or b:\ in the Directories list box. Double-click UNIT_03.WPS in the File Name list box.

   d. Click File, then click Save As. In the Save As dialog box, type **my_files\skisack3** in the File Name text box and click OK.

   e. When the dialog box asks if you will be saving to a different floppy disk, click No to save the file with a new name.

2 Format the top two lines of the document to Courier New font, then change the font size to 18 points and the style to underline. Format the five headings in the document with italic.

a. Select the top two lines with the mouse, then change the font to Courier New with the Font Name drop-down list box on the toolbar.

b. Change the font size to 18 points, using the Font Size drop-down list box on the toolbar.

c. With the top two lines still selected, change the font style to underline with the underline button on the toolbar.

d. Select each of the five header lines in the document one at a time and change the font style to italic.

3 Right align the top two lines of the document and format the Description paragraph with justified alignment.

a. Select the top two lines of the document and click the Right align button on the toolbar.

b. Select the Description paragraph, click Format on the main menu bar, then click Paragraph. Click the Indents and Alignments tab and click the Justified option button.

4 Change the top, bottom, left, and right margins in the document to 1.5 inches.

a. Click File on the main menu bar, then click Page Setup and click the Margins tab.

b. Type **1.5"** in the top four text boxes and click OK.

c. Verify the margin settings with the Page Layout command on the View menu and the ruler.

5 Change the paragraph style of the Description paragraph to hanging indent, and format the Competitive Products paragraph as a bulleted list.

a. Select the paragraph under the Description heading and choose the Paragraph command from the Format menu. Click the Quick Format tab to display the paragraph style options.

b. Click the Hanging indent option button, then click OK to format the Description paragraph with hanging indent style.

c. Select the paragraph under the Competitive Products heading and click the Bulleted List button on the toolbar to format the lines as a bulleted list.

6 Insert a page break into the document after the Description paragraph, then view the document with Print Preview.

a. Move the cursor to the blank line beneath the Description paragraph.

b. Click Insert on the main menu bar, then click Page Break. A page break is inserted into the document beneath the cursor, indicated by the dotted line.

c. Click the Print Preview button on the toolbar and examine the first page of the document. Click the Next button to view the second page, then click Cancel to return to Normal view.

d. Select the page break and press [Del] to remove it from the document.

7 Insert *Cascade Ski Sack* as a header in the document, printed in the center at the top of the page. Insert *Page* and the page number as a footer in the document, printed in the center at the bottom of the page.

a. Click View on the main menu bar, then click Headers and Footers.

b. Type **&cCascade Ski Sack** in the header text box and type **&cPage &p** in the footer text box. Click OK to add the header and footer to the document.

c. View the document in Print Preview to be sure you typed the headers and footers correctly.

INDEPENDENT
CHALLENGE

The Options command on the Tools menu displays a dialog box that lets you choose how Works appears on the computer. For example, you can choose the units of measure on the ruler (inches, centimeters, picas, etc.), the dictionary used by the spell checker (American or British English), and the characteristics of several keyboard and mouse operations, as well as key parameters for each Works application. If you have any questions about which settings to use, ask your lab instructor or your dealer.

To complete this Independent Challenge:

1 Open the Options dialog box to see the choices in each category.

2 Use the Works on-line help if you don't understand any category. If you aren't sure how an option affects an application, just select the option, then open the application and watch carefully to see how it works. (Make sure you make a note of the original settings, so you can return to them when you finish.)

UNIT 4

OBJECTIVES

▶ Open the Outdoor Designs kite flyer

▶ Create multiple columns

▶ Place borders around text

▶ Insert WordArt

▶ Insert ClipArt

▶ Insert footnotes

▶ Search for text

▶ Verify page layout and print

Getting STARTED WITH DESKTOP PUBLISHING

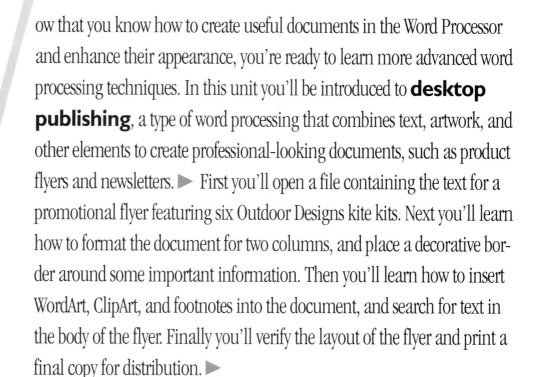

Now that you know how to create useful documents in the Word Processor and enhance their appearance, you're ready to learn more advanced word processing techniques. In this unit you'll be introduced to **desktop publishing**, a type of word processing that combines text, artwork, and other elements to create professional-looking documents, such as product flyers and newsletters. ▶ First you'll open a file containing the text for a promotional flyer featuring six Outdoor Designs kite kits. Next you'll learn how to format the document for two columns, and place a decorative border around some important information. Then you'll learn how to insert WordArt, ClipArt, and footnotes into the document, and search for text in the body of the flyer. Finally you'll verify the layout of the flyer and print a final copy for distribution. ▶

Opening the Outdoor Designs kite flyer

You have been assigned the project of desktop publishing a one-page promotional flyer for Outdoor Designs' six kite kits. To help you out, Frasier has given you a disk with the text of the flyer on it (the name of the file is UNIT_04.WPS), and has requested that the flyer be in two-column format. He has also inserted reminders in the document where you should add borders and art to enhance the appeal of the flyer. You'll open UNIT_04.WPS from your Student Disk now and save it under a different filename.

1 **Start Works from the Program Manager**
The Startup dialog box displays.

2 **Put your Student Disk in drive A (or drive B), then click the Open an Existing Document button**
The Open dialog box displays.

3 **Click a: (or b:) in the Drives drop-down list box**

4 **Double-click a: (or b:) in the Directories list box**
Works displays the files in the root directory of drive A in the File Name list box. UNIT_04.WPS displays in the list.

5 **Double-click UNIT_04.WPS to open the file in the Word Processor**
The dialog box closes and after a moment the text for the kite kit promotional flyer displays in a window in the Word Processor, as shown in Figure 4-1. Now save the file with a different name to protect the original.

6 **Click the File menu, then click Save As**
The Save As dialog box displays.

7 **Type kites2 in the File Name text box, then double-click the my_files directory in the Directories list box and press [Enter]**
Works displays a dialog box asking if you want to save the file to a different floppy disk.

8 **Click No**
Works saves the new file, KITES2.WPS, on your Student Disk in the MY_FILES directory.

FIGURE 4-1:
The text for the
kite flyer

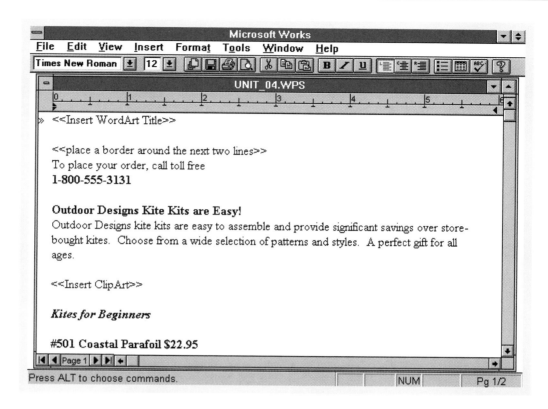

The File Organizer WorksWizard

If you have trouble locating a file you want to open, click the **Find File button**
in the Open dialog box and search for the file with the File Organizer WorksWizard.
The File Organizer WorksWizard prompts you for part or all of the filename you're
looking for, the drive you want to search on, and the approximate time the file was
last worked on, as shown in Figure 4-2. The File Organizer WorksWizard uses this
information to locate the file on disk (if possible), and to let you preview, open,
rename, move, copy, or delete it.

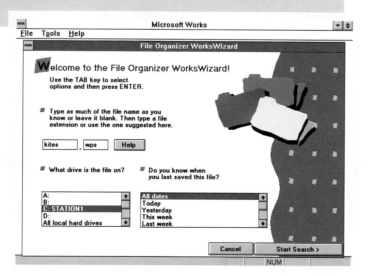

FIGURE 4-2: The File Organizer WorksWizard

QUICK TIP

To open a file and
prevent it from being
modified, click the
**Read Only check
box** in the Open dia-
log box before you
open the file. When a
file has been opened
as read only, you can
edit the file, but your
changes can only be
saved under a new
filename.■

Creating multiple columns

The Word Processor lets you divide your document vertically into two or more **columns** of text. Each page in your document must have the same number of columns, and they can be viewed in their proper orientation in Page Layout view and in Print Preview. You'll format the kite flyer for two columns now.

STEPS

1   Click the Format menu, then click Columns
The Columns dialog box displays, as shown in Figure 4-3. It lets you specify the number of columns in your document, the distance between the columns, and the presence of a dividing line between the columns. A Sample window gives you an indication of how your document will look after column formatting.

2   Type 2 and press [Tab]
The number *2* displays in the Number of columns text box and the highlight moves to the Space between text box. A two-column document displays in the sample window.

3   Press [Tab] to accept the measurement between the columns
The highlight moves to the Line Between check box.

4   Click the Line Between check box to remove the line between the columns
The dividing line disappears from the sample window.

5   Click OK to format the document with the column selections you have indicated
Works displays a dialog box recommending that you work with the document in Page Layout view so you can see the columns as they will be printed (in Normal and Draft views you don't see the columns side by side).

6   Click Yes to switch to Page Layout view now
The dialog box closes and the document displays in two-column format in Page Layout view, as shown in Figure 4-4. Notice that the margins in the document have changed (indicated by the right and left margin markers on the Ruler). Text now wraps within the columns and flows from the bottom of the first column to the top of the second column.

7   Read the kite flyer
Take a few moments to read the kite flyer, using the scroll bars to read parts of the document that don't display in the window. Notice the four instructions surrounded by double arrows. These are the layout and art requests from Frasier, which you'll be working on throughout the unit.

8   Click 🖫 to save your formatting changes

FIGURE 4-3: The Columns dialog box

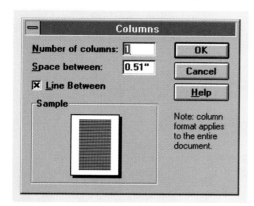

FIGURE 4-4: The kite flyer in two-column format

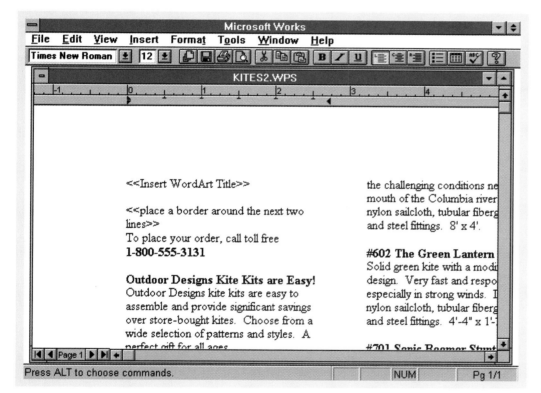

QUICK **TIP**

Works requires that your entire document have the same number of columns. However, you can create a report containing different column types by creating the columns in separate documents and assembling them later.■

Placing borders around text

The Word Processor lets you add decorative borders that emphasize words and paragraphs in your document. Selected text can be surrounded with one or more lines on the top, bottom, left, or right edges of the text, or boxed with a frame that outlines the text. Now you'll place a box around the two lines Frasier indicated at the top of the kite flyer, then center the text inside the box.

1 Use the **line pointer** to select the two lines with the toll-free phone number information
Scroll to the top of the document if it is not already visible. The words *To place your order, call toll free 1-800-555-3131* highlight. Before you format text with a border, you must select it. Table 4-1 includes some useful shortcuts for selecting blocks of text with the keyboard.

2 Click the **Format menu**, then click **Border**
The Border dialog box displays, as shown in Figure 4-5. It lets you select the border and line styles you want to include around the selected text. You can click one or more Border check boxes, but only one Line Style option button. Note that clicking the Outline check box is equivalent to clicking the Top, Bottom, Left, and Right check boxes. The gray setting in the Border check boxes means that multiple paragraphs have been selected, and they have different borders.

3 Click the **Outline check box**
An *x* appears in the Outline check box.

4 Click the **Bold Line Style option button**
The Bold option button is selected.

5 Click **OK** to place the border around the selected text
The Border dialog box disappears and a bold box displays around the selected text. Now center-align the selected text in the box.

6 Click the **Center-Align button** 🖺 on the toolbar
The selected text aligns to the center of the column, which is also the center of the box. Now delete the reminder tag Frasier left for you above the box (the tag beginning with the words *place a border around*).

7 Select the **reminder tag** and press **[Del]**
The reminder tag is deleted. The completed text border is shown in Figure 4-6.

8 Click 💾 to save the border formatting

TABLE 4-1:
Shortcuts for selecting blocks of text with the keyboard

TO SELECT	PRESS
A word	[F8] twice
A sentence	[F8] three times
A paragraph	[F8] four times
The entire document	[F8] five times
Previous selection level	[Shift][F8]

FIGURE 4-5: The Border dialog box

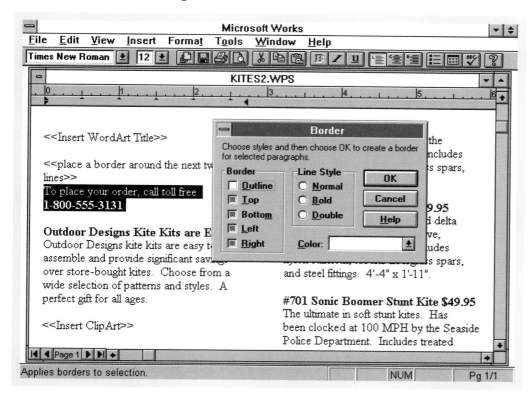

QUICK **TIP**

The Border dialog box includes a Color drop-down list box that lets you change the color of the border. This formatting option is useful if you have a color printer or if you want to emphasize part of your document on the screen.■

FIGURE 4-6: Text emphasized with a bold outline border

Completed text border

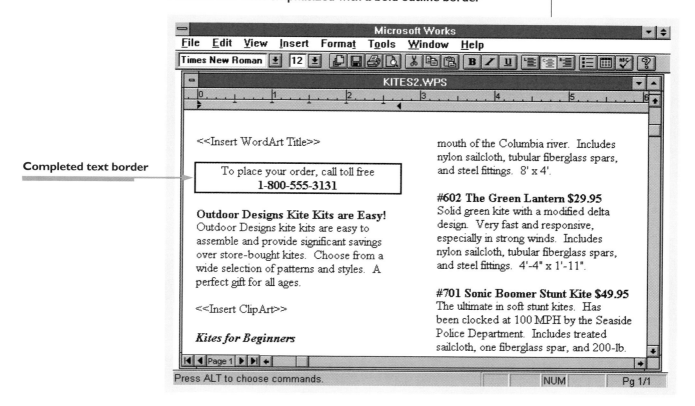

Inserting WordArt

The Word Processor allows you to insert several types of electronic art into your document. In this lesson you will learn how to insert **WordArt**, a type of stylized text created by the WordArt accessory, into the Outdoor Designs kite flyer. The WordArt accessory provides sophisticated text formatting features that aren't available in the Word Processor. In this lesson you'll learn how to add shadow to text, and change the text point size and style. The WordArt accessory contains several additional features that we won't discuss in this lesson; to learn more about them consult the WordArt on-line help. Now you'll use the WordArt accessory to add a title to the Outdoor Designs kite flyer.

1   Select the reminder tag **<<Insert WordArt Title>>** and press **[Del]**
    The reminder tag is deleted from the document and the cursor blinks on the blank line at the top of the flyer.

2   Click the **Insert menu,** then click **WordArt**
    The WordArt accessory starts and the WordArt window displays on the screen, as shown in Figure 4-7. Notice that the Word Processor menu bar and toolbar have been replaced by the WordArt menu bar and toolbar. The interface elements of the WordArt accessory are labeled in Figure 4-7. The WordArt window appears in the document, near the place where the WordArt will be inserted. This window is where you type the text you want to use as a title for the flyer. The text in both the window and in your document is currently *Your Text Here*.

3   Type **Outdoor Designs Kite Kits** and click the **Update Display button** in the WordArt window
    The text you entered into the WordArt window is inserted at the top of your document.

4   Click the **Bold button** ▣ on the toolbar
    The style of the WordArt text changes to boldface.

5   Click the **Shadow button** ▣ on the toolbar, then click the shadow style in the center of the right-hand column
    A 3D shadow displays behind the WordArt text.

6   Click the **Font Size drop-down list box,** then click **16**
    The font size 16 points is selected, and a dialog box displays asking if you'd like to resize the WordArt text frame to fit the enlarged text.

7   Click **Yes** to resize the WordArt frame
    The font size of the WordArt changes to 16 points and the resized WordArt displays at the top of the document.

8   Click in the text of the flyer, somewhere outside of the WordArt window and the WordArt text frame
    The WordArt window disappears and the Word Processor menu and toolbar display again, as shown in Figure 4-8. When you finish designing your WordArt, simply click somewhere else in the document and continue working. When you want to work on the WordArt again, double-click on the WordArt text and the WordArt accessory will start again.

9   Click ▣ to save your document to disk with the new WordArt

Font Size drop-down list box

FIGURE 4-7: The WordArt accessory

WordArt menu bar

WordArt toolbar

WordArt window

WordArt text

Bold button

Shadow button

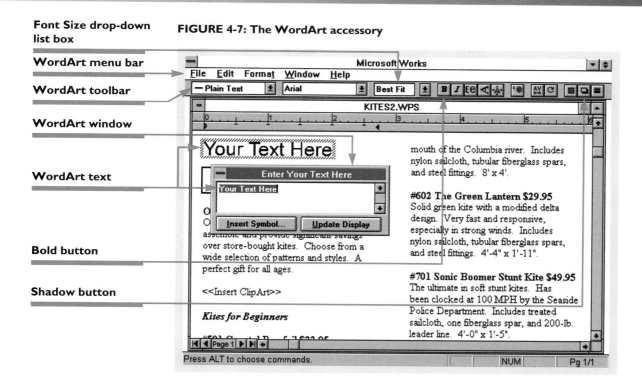

FIGURE 4-8: The completed WordArt in the kite flyer

Completed WordArt

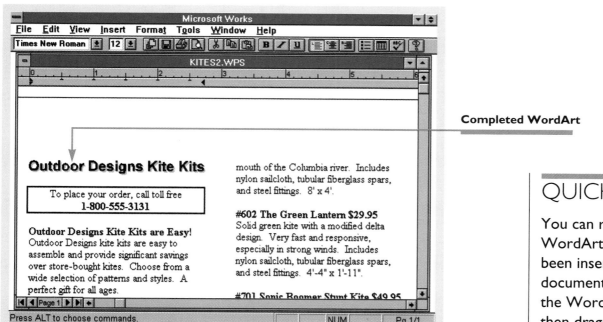

QUICK **TIP**

You can resize WordArt that has been inserted into a document by clicking the WordArt frame, then dragging the right or left edge of the frame with the sizing pointer. To remove unwanted WordArt from a document, highlight the WordArt and press **[Del]**.■

Inserting ClipArt

Another type of electronic art that you can insert into a document is **ClipArt**. ClipArt is ready-to-use art stored in the ClipArt Gallery. Works includes about three dozen of these graphic images in different shapes, sizes, and colors. Several of them are related to seasons, holidays, and business activities, and many are general-purpose enough to add appeal to almost any document. You can also purchase additional ClipArt images and add them to the ClipArt Gallery to increase your selection. Now you'll add two pieces of ClipArt to the Outdoor Designs kite flyer.

I Select the reminder tag **<<Insert ClipArt>>** in the first column and press **[Del]**
Scroll to the reminder text if it is not visible on the screen. This reminder tag, about one-third of the way down the first column, is Frasier's note to insert ClipArt related to the beginners' kite kits. After you have deleted the reminder, the cursor should be blinking on a blank line, with a blank line above it and below it. (If it is not this way now, make it so.)

2 Click the **Insert menu,** then click **ClipArt**
The ClipArt Gallery displays, as shown in Figure 4-9. The ClipArt Gallery gives you access to all the ClipArt images stored in the \msworks\clipart directory on your hard disk. Works normally includes 36 images in the ClipArt Gallery, accessible through the ClipArt list box. By default the images in all subject categories are displayed, but you can narrow the selection by clicking a different category in the Category list box. You'll select the summer ClipArt in the ClipArt Gallery. (The summer ClipArt is in the shape of a diamond, and has a sailboat on it.)

3 Click the **down scroll arrow** on the ClipArt list box scroll bar
The ClipArt list box scrolls and the summer ClipArt appears at the bottom of the ClipArt list box.

4 Double-click the **summer ClipArt**
The ClipArt Gallery closes and the summer ClipArt displays in the document, as shown in Figure 4-10. The image displays in the first column (where the cursor was), with text above and below it, and in full color. (When it is printed it will appear in black and gray, unless you have a color printer.) To change the alignment of the ClipArt in the column, you would click one of the alignment buttons on the toolbar. Now add the second ClipArt image to the document.

5 Scroll up and to the right, until the second **<<Insert ClipArt>>** reminder tag appears
The reminder tag is at the top of the second column.

6 Select the reminder tag and delete it, then place the cursor at the top of the second column
The blinking cursor appears at the top of the second column.

7 Click **Insert**, click **ClipArt**, then click the **down scroll arrow** on the **ClipArt list box scroll bar** three times
The ClipArt Gallery displays and the ClipArt list box scrolls. Now you'll insert the ClipArt image that looks like a fireworks rocket (the second image from the left on the bottom row).

8 Double-click the **fireworks ClipArt**
The ClipArt Gallery closes and the fireworks ClipArt displays in the document, at the top of the second column.

9 Click 🖫 to save the ClipArt in the document

FIGURE 4-9: The ClipArt Gallery

Category list box

ClipArt list box

FIGURE 4-10: The summer ClipArt in the Outdoor Designs kite flyer

Summer ClipArt in flyer

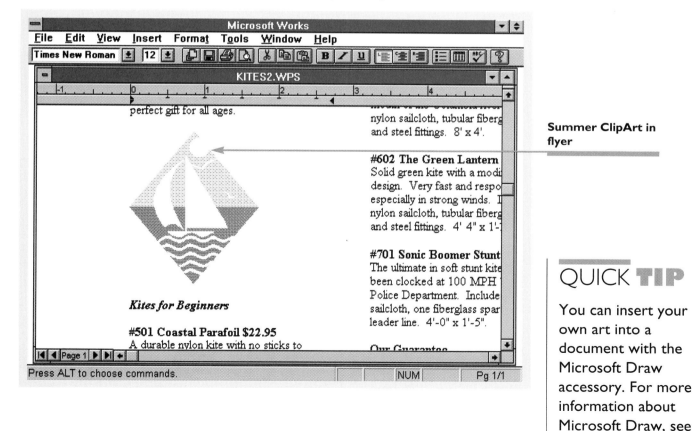

QUICK TIP

You can insert your own art into a document with the Microsoft Draw accessory. For more information about Microsoft Draw, see Unit 12.■

Inserting footnotes

Did you ever want to add some "fine print" at the bottom of a page in a document? Works lets you add margin notes or citations to the bottom of a page with the Footnote command. Works adds the footnote to your document automatically and handles all layout issues related to the footnote at the bottom of the page and the footnote reference in the text. You can also format the font and style of the footnote after it has been entered in Page Layout view. You'll use the Footnote command now, to add some "fine print" to the kite flyer.

STEPS

1 Scroll to the description of the Sonic Boomer Stunt Kite, near the end of the second column

The paragraph describing the Sonic Boomer displays on the screen. Lucinda in the Outdoor Designs legal department has suggested that the statement *Has been clocked at 100 MPH by the Seaside Police Department* could be construed as a product endorsement by the Seaside Police Department and the City of Seaside. To clarify this issue, you have been asked to add a footnote that acts as a disclaimer to the sentence in question.

2 Click directly after the period in the sentence *Has been clocked at 100 MPH by the Seaside Police Department*

The cursor blinks after the period in the sentence.

3 Click the **Insert menu,** then click **Footnote**

The Footnote dialog box displays on the screen. If you use numbered footnotes in a document such as a term paper, Works automatically keeps track of the numbering for you. (The Footnote WorksWizard, accessed through the Use WorksWizard button, is also helpful for term papers. It prompts you for information about your source, then creates the footnote using accepted footnote conventions.) Because you're just inserting one footnote into this flyer, you'll use the Character mark option button to supply a custom footnote reference.

4 Click the **Character mark option button** and press **[Tab]**

The Character mark option button is selected and the cursor blinks in the Mark text box.

5 Type ***** and click **OK** to use the asterisk (*) as the footnote reference

The Footnote dialog box closes, and a superscript (slightly raised) asterisk is inserted into the document at the insertion point. The cursor displays at the bottom of the screen in the footnote area. This is where you'll enter the text of your footnote. (Note that the footnote area only displays in Page Layout view and Print Preview.) To have all your footnotes printed at the end of your document as **endnotes**, you would click **Page Setup** on the File menu, click the **Other Options tab**, then click the **Print Footnotes at End of Document check box**.

6 Type **Kite not endorsed by the Seaside Police Department**

The text of the footnote displays in the footnote area. Next you'll change the size of the footnote to 8 point and the style of the footnote to italic.

7 Select the footnote with the mouse, then click the **Italic button** 📐

The footnote style changes to italic.

8 Change the point size to **8** with the **Size drop-down list box** on the toolbar

The point size is reduced to 8 point. (Good fine print, just like in the car ads.) The completed footnote (with the reference character in text) is shown in Figure 4-11.

9 Click 💾 to save your footnote changes to disk

FIGURE 4-11: The completed footnote in the kite flyer

Footnote reference character

Completed footnote

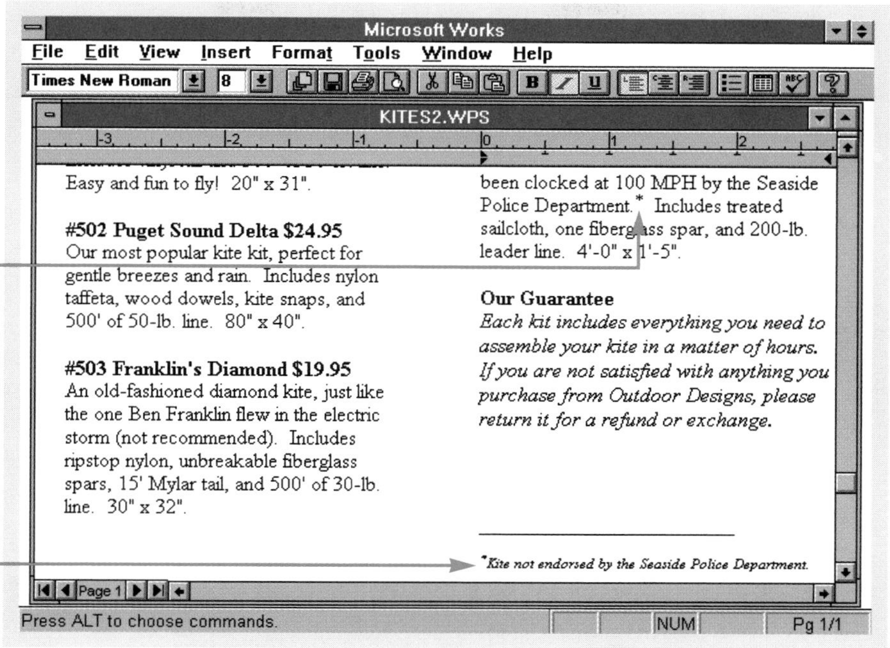

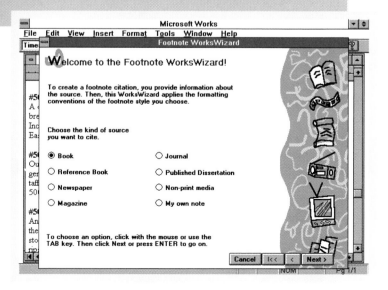

The Footnote WorksWizard

The Footnote WorksWizard helps you style your footnote according to accepted footnote conventions. If you don't have a style manual handy, the Footnote WorksWizard helps you get it right automatically. To use the Footnote WorksWizard, place the cursor where you want the footnote reference to appear in the text, choose Footnote from the Insert menu, then click the Use WorksWizard button in the Footnote dialog box. The Footnote WorksWizard displays, as shown in Figure 4-12. Provide the information requested by each screen in the WorksWizard, then click the Done button to insert the footnote into the document.

FIGURE 4-12: The Footnote WorksWizard

QUICK **TIP**

To delete a footnote from a document, select the **footnote reference mark** in the body of the text and delete it. The corresponding footnote is deleted and the remaining footnotes are renumbered automatically.■

Searching for text

Frasier, Outdoor Designs' marketing manager, has decided to change the pricing scheme for all kite kits so that prices end with 99 cents, rather than 95 cents. The pricing label for each of the kite kits is being changed, and Frasier has asked you to update the pricing in the kite flyer. To make this comprehensive change in the document, you will use the Word Processor Replace command to find each occurrence of 95 in the document and change it to 99.

1 **Move the cursor to the top of the document, right before the WordArt title**
Use the scroll bars if necessary to bring the top of the first column into view, then click before the WordArt.

2 **Click the Edit menu, then click Replace**
The Replace dialog box displays. It contains the Find What and Replace With text fields, the Match Whole Word Only and Match Case check boxes, and several command buttons.

3 **Type 95 in the Find What text field and press [Tab]**
You enter the text you are searching for in the Find What text field. The text can be several words in a sentence or, as in this case, a few numbers from a price.

4 **Type 99 in the Replace With text field**
You enter the text you want to use in the Replace With text field. Typing 99 means you want to replace 95 with 99.

5 **Click the Find Next button**
Works starts searching for 95 in the document, beginning at the top of the flyer where you placed the cursor. The first 95 it finds is in the description for the Coastal Parafoil kite, as shown in Figure 4-13.

6 **Click the Replace button to replace 95 with 99**
The price of the Coastal Parafoil kite changes from $22.95 to $22.99, and Works highlights the next 95 in the document. Now you'll change the remaining prices in the document.

7 **Click the Replace button five more times, pausing after each click to verify that you are changing a price in the document and not something else**
Each time you click Replace, the price changes and the next occurrence of 95 highlights. After the last price has been changed, the Replace button in the dialog box dims, indicating there are no more occurrences of 95 in the document.

8 **Click the Close button to end the search**
The Replace dialog box closes and the search ends. Take a moment to scroll through the document and verify that the prices have changed.

9 **Click 🖫 to save your price changes**

FIGURE 4-13: Changing 95 to 99 with the Replace dialog box

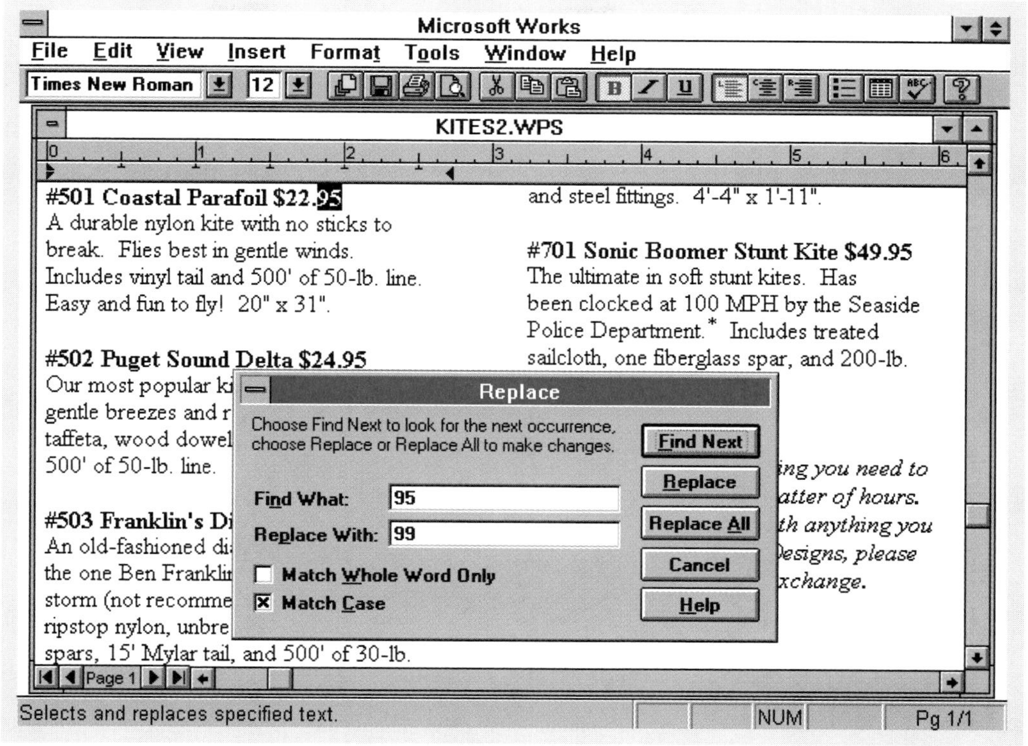

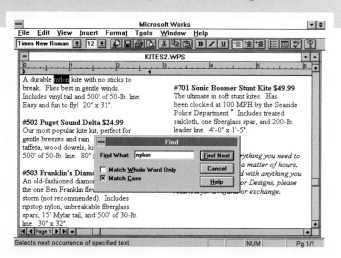

The Find command

The **Find command** on the Edit menu is similar to the Replace command, but it searches for text without replacing it with anything. The Find command is useful when you want to locate a particular word or phrase in a document, but you don't know where it is. To use the Find command, click **Find** on the Edit menu, type the word you're looking for in the Find What text box, then click **Find Next**. If Works finds the word, it highlights it in the document window. To search for the word again in the document, click **Find Next** again. The Find dialog box is shown in Figure 4-14.

TROUBLE?

Be careful with the Replace All button in the Replace dialog box. When you click Replace All, Works makes all the substitutions in your document at once, without letting you preview them first. Use the Replace button instead, so you know just what changes you're making.■

FIGURE 4-14: The Find dialog box

Verifying page layout and printing

When you finish desktop publishing a document, it is often useful to spend a few minutes examining the column breaks and page breaks in the document, just to make sure that everything fits and looks good. After all, when you add sophisticated art, borders, and footnotes to your creation, you want to make sure everything is correct before you print a final copy. You'll take a few minutes now to verify the page layout of the finished kite flyer, then print a final copy for distribution.

1 Click the **Print Preview button** 🖺 on the toolbar
The Outdoor Designs kite flyer appears in Print Preview, as shown in Figure 4-15. Take a moment to size up the layout of the document, evaluating how the various elements work together on the page. Page layout can be very subjective, so sometimes it helps to ask yourself a few questions about how the document looks. How do the different elements work together on the page? Will the reader's attention be drawn to the right things? Should any of the items be rearranged?

2 Verify that the entire flyer fits on one page
You want the contents of the kite flyer to fit on one page, without any text wrapping to subsequent pages. Check to see if the Next and Previous buttons are dimmed. If they are, then the document is exactly one page long. If everything doesn't fit, this would be a good time to edit it down to size.

3 Verify that the margins and columns are appropriate for the flyer
If the text looks out of proportion on the page, a solution could include changing the width of the margins or columns. Changing these variables can also help you fill up a short page or make room for extra text. To change document margins, you would use the Page Setup command. To change column margins, you would use the Columns command.

4 Verify that the footnotes and other items are in the right places
Use the zoom pointer to examine the document and verify that the footnote is in the right place. After you've verified the page layout of your document, you're ready to print!

5 Turn on your printer and prepare it for printing
If necessary, ask your instructor or lab manager for help.

6 Click the **Print button** in Print Preview
The printer produces the final copy of the kite flyer, shown in Figure 4-16.

7 Click 🖫 to save any changes

8 Click **File** on the main menu bar, then click **Exit Works**
The KITES2.WPS document closes and the Works program exits. The Program Manager displays, with the Microsoft Works for Windows group highlighted.

FIGURE 4-15: The final kite flyer in Print Preview

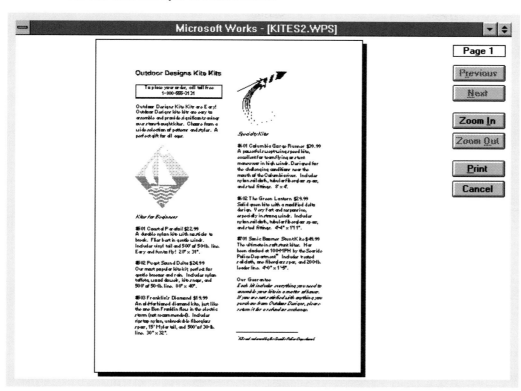

FIGURE 4-16: Printout of the Outdoor Designs kite flyer

QUICK TIP

To change the size of a piece of art in the Word Processor, select the art, then click the **Picture/Object command** on the Format menu. When the Picture/Object dialog box displays, click the **Size tab** and type the specific size or scaling percentage you want.∎

CONCEPTSREVIEW

**Label each of the elements
of the WordArt accessory,
as shown in Figure 4-17.**

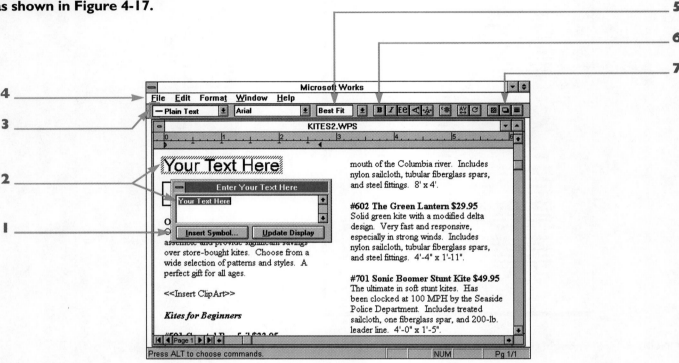

FIGURE 4-17

**Match each keyboard operation with the
amount of text it selects in the document
window.**

8 Press [F8] twice

9 Press [F8] three times

10 Press [F8] four times

11 Press [F8] five times

12 [Shift][F8]

a. A sentence

b. A paragraph

c. The previous selection level

d. The entire document

e. The word in which the cursor
is located

Select the best answer from the list of choices.

13 Which of the following should *not* be considered a desktop
publishing activity?

a. Adding electronic art to a document

b. Combining text, art, and footnotes in multiple columns

c. Using Print Preview to verify page layout and design

d. Opening a document created by another user

14 Which of the following file operations *cannot* be accom-
plished with the File Organizer WorksWizard?

a. Searching for a file

b. Opening a file

c. Creating a subdirectory

d. Deleting a file

15 Which of the following column characteristics *cannot* be
changed with the Columns dialog box?

a. Number of columns in the document

b. Distance between the outside column margins and the edge
of the page

c. Distance between the columns

d. Presence of a dividing line between the columns

16 Which document view is best suited for creating multiple-
column documents?

a. Normal view

b. Page Layout view

c. Draft view

d. Print Preview

17 How would you place a box around text that had been selected in the Word Processor?

   a. Click the Outline check box in the Border dialog box

   b. Click the Top check box in the Border dialog box

   c. Click the Bulleted check box in the Indents and Alignments tab in the Paragraph dialog box

   d. Hold down [Shift] and click the Center-align button on the toolbar

18 Which of the following is *not* a Line Style option in the Border dialog box?

   a. Normal

   b. Bold

   c. Dotted

   d. Double

19 Which of the following buttons would you click in WordArt to add shadow styling to text?

   a. **B**

   b.

   c.

   d.

20 When you have finished creating your WordArt, how do you return to your document?

   a. Double-click the WordArt window

   b. Click in your document where you want to work next

   c. Click Close on the File menu

   d. Click Exit Works on the File menu

21 Which of the following images is *not* included in the ClipArt Gallery?

   a. A soccer ball

   b. A valentine

   c. A light bulb

   d. A portrait of David Letterman

22 Which toolbar button would you click to center a ClipArt image in a column?

   a.

   b.

   c.

   d.

23 What button would you click in the Footnote dialog box to specify a custom footnote reference character?

   a. The Numbered option button

   b. The Cancel command button

   c. The Character mark option button

   d. The Use WorksWizard button

24 What button would you click in the Replace dialog box to end a search-and-replace operation?

   a. Find Next

   b. Replace

   c. Replace All

   d. Cancel

25 What is the difference between the Find command and the Replace command?

   a. The Find command can't be used to replace one word with another

   b. The Find command only works with numbers

   c. The Find command doesn't have a Help button

   d. The Find dialog box is bigger than the Replace dialog box

APPLICATIONSREVIEW

1 Start Works and load the file UNIT_04.WPS from your Student Disk in drive A.

   a. Click the Open an Existing Document button in the Startup dialog box.

   b. Click a: in the Drives list box, then double-click UNIT_04.WPS in the File Name list box.

   c. Save the file in the my_files directory on your Student Disk.

2 Format the document for two columns.

   a. Click Columns on the Format menu.

   b. Type **2** in the Number of columns text box, then click the Line Between check box.

   c. Click OK to close the Columns dialog box and click Yes to switch to Page Layout view.

3 Place a box around the guarantee paragraph at the bottom of the second column.

   a. Use the line pointer to select the six lines of the guarantee paragraph (including the title).

   b. Click Border on the Format menu.

   c. Click the Outline check box and the Double Line Style option button.

   d. Click OK to place the border around the guarantee paragraph.

4 Insert the word Kites! as a WordArt title at the top of the document.

  a. Delete the reminder tag <<Insert WordArt Title>> at the top of the document, then position the cursor on the first line of the document.

  b. Click WordArt on the Insert menu.

  c. Type **Kites!** in the WordArt window and click the Update Display button.

  d. Click the Bold and Shadow buttons to format the text with bold and shadow styles (specify background shading).

  e. Click anywhere in the kite document to exit the WordArt accessory and continue working with the document.

5 Insert two ClipArt images into the kite document.

  a. Delete the two <<Insert ClipArt>> reminder tags from the document.

  b. Place the cursor where the first reminder tag was, then click ClipArt on the Insert menu.

  c. Double-click the palm trees ClipArt image.

  d. Place the cursor where the second reminder tag was, then click ClipArt from the Insert menu.

  e. Double-click the smiling sun ClipArt image.

  f. Delete any remaining reminder tags in the document.

6 Insert a footnote into the document.

  a. Place the cursor after the name Ben Franklin in the first column of the document.

  b. Click Footnote on the Insert menu.

  c. Click the Character mark option button and press [Tab].

  d. Type ***** and click OK to use the asterisk (*) as the footnote reference.

  e. Type **Kite not endorsed by the Franklin family**.

  f. Format the footnote text for 8 point italic.

7 Change all the prices in the document so that they end with 50 cents (Frasier has changed his mind again).

  a. Move the cursor to the top of the document.

  b. Click Replace on the Edit menu.

  c. Type **95** in the Find What text field and press [Tab].

  d. Type **50** in the Replace With text field and click the Find Next button.

  e. Click the Replace button six times to replace each occurrence of 95 with 50.

  f. Click the Close button to end the search.

8 Verify the page layout of the document and print it

  a. Click the Print Preview button on the toolbar to view the document in Print Preview.

  b. Verify that the flyer fits on one page, that the margins and columns are sized correctly, and that the footnote is placed correctly.

  c. Turn on your printer and prepare it for printing.

  d. Print the document, save your changes, and exit Works.

INDEPENDENT
CHALLENGE

Dianne Finn in Human Relations has asked you to prepare a flyer for Outdoor Designs' annual Beach Bash on Saturday, June 14. The picnic will take place at Glass Lake from 2 p.m. until dusk. The company will provide lobster and chicken dinners, hot dogs and hamburgers for the children, and build-your-own ice cream sundaes for all. Activities will include swimming, windsurfing, and volleyball, as well as team sandcastle building and a treasure hunt for the children. The flyer should contain an RSVP section that asks for employee name, number of adults attending, and number of children attending.

To complete this Independent Challenge:

1 Prepare a poster based on the information supplied. Use the toolbar or menus in the WordArt accessory to rotate text, create shaped text or sideways text, adjust spacing between characters, add shading, shadows, or borders.

2 Use Print Preview as you work to produce an effective layout.

3 Print a copy of your flyer and save the file as BASH94.

UNIT 5

OBJECTIVES

▶ Start the Spreadsheet

▶ Enter numbers and labels

▶ Save your work

▶ Change column widths and row heights

▶ Use formulas

▶ Edit the spreadsheet

▶ Change alignment and number format

▶ Change the font

▶ Print the spreadsheet

Building
A SPREADSHEET

*I*n Units 2 through 4 you learned how to use the Works Word Processor to create useful business documents. In this unit you'll be introduced to the Works **Spreadsheet** application, an electronic ledger you can use to organize rows and columns of information and create colorful business charts. The Spreadsheet is useful for financial planning, calculating, data analysis, and creating business forms. Outdoor Designs uses the Spreadsheet to track orders and sales. Your first assignment with the Spreadsheet will be to record this month's product orders as they come in from the sales reps. ▶ In this unit you'll learn how to start the Spreadsheet and enter order information in spreadsheet cells. Next you'll change the size of cells, save your work in a file, use formulas, and edit your spreadsheet. Finally, you'll adjust the alignment, borders, and fonts in spreadsheet cells, then print the product order spreadsheet. ▶

Starting the Spreadsheet

You start the Spreadsheet application from the Works Startup dialog box. The Spreadsheet has a graphical interface similar to the one in the Word Processor application. If you worked through Units 2 through 4 you'll recognize many of the toolbar buttons and menu commands. Unlike the Word Processor, however, the Spreadsheet document window is divided into rows and columns of **cells** that can contain numbers, text, and formulas. Figure 5-2 identifies the important elements of the Spreadsheet interface, and Table 5-1 lists the buttons unique to the Spreadsheet toolbar. You'll start Works and the Spreadsheet application now.

1   Double-click the **Microsoft Works program icon** to start the Works program
The Startup dialog box displays, as shown in Figure 5-1. The Startup dialog box contains buttons that start the Word Processor, Spreadsheet, Database, and Communications applications.

2   Click the **Spreadsheet button** to start the Works Spreadsheet application
The Startup dialog box disappears and the Spreadsheet application opens in a window, as shown in Figure 5-2. The Spreadsheet contains the interface elements found in every Works application: a menu bar, toolbar, document window, scroll bars, toggle indicators, sizing buttons, and control menu boxes. The mouse pointer becomes a cross in the Spreadsheet. Unique to the Spreadsheet interface are a document window divided into **rows** and **columns** that intersect to form **cells**, the **cell reference box** that shows the currently highlighted cell, and a **formula bar**, where you enter equations that perform Spreadsheet calculations.

Use Figure 5-2 to identify the interface elements of the Spreadsheet. Refer to Table 5-1 to identify the toolbar buttons that are unique to the Spreadsheet.

TABLE 5-1: Toolbar buttons unique to the Spreadsheet

BUTTON	FUNCTION
Σ	Sums the numbers in the highlighted cells
$	Formats the highlighted cells in currency format
📊	Creates a chart using the highlighted cells

FIGURE 5-1: The Works Startup dialog box

Spreadsheet button

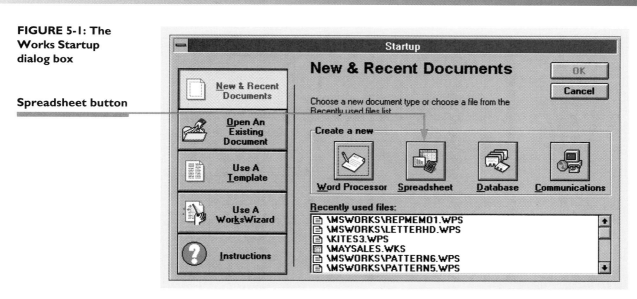

FIGURE 5-2: The Works Spreadsheet with unique elements labeled

Cell reference box

Cell A1

Formula bar

Rows

Sum button

Currency button

Chart button

Columns

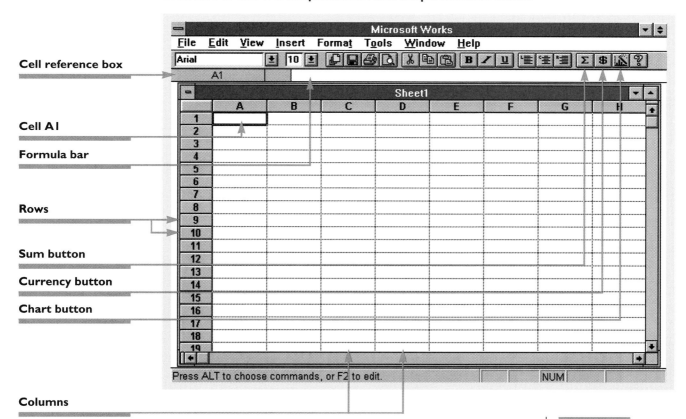

QUICK **TIP**

Press **F1** when the Spreadsheet is running for a detailed on-line introduction to the Spreadsheet application.■

Entering numbers and labels

You enter numbers and labels in the Spreadsheet by typing in spreadsheet cells. A **cell** is the rectangular area formed where a row and column intersect. When you open a new spreadsheet, Works highlights the cell in the upper left corner of the document window. This cell is referred to as "A1," or the cell where column A and row 1 intersect. You can move the highlight to other cells by clicking them with the mouse, or by moving to them with the direction keys. You'll practice entering numbers and labels into the Spreadsheet now by typing in a product order from one of the Outdoor Designs sales reps. The completed product order serves as an internal tracking sheet that the Outdoor Designs fulfillment and billing staff will use to process the order.

STEPS

1 Type Outdoor Designs Product Order in cell A1
As you type, the text displays in cell A1 and in the formula bar.

2 Press [Enter]
The text in the formula bar is entered into the spreadsheet, as shown in Figure 5-3. Because the text you typed began with a letter (rather than a number), Works considers it to be a **label**, a piece of text used for description, not calculation. Works lets labels extend into neighboring cells that don't contain data, so the text *Outdoor Designs Product Order* extends into cells A1, B1, and C1. The text is identified as a label in the formula bar by the presence of a double quotation mark (") at the beginning of the formula bar.

3 Press ↓ twice to move to cell A3
Cell A3 highlights and *A3* appears in the cell reference box, which identifies your current location. You can use the direction keys to highlight different cells in the Spreadsheet and to enter information into cells, as you'll see in the following step.

4 Type the following four lines, pressing ↓ after each line
Sales rep: Kimberly Ullom ↓
Store: Mountain Air, North Bend, WA ↓
Order date: June 30, 1994 ↓
Terms: Payment 30 days after receipt (Net 30) ↓

5 Press ↓ to move to cell A8, then type the following text into columns A through D of rows 8 through 13. Press → and click new cells at the points indicated (see Figure 5-4).

Kit num	Kit name	Price	Quantity	
#401	Cascade Ski Sack	19.95	5	[click A9]
#501	Coastal Parafoil Kite	22.95	1	[click A10]
#502	Puget Sound Delta Kite	24.95	2	[click A11]
#801	Olympic Rain Tent	79.95	2	[click A12]
#802	Tent Vestibule	19.95	1	[click A13]
				[Enter]

Works enters the labels and numbers into the spreadsheet, as shown in Figure 5-4. The text in row 8 and in columns A and B are considered labels, but are not allowed to overlap neighboring cells because the neighboring cells contain data. The numbers in columns C and D are considered **numeric values** by Works. You'll use these numbers in calculations later in the unit.

FIGURE 5-3: Spreadsheet text in the formula bar and in neighboring cells

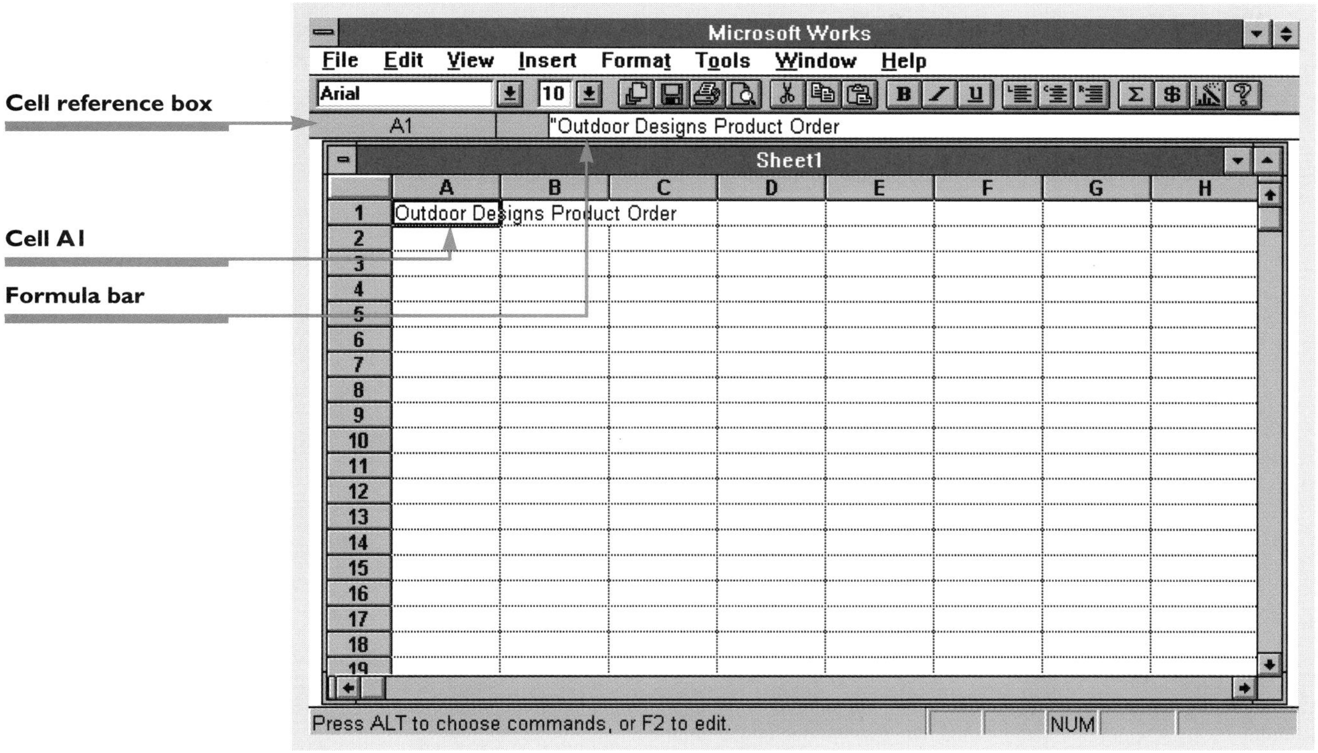

Cell reference box

Cell A1

Formula bar

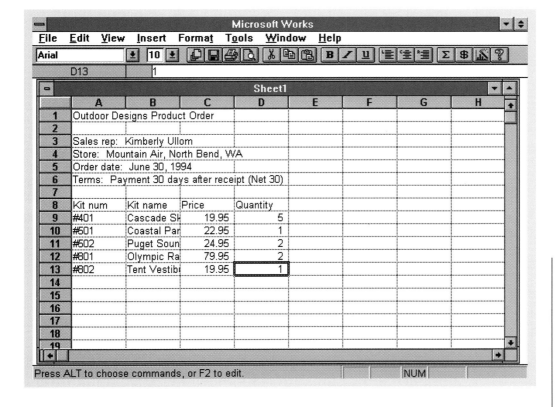

FIGURE 5-4: The spreadsheet after the product order data has been entered

QUICK **TIP**

Pressing [Tab] is the same as pressing → in the Spreadsheet, and you may find it more convenient when entering multiple columns of data.■

Saving your work

The process of saving a document in the Spreadsheet is identical to saving a document in the Word Processor. To save a new document and give it a unique filename on disk, use the Save As command on the File menu. To save changes to a document that has already been named and saved, use the Save command on the File menu or click the Save button on the toolbar. You'll save the product order spreadsheet to disk now with the name SALE6-30.WKS.

1   Put your Student Disk in drive A

2   Click the **File menu**, then click **Save As**
The Save As dialog box displays, as shown in Figure 5-5
Several of the dialog box elements contain suggested or **default** values to help you save your file. The Save File as Type drop-down list box contains a default value of *Works Spreadsheet*, but you can request that Works save the file in another format, so that other spreadsheet programs, such as Lotus 1-2-3, can use the file too. Table 5-2 lists the different spreadsheet file formats supported by Works 3.0. To save your spreadsheet so that it can be opened in one of the programs listed in Table 5-2, you would click the Save File as Type drop-down list box, then click the name of the spreadsheet program where you'll load your file. The employees at Outdoor Designs use this technique when they give their spreadsheet files to a consulting accountant who uses the Lotus 1-2-3 for Windows program.

3   Type **sale6-30**
The filename sale6-30 displays in the File Name text box. Now you need to indicate that Works should save your product order spreadsheet to your Student Disk.

4   Click the **Drives drop-down list box**, then click **a:** to select drive A
A list of your Student Disk files displays in the File Name list box, and the MY_FILES directory that you created in Unit 1 displays in the Directories box.

5   Double-click my_files in the Directories list box
The my_files directory opens, indicating that your file will be saved to this directory.

6   Click OK
The Save As dialog box disappears and the spreadsheet window reappears with SALE6-30.WKS in the title bar. Works has added the three-character extension .WKS to your filename to identify the document as a Works Spreadsheet file.

TABLE 5-2:
Spreadsheet formats included in the Save File as Type drop-down list box

SPREADSHEET FORMAT	DESCRIPTION
Works for Windows 2.0	A format that version 2.0 of Works for Windows can read
Text and Commas	Unformatted spreadsheet with entries separated by commas
Text and Tabs	Unformatted Windows spreadsheet with entries separated by tabs
Text and Tabs (DOS)	Unformatted DOS spreadsheet with entries separated by tabs
Excel 4.0/5.0	A format that Excel for Windows versions 4.0 and 5.0 can read
Lotus 1-2-3	A format that Lotus 1-2-3 versions 2.0 and later can read
Works 3.0 for Macintosh SS	A format that Works for the Apple Macintosh can read

FIGURE 5-5: The Save As dialog box

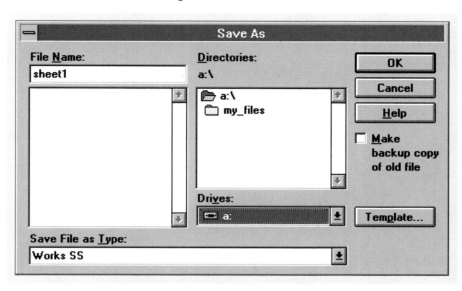

Using the Spelling Checker

After you save your document, it is a good idea to check the spelling of the words and labels you've entered. The Spelling Checker in the Spreadsheet is identical to the one in the Word Processor. (However, the Thesaurus is not available in the Spreadsheet.) To run the Spelling Checker in the Spreadsheet, click **Spelling** on the Tools menu. The Spelling dialog box displays and Works starts checking the spelling of the text in the spreadsheet, starting with cell A1. (The Spelling Checker ignores all numeric values.) Figure 5-6 shows the Spelling Checker at work in the SALE6-30.WKS spreadsheet.

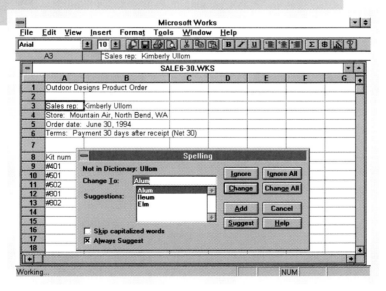

FIGURE 5-6: The Spreadsheet Spelling Checker

QUICK TIP

[Ctrl][S] is the keyboard shortcut for saving a file in Works.■

Changing column widths and row heights

Earlier in this unit you created a spreadsheet with several rows and columns of data. Now spend a few minutes adjusting the column widths so that all the information in each cell is visible. Spreadsheet column widths and row heights can be adjusted in two ways: you can choose the Column Width or Row Height commands from the Format menu, or you can drag the column or row borders with the mouse. You'll try changing column width and row height in the spreadsheet now.

1 Select **column B** in the spreadsheet by clicking the letter **B** at the top of the column
Column B highlights. Before you resize or format one or more cells in a spreadsheet, you must first **select** them. Table 5-3 lists several methods for selecting cells in a spreadsheet with the mouse or keyboard.

2 Click the **Format menu**, then click **Column Width**
The Column Width dialog box displays. The Column Width dialog box contains a Width text box where you can specify the column width (in characters), and a Best Fit check box, which will (when selected) automatically resize the column so that it is slightly wider than the longest item in the column.

3 Click the **Best Fit check box** and click **OK**
The Column Width dialog box closes and column B is resized. Notice that the complete description for each kit name now appears in the column. Next you'll increase the height of row 7, to add a little more distance between the two blocks of text in the spreadsheet.

4 Select **row 7** in the spreadsheet by clicking the number **7** to the left of row 7
The row highlights.

5 Click the **Format menu**, then click **Row Height**
The Row Height dialog box displays. Works automatically adjusts the height of each row to be at least as large as the biggest font in the row, so you'll only need to use the Row Height dialog box if you want to intentionally increase or decrease the row height. Here you'll change the height of the row to 20 points.

TABLE 5-3:
Methods for selecting cells in spreadsheets

6 Type **20** in the **Row Height text box** and press **[Enter]**
The row height of row 7 changes from 12 to 20 points, as shown in Figure 5-7.

TO SELECT	WITH THE MOUSE	WITH THE KEYBOARD
A cell	Click the cell	Use direction keys
A row	Click the row number	Select a cell in a row, then press [Ctrl][F8]
A column	Click the column number	Select a cell in a column, then press [Shift][F8]
Group of cells	Drag across the cells	Press [F8], then use direction keys
Spreadsheet	Click the box above row 1	Press [Ctrl][Shift][F8]

FIGURE 5-7: The product order spreadsheet with row and column changes

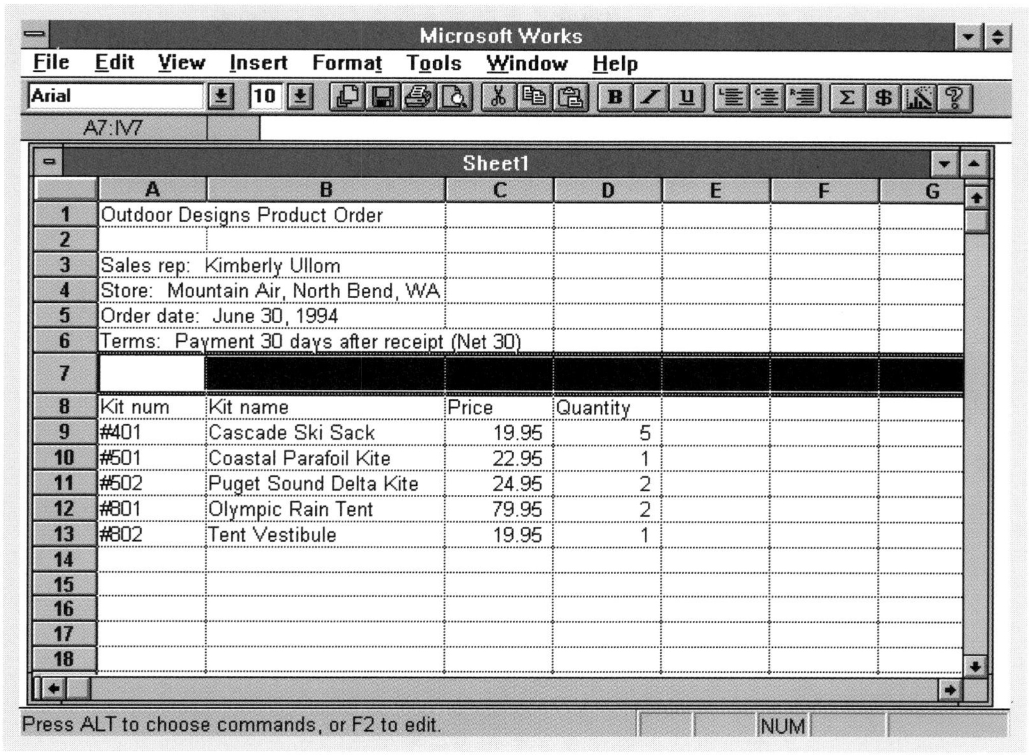

	A	B	C	D	E	F	G
1	Outdoor Designs Product Order						
2							
3	Sales rep: Kimberly Ullom						
4	Store: Mountain Air, North Bend, WA						
5	Order date: June 30, 1994						
6	Terms: Payment 30 days after receipt (Net 30)						
7							
8	Kit num	Kit name	Price	Quantity			
9	#401	Cascade Ski Sack	19.95	5			
10	#501	Coastal Parafoil Kite	22.95	1			
11	#502	Puget Sound Delta Kite	24.95	2			
12	#801	Olympic Rain Tent	79.95	2			
13	#802	Tent Vestibule	19.95	1			
14							
15							
16							
17							
18							

Microsoft Works — File Edit View Insert Format Tools Window Help — Arial 10 — A7:IV7 — Sheet1

Press ALT to choose commands, or F2 to edit.　　NUM

Dragging cell borders

You can also change column width and row height in the spreadsheet by dragging the cell borders with the mouse. To drag a cell border, position the mouse pointer over the line to the right of a column heading or below a row number, until the mouse pointer changes shape and the word *Adjust* appears below it. When the pointer changes, drag the border in the direction you want to change. Changing column width and row height with the mouse is fast, but the technique is limited because you can only change one row or column at a time, and you can't specify an exact value.

QUICK **TIP**

If you make a mistake, press **[Ctrl][Z]** or click **Undo** on the Edit menu to cancel your most recent column width or row height adjustment.■

Using formulas

To perform a calculation in the Spreadsheet, you enter a formula in a cell. A **formula** is an equation that calculates a new value from existing values. For example, a simple formula could calculate the total cost of an item by adding its price, sales tax, and shipping costs. Formulas can contain numbers, mathematical operators, cell references, and built-in equations called **functions**. Table 5-4 lists some of the mathematical operators that can be used in a formula. You'll use a formula now to calculate subtotals in the product order sheet. The formula will multiply the cost of an item by the quantity ordered.

1   Click cell **E8** and type **Subtotal**, then press [↓]

2   Type **=**
The equal sign (=) lets Works know you're about to enter a formula in cell E9. From this point on any numbers, mathematical operators, cell references, or functions you type will be included in the formula.

3   Press ← twice to move to cell **C9**
Cell C9 highlights and appears as a **cell reference** in the formula. When the formula is calculated, Works will use the number in cell C9 to perform its calculation. To help you keep track of the formula as you build it, Works displays the formula in both the formula bar and in cell E9.

4   Type *****
The asterisk (*) is the multiplication operator in Works (see Table 5-4). When the formula is calculated, Works will use the asterisk to multiply the number in cell C9 with the next cell reference you select.

5   Press [←] once to move to cell **D9**
Cell D9 highlights and appears as the last cell reference in the formula. When the formula is calculated, Works will multiply the product price in cell C9 by the quantity in cell D9 and place the result in cell E9.

6   Press [**Enter**] to enter the formula
Works enters the formula, multiplies the two numbers, and displays the result (*99.75*) in cell E9. Notice that although the result of the calculation appears in cell E9, the original formula still appears in the formula bar. Now use the Fill Down command to **replicate** the formula in cells E10 through E13.

7   Select cells **E9** through **E13** with the mouse
You select multiple cells or **cell ranges** in the Spreadsheet by dragging across the cells with the mouse, or holding down the shift key and pressing the direction keys to highlight the cells. When a range of cells is selected, you can use the Fill Down command to replicate the contents of the top cell into the selected cells.

8   Click the **Edit menu**, click **Fill Down**, then click 💾
The Subtotal formula is replicated in cells E10 through E13 and the subtotal for each product appears, as shown in Figure 5-8.

FIGURE 5-8:
The Subtotal formula
replicated in cells E10
through E13

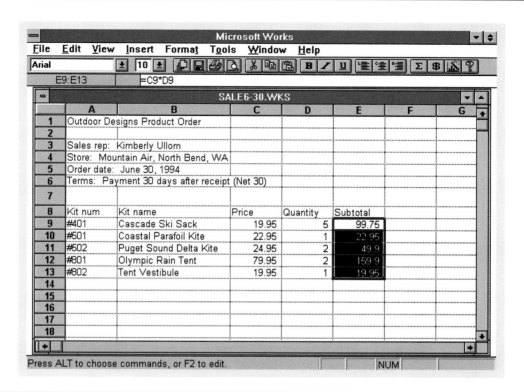

How Works calculates formulas

When you enter a formula that contains more than one mathematical operator, Works follows standard algebraic rules to determine which calculation in the formula to accomplish first. These rules dictate that exponential calculations are performed first, multiplication and division calculations second, and addition and subtraction calculations last. If there is more than one calculation in the same category, Works evaluates them left to right. Therefore, when evaluating the formula 6–5+3*4, Works always produces the answer 13. When you are typing your own formulas, you may want to include parentheses around calculations for clarity. Works recognizes them and evaluates the calculations between parentheses first.

TABLE 5-4: Useful mathematical operators (in order of evaluation)

OPERATOR	DESCRIPTION	EXAMPLE	RESULT
( )	Parenthesis	(3+6)*3	27
^	Exponential	10^2	100
*	Multiplication	7*5	35
/	Division	20/4	5
+	Addition	5+5	10
–	Subtraction	12–8	4

QUICK **TIP**

Use cell references, rather than actual numbers, in formulas. This makes your calculations easier to replicate.■

Editing the spreadsheet

There are several ways to edit cells in a spreadsheet. You can revise a single cell by clicking the cell and editing its contents in the formula bar. You can cut, copy, and paste blocks of cells with the editing commands on the Edit menu and the editing buttons on the toolbar. (Cut, Copy, and Paste operations in the Spreadsheet work as they do in the Word Processor.) You can also move cells from one place to another with the mouse using drag-and-drop editing. Finally, you can use the Replace command to exchange one word for another throughout the spreadsheet. You'll practice editing the product order spreadsheet now.

1   Select cell **D10** and type **3**, then press **[Enter]**
The number in cell D10 changes from *1* to *3*, and the subtotal in cell E10 changes from *22.95* to *68.85*. Now you'll edit the contents of cell A6 on the formula bar.

2   Select cell **A6**
The cell highlights and the label *Terms: Payment 30 days after receipt (Net 30)* appears in the formula bar. The accounting department has notified you that the payment grace period for the Mountain Air store has been extended to 60 days. You'll make that change in this cell.

3   Select the first **3** in the label, then type **6**
The number *3* is selected, then replaced with a *6* when you type the new number. This is a feature that applies to all Works applications: when text is selected, the new text replaces the selected text as you type.

4   Select the second **3** in the formula bar, then type **6**
The second number *3* is replaced with the number *6*. The formula bar now contains *Terms: Payment 60 days after receipt (Net 60)*.

5   Press **[Enter]** to confirm your formula bar edits
The updated label appears in the spreadsheet at cell A6. Now you'll use **drag-and-drop** to move the sales rep name from row 3 to row 6.

6   Select **row 3** in the spreadsheet by clicking the number **3** to the left of row 3

7   Move the mouse pointer to the bottom edge of the selected row, until it changes to the **drag pointer**
The mouse pointer changes to the drag pointer, containing a diagonal arrow with the word *Drag* beneath it.

8   Click the row and drag it down until row **7** highlights, then release the mouse button
The word *Move* appears beneath the mouse pointer, and the contents of row 3 move to row 6, as shown in Figure 5-9. Notice that the contents of rows 4, 5, and 6 each move up a row to fill in the gap left by row 3. When you move a row or column in a spreadsheet, the other rows and columns adjust after the move is finished (this ensures there are never any "missing" rows or columns in the spreadsheet). However, when you move individual cells, they replace the cells they move onto.

9   Click 🖫 to save your editing changes

FIGURE 5-9:
The product order
spreadsheet after
editing

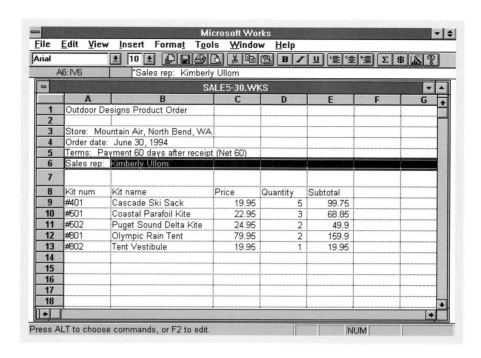

Making changes with the Replace command

If you need to replace several instances of the same word or number in the spreadsheet, use the Replace command on the Edit menu. The Replace command works the same in the Spreadsheet as it does in the Word Processor: you specify the text you want to search for in the Find What text box and the text you want to substitute in the Replace With text box, then click the Find Next button. You can replace one word at a time by clicking the Replace button (the recommended technique), or replace everything in the spreadsheet at once with the Replace All button. Figure 5-10 shows the Replace command at work in the Spreadsheet.

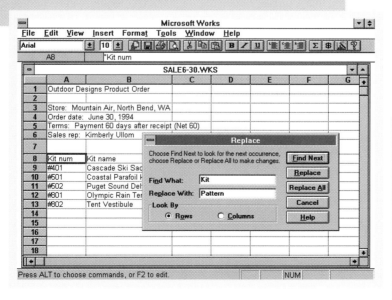

QUICK **TIP**

To edit a cell from the keyboard, use the direction keys to select the cell you want to edit, then press **[F2]** to move the edit cursor to the formula bar.■

FIGURE 5-10: The Replace command

Changing alignment and number format

Works can right align, center align, or left align the information in cells, and can format numbers so that they appear in one of several standard formats, including dollars and cents, percentages, and exponential values. Changing the alignment and number format can make your spreadsheet look better and easier to read. You'll practice changing the alignment and number format now in the Outdoor Designs product order spreadsheet.

1 Select **row 8** in the spreadsheet
The row of column labels highlights.

2 Click the **Format menu**, then click **Alignment**
The Alignment dialog box, which contains an option button for each of the cell alignment options available in the Spreadsheet, displays. General (the default) aligns labels to the left of the cell and numbers to the right, Left aligns everything to the left, Right aligns everything to the right, Center aligns everything to the center, Fill repeats the characters in the cell until the cell is full (useful for repeating a dash or another symbol), and Center across selection centers text horizontally across several selected cells.

3 Click the **Center option button**, then click **OK**
Each of the labels in row 8 is centered in its cell. Now you'll center the title of the spreadsheet.

4 Select cells **A1** through **E1**
The title *Outdoor Designs Product Order* highlights.

5 Click the **Format menu**, then click **Alignment**
The Alignment dialog box displays.

6 Click the **Center across selection option button**, then click **OK**
The spreadsheet title is centered across the five highlighted cells. (Note that the cell reference of the title is still A1, however.) Now you'll change the alignment in two columns using the alignment buttons on the toolbar.

7 Select cells **A9** through **A13** and click the **Center-align button** 🗐 on the toolbar
The five cells in the *Kit num* column highlight and Works centers the contents of the five cells in the column.

8 Select cells **D9** through **D13** and click 🗐 on the toolbar
The five cells in the *Quantity* column highlight and Works centers the contents of the five cells in the column, as shown in Figure 5-11.

9 Click 🖫 to save your alignment changes

FIGURE 5-11:
Changing the alignment
of information in cells

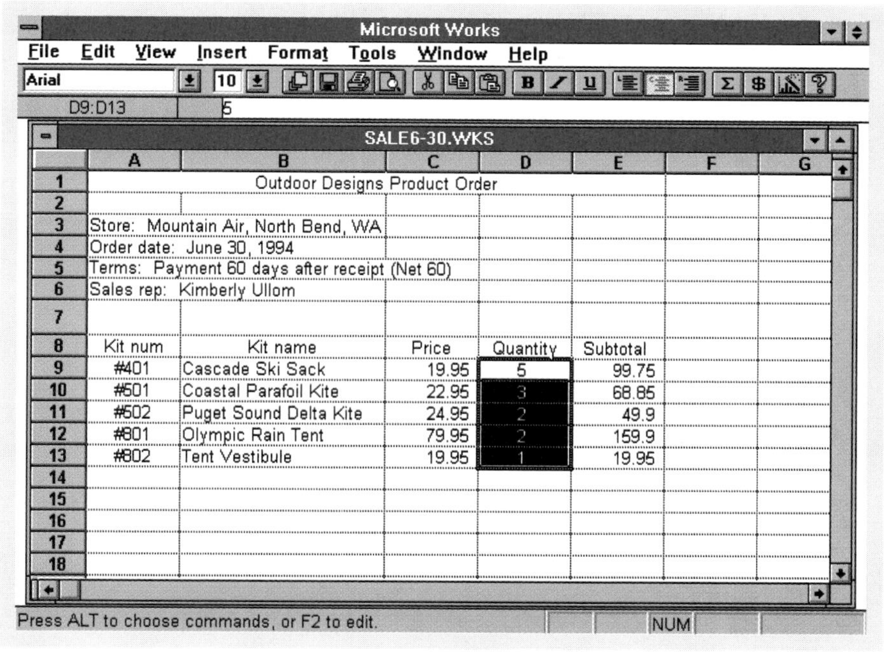

Changing the number format

To change the number format in a cell, click the Number command on the Format menu and click the format you want in the Number dialog box. The most popular option is **Currency**, which formats the selected numbers with dollar signs ($) and two decimal places representing cents (you can also specify a different number of decimal places). Because the Currency format is used so often in the Spreadsheet, the designers of Works placed a **Currency button** ⊞ on the toolbar that accomplishes the same task. Use the Currency button on the toolbar now to change the number format in columns C and E to currency. When you've finished, your spreadsheet should look like the one in Figure 5-12.

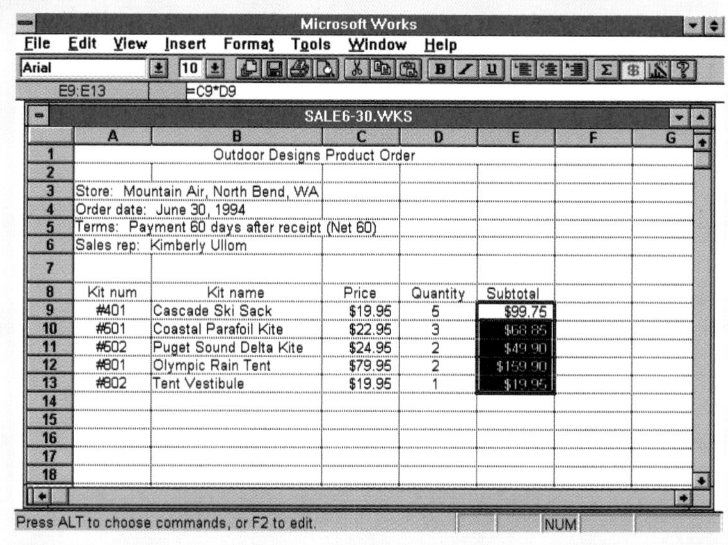

FIGURE 5-12: The spreadsheet after formatting numbers for currency

QUICK TIP

If you ever see ######## in a cell, it means that the cell is not wide enough to display the information in the format you have chosen. Use the Column Width command on the Format menu to increase the column width, or choose a different format.■

Changing the font

Works can change the font and font style of text in the spreadsheet, and add borders and shading to make important information stand out. The font and font style commands are identical to the commands in the Word Processor, and several of them are also available as toolbar buttons. The Borders and Patterns commands on the Format menu help you take advantage of the unique rectangular design of spreadsheet cells, and can produce impressive formatting effects. You'll try working with the font, Borders, and Patterns formatting commands now.

1 Select cell **A1** and click the **Bold** 🅱 and **Italic** 🅸 **buttons** on the toolbar
The title *Outdoor Designs Product Order* appears in bold italic style.

2 Click the **Font size drop-down list box** and click **16**, then click the Font name drop-down list box and click **Times New Roman**
The size of the title is changed to 16 points. The font of the title changes from Arial to Times New Roman. Notice that the sizing buttons work exactly as they do in the Word Processor. You can also use the Font and Style command on the Format menu to accomplish these formatting changes.

3 Select **row 8** in the spreadsheet, then click 🅱
The font style of the row of column labels changes to bold. Now you'll add a border around the sales information in rows 3 through 6.

4 Select cells **A3** through **C6** (a block of cells three cells wide and four cells long)
The block of cells highlights and the cell range A3:C6 appears in the cell reference box.

5 Click the **Format menu**, then click **Border**
The Border dialog box displays. It lists the border options for the selected block of cells. The Border and Line Style options let you control the type of border and type of line, respectively.

6 Click **double line** (the third from the bottom) under Line Style, then click **OK**
A selection rectangle is placed around the double line style and a double line appears in the Outline Border option. (Outline is the style you want.) When you click OK, the dialog box closes and a double line border appears around the block of highlighted cells.

7 Select cells **A8** through **E13** (a block of cells five cells wide and six cells long), click the **Format menu**, then click **Border**
The block of cells highlights and the cell range A8:E13 appears in the cell reference box. When you click Border, the Border dialog box displays.

8 Click the **Top, Bottom, Left**, and **Right Border options**, then click **OK**
The dialog box closes and a single line border is placed around each cell in the selection, as shown in Figure 5-13.

9 Click 💾 to save your formatting changes

FIGURE 5-13:
The spreadsheet after font style and border formatting

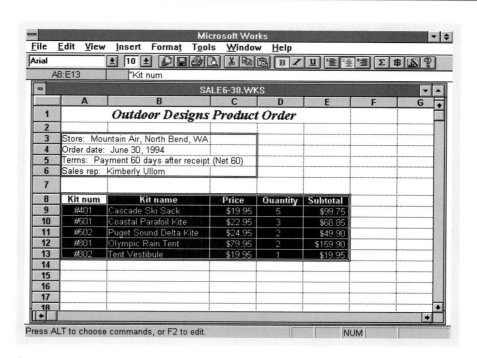

Adding shading to cells

You can fill one or more spreadsheet cells with a shading pattern using the Patterns command on the Format menu. Pattern formatting works like other types of formatting: first you select the cells you want to format, then you click the formatting options you want in the Patterns dialog box. The Patterns drop-down list box contains 14 different shading patterns for you to choose from. The patterns range from slight shading to stripes to solid black. The lightest shading patterns usually work best when you're trying to emphasize a cell with text in it. Figure 5-14 shows the Patterns dialog box and a range of cells in column E formatted with light gray shading.

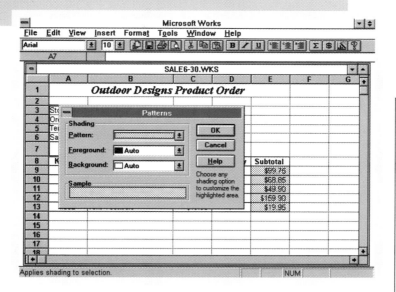

FIGURE 5-14: The Patterns dialog box and shaded cells

QUICK **TIP**

The AutoFormat command on the Format menu combines several formatting operations into one command and can be an effective way to format a range of cells in several different styles.■

Printing the spreadsheet

When you've finished working with your spreadsheet and are ready to print, you can examine your document in Print Preview and verify the page layout with the zoom pointer. After you have previewed your document, you're ready to print a copy with the Print command. Ask your instructor or lab manager for specific instructions on how to print from your classroom printer. After you have printed the product order spreadsheet, you'll save your changes and exit Works.

1 Click the **File menu,** then click **Print Preview**
The Print Preview window opens and the product order spreadsheet displays as it will appear on the printed page. Several command buttons that control the operation of the Print Preview window appear on the right side of the window.

2 Move the mouse pointer onto the document page
The pointer changes to the **zoom pointer**, a magnifying glass with the word *zoom* below it. The zoom pointer lets you examine parts of the document closely in Print Preview.

3 Click the top half of the spreadsheet with the zoom pointer
The document enlarges to half size in the Print Preview window.

4 Click the **title** of the spreadsheet with the zoom pointer
The spreadsheet enlarges to full size in the Print Preview window, as shown in Figure 5-15. Your last column might not have shading if you did not do the tasks described in the "Adding shading to cells" section on the preceding page.

5 Click the **Cancel button**
The Print Preview window closes and the Sales Rep document displays.

6 Click the **File menu,** then click **Print**
The Print dialog box displays. It lets you specify the number of copies you want to print, the printing page range (if you don't want to print the entire document), and whether the printing should be best quality (the default) or draft quality.

Take a moment now to verify that your printer is on-line and properly connected to your computer. If you have any questions, ask your instructor or lab manager for help.

7 Click **OK** to print the spreadsheet
The Print dialog box closes. After a few moments the completed product order emerges from your printer. Now save your changes and exit Works.

8 Click 🖫 to save your changes

9 Click the **File menu,** then click **Exit Works** to exit Works
The SALE6-30.WKS document closes and the Works program exits. The Program Manager displays, with the Microsoft Works for Windows group highlighted.

FIGURE 5-15:
The spreadsheet in
Print Preview

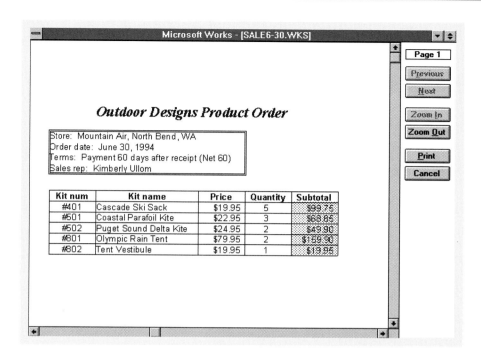

Adding headers and footers

When you print your document, you may want to add page numbers, the current date, or some other text to the top or the bottom of each page. You can add this information to your document with the Headers and Footers command on the View menu. The Headers and Footers dialog box is shown in Figure 5-16. A standard header or footer in Works is one line long and can contain one or several **header and footer codes**. The header and footer codes in the Spreadsheet are identical to the header and footer codes in the Word Processor, listed in Table 3-3. Headers and footers don't appear in your document in Normal view, but can be examined in Print Preview.

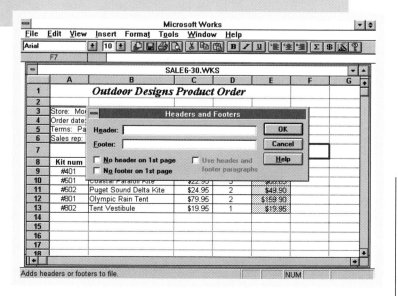

FIGURE 5-16: The Headers and Footers dialog box

QUICK **TIP**

Use the Page Setup command on the File menu to change page margins and other printing options.■

CONCEPTSREVIEW

Label each of the elements of the Spreadsheet, as shown in Figure 5-17.

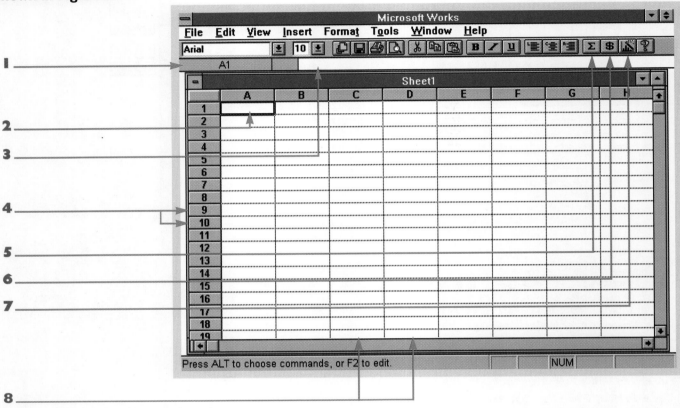

FIGURE 5-17

Match the mathematical operators with their uses in spreadsheet formulas.

9 ^   a. Multiplication

10 /   b. Division

11 *   c. Addition

12 –   d. Exponential

13 +   e. Subtraction

Select the best answer from the list of choices.

14 The Spreadsheet application is started from the:

    a. DOS Prompt

    b. Program Manager

    c. Help system

    d. Works Startup dialog box

15 Spreadsheet rows and columns intersect to form:

    a. The toolbar

    b. Cells

    c. Paragraphs

    d. Selected text

16 The name of a cell in column B and row 2 is:

    a. A1

    b. 1A

    c. B2

    d. 2B

17 If text in the formula bar has a double quotation mark (") in front of it, it is a:

    a. Label

    b. Number

    c. Formula

    d. Function

18 How do you select an entire column in the spreadsheet?

a. Press [Esc]

b. Press [Ctrl][B]

c. Click the row number to the left of the column

d. Click the column letter at the top of the column

19 What does the Best Fit check box in the Column Width dialog box do?

a. Lets you specify the width (in characters) of the column

b. Automatically resizes the column so that it is slightly wider than the longest item

c. Picks the best TrueType font for the cell

d. Places a border around the column

20 Which of the following items *cannot* be included in a spreadsheet formula?

a. Mathematical operator

b. Cell reference

c. Built-in function

d. Italic type

21 What answer does Works give after calculating the formula 4+3*2–2?

a. 12

b. 8

c. 6

d. 4

22 What word is part of the drag-and-drop pointer?

a. Drag

b. Drop

c. Copy

d. There is no word in the drag-and-drop pointer

23 Which of the following is *not* an option button in the Alignment dialog box?

a. Default

b. Left

c. Right

d. Center across selection

24 What does ######## mean if it appears in a cell?

a. The cell has been formatted for currency

b. The cell contains shading

c. The cell is not wide enough to display the information in the cell

d. The cell is busy

25 Imagine that cell B5 is selected in your spreadsheet. What happens when you press [Shift][F8]?

a. Row 8 is selected

b. Column B is selected

c. The entire spreadsheet is selected

d. The contents of cell B5 are formatted for italic

APPLICATIONSREVIEW

1 Start the Spreadsheet application and identify the elements of the interface.

a. Double-click the Microsoft Works program icon in the Program Manager.

b. Click the Spreadsheet button.

c. Identify the elements of the Spreadsheet interface, referring to Figure 5-2 and Table 5-1.

2 Type in the labels and numbers for a second Outdoor Designs product order spreadsheet.

a. Type the following information (starting in cell A1), pressing [↓] as indicated.

Outdoor Designs Product Order [↓][↓]

Sales rep: Kimberly Ullom [↓]

Store: Pam's Kites, Edmonds, WA [↓]

Order date: June 29, 1994 [↓]

Terms: Payment 30 days after receipt (Net 30) [↓][↓]

Kit num	Kit name	Price	Quantity	[click A9]
#401	Cascade Ski Sack	19.95	2	[click A10]
#501	Coastal Parafoil Kite	22.95	2	[click A11]
#503	Franklin's Diamond	19.95	3	[click A12]
#701	Sonic Boomer Kite	49.95	2	[click A13]
#801	Olympic Rain Tent	79.95	1	[Enter]

3 Adjust the column widths so that all the information appears in the spreadsheet.

   a. Select column B, click the Format menu, then click Column Width.

   b. Click the Best Fit check box and press [Enter].

   c. Select row 7 and click Row Height on the Format menu.

   d. Type **20** in the Row Height text box and press [Enter].

4 Save the spreadsheet in the my_files directory on your Student Disk with the name SALE6-29.WKS.

   a. Click the File menu, then click Save As.

   b. Type **sale6-29** , then select Drive A and my_files directory, and click OK.

   c. Click the Tools menu, then click Spelling to run the Spelling Checker.

   d. Verify the spelling in the spreadsheet, then click OK when the spelling check has finished.

5 Enter a formula in cell E9 that calculates the value of the product price times the product quantity, then replicate the formula in cells E10 through E13.

   a. Click cell E8 and type Subtotal, then press [↓].

   b. Type **=C9*D9** in cell E9, then press [Enter].

   c. Select cells E9 through E13.

   d. Click the Edit menu, then click Fill Down.

6 Practice editing the contents of cells in the formula bar and using the mouse to drag and drop text.

   a. Select cell A6, then click the formula bar.

   b. Change the 30 to 45 twice in the formula bar, then press [Enter].

   c. Select rows 9 and 10 and drag them to row 14.

7 Change the cell alignment and number formats.

   a. Center-align row 8 with the Center option button in the Alignment dialog box.

   b. Select cells A1 through E1, click the Format menu, then click Alignment.

   c. Click the Center across selection option button, then click OK.

   d. Center-align the cells in the *Kit num* and *Quantity* columns with the Center-align button on the toolbar.

   e. Change the number format of the *Price* and *Subtotal* columns to currency with the Currency button on the toolbar.

8 Emphasize the important points of the document with font and border changes.

   a. Select cell A1 and click the Underline button on the toolbar.

   b. Change the font to Courier New and the font size to 18 point.

   c. Select cells A3 through C6.

   d. Click the Format menu, then click Border.

   e. Click Thick Line under Line Style (the bottom style), then click OK.

9 Examine the document in Print Preview, then print out a final copy.

   a. Click the File menu, then click Print Preview.

   b. Click the spreadsheet twice with the zoom pointer.

   c. Click the Cancel button, click the File menu, then click Print.

   d. Verify your printer is turned on, then click OK to print the spreadsheet on your printer.

   e. Click the Save button on the toolbar, click the File menu, then click Exit Works.

INDEPENDENT
CHALLENGE

Number formatting commands in Works save you typing time, insure consistent formatting across a range of cells, and allow you to switch the data at will to a different format. Open a new spreadsheet now and type four or five 6-digit numbers in adjacent cells. To complete the Independent Challenge, highlight the cells containing the numbers and explore what happens when you apply different formats.

1 Use the Number command on the Format menu to view the General, Fixed, Comma, Percent, and Exponential formats.

2 To look at Leading Zeros format, change the number of digits to 9.

3 To examine the Fraction format, type some whole numbers with decimal extensions. Choose Fraction format and watch how Works converts them.

4 For True/False format, type a few more numbers, including several numbers that are equal to zero (0, 0.0, 0.000, 0000, etc.). Notice that zero values display FALSE, and nonzero values display TRUE.

5 To explore Date and Time formats, type today's date and time, select the cells that contain the date or time, then choose the number format you want to see.

When you finish, close the file without saving it.

UNIT 6

Working

WITH SPREADSHEET FUNCTIONS

n Unit 5 you learned how to use the basic features of the Spreadsheet to create the Outdoor Designs product order spreadsheet. In this unit you'll learn about **functions**, built-in calculations you can use in spreadsheet formulas. Spreadsheet functions help you accomplish sophisticated numerical and text processing operations automatically. For example, you can use a function to find the average of a group of numbers, or to calculate the monthly payments on a loan. In this unit you'll learn how functions are used in formulas. You'll also put them to work in the Outdoor Designs product order spreadsheet. You'll learn how the Sum function is used to add up a column of numbers, and how to use date and time functions to determine when an account balance is overdue. Then you'll use statistical, financial, and text functions to add some useful account information (as well as some interesting special effects) to the spreadsheet. Finally, you'll learn to sort the rows in the product order spreadsheet, then print out a final copy for the order processing department. ▶

Learning about functions

A **function** is a calculation used in a formula. Each function includes the function name, a set of parentheses, and function **arguments** separated by commas and enclosed in the parentheses. Arguments are the information the function needs to perform the task. Figure 6-1 shows the anatomy of a Works function named AVG, used to calculate the average of a set of numbers in a spreadsheet. AVG accepts one or more numbers or **range references** as arguments. Table 6-1 lists the different categories of functions that can be used in the Spreadsheet. ▶ Sue Ellen has asked you to use AVG and several other functions to add information to the Outdoor Designs product order spreadsheet. She and Frasier will use this information to evaluate how the Outdoor Designs products are selling in each of the stores. In the steps that follow, you'll open the product order spreadsheet (UNIT_06.WKS), save a copy under a new name, and prepare to use functions to add useful information to the spreadsheet.

1　Make sure your Student Disk is in drive A or drive B, start Works from the Program Manager, and click the **Open an Existing Document button**
The Open dialog box shows the contents of the current directory in the File Name list box. If the drive containing your Student Disk is active, locate the file UNIT_06.WKS in the File Name list box, using the scroll bars if necessary. You may need to change the current drive to see the contents of the Student Disk; if you do, perform step 2.

2　Click the **Drives drop-down list box**, click **a:** to select drive A (or **b:** if your Student Disk is in drive B)
The Works files on your Student Disk display in the File Name list box.

3　Double-click **UNIT_06.WKS** to open the file in the Spreadsheet
The sales data spreadsheet opens in a window. First save a copy of this file with a new name to avoid changing the original file.

4　Click the **File menu**, click **Save As**. Type **function** in the File Name text box, double-click the **my_files** directory in the Directories list box, then click **OK**
You are now ready to enhance your spreadsheet with functions.

FIGURE 6-1: The anatomy of the AVG function

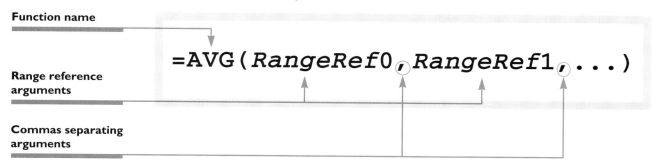

Function name

Range reference arguments

Commas separating arguments

$$=AVG(RangeRef0, RangeRef1, ...)$$

Planning to use functions

Using functions in a spreadsheet takes some advanced planning, because many of the arguments used in functions come from cells in the spreadsheet. Before you start entering your spreadsheet data, think about how you will enter your functions and formulas later, so the information can make best use of the spreadsheet contents. Because spreadsheet ranges can be included as arguments, organize your rows and columns so they can be selected and included in functions. Before you start, you should also determine what results you want from your spreadsheet data and examine the list of Works functions in the on-line help to see if any of them can handle the calculations for you. You might find it useful to draw out a rough sketch of your spreadsheet on paper, before you start entering data and formulas.

QUICK **TIP**

Many of the 76 Spreadsheet functions can also be used in the Database application.■

TABLE 6-1: Categories of Spreadsheet functions

CATEGORY	USED FOR
Date and time	Calculations involving dates and times
Financial	Loan payments, appreciation, and depreciation
Statistical	Average, sum, variance, and standard deviation calculations
Mathematical	Mathematical and trigonometric calculations like those found on a scientific calculator
Informational	Determining if an error has occurred in a calculation
Lookup and reference	Used for calculations involving tables of data
Logical	Calculations that produce the result TRUE or FALSE
Text	Comparing, converting, and reformatting text in cells

Using the SUM function

The SUM function is the most popular spreadsheet function. SUM gives the total of all the numbers and cell references included as function arguments. To add the SUM function to a formula, choose the Function command on the Insert menu, select the SUM function, then edit the function arguments in the formula bar. You can also sum highlighted cells by clicking the Autosum button on the toolbar. You'll use the SUM function now to total the Quantity and Subtotal columns in the product order spreadsheet.

1   Click **cell C14**

2   Type **Totals** and press **[Enter]**, then click ▤ and **B**
    The label *Totals* is entered into cell C14, then formatted for right alignment and boldface.

3   Click **cell D14**, then type **=**
    An equals sign (=) appears in the formula bar, indicating you're about to enter a formula.

4   Click the **Insert menu**, then click **Function**
    The Insert Function dialog box displays, as shown in Figure 6-2. It contains Category option buttons that let you select the type of function you want to insert, a Functions list box that lets you select a template for the function, and a Description window that describes the function highlighted in the Functions list box.

5   Click the **Statistical option button,** then double-click the **SUM function template**
    The Insert Function dialog box closes and the SUM function template displays in the formula bar. The template lists the arguments required by the SUM function. These arguments will be replaced with the actual cell references from your spreadsheet.

6   In the formula bar, select the text **RangeRef0,RangeRef1,...** and press **[Del]**
    The arguments for the SUM function are deleted, and the formula bar displays =SUM ().

7   Select **cells D9 through D13** in the spreadsheet, then press **[Enter]**
    After you select the five cells in the Quantity column, the range *D9:D13* appears in the formula bar as the argument in the SUM function. When you press [Enter], the formula is entered into the spreadsheet; Works also calculates the sum of cells D9 through D13 and displays the number 13 in cell D14. Next you'll use the Autosum button to total the dollar amounts in the Subtotals column.

8   Click **cell E14**, then click the **Autosum button** Σ on the toolbar
    The Autosum button automatically places the SUM function in the formula bar. To complete the function, you'll select the range of numbers you want to total.

9   Select the **cell range E9:E13,** then press **[Enter]**
    The range is entered into the SUM function, the results are calculated, and the amount 398.35 displays in cell E14, as shown in Figure 6-3.

10 Format **cells D14 and E14** to match the formatting in the cells above them, then click 🖫

FIGURE 6-2: The Insert Function dialog box

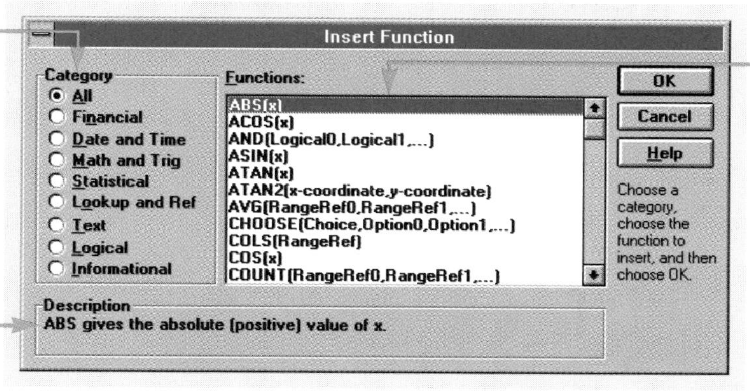

Category option buttons

Functions list box

Description window

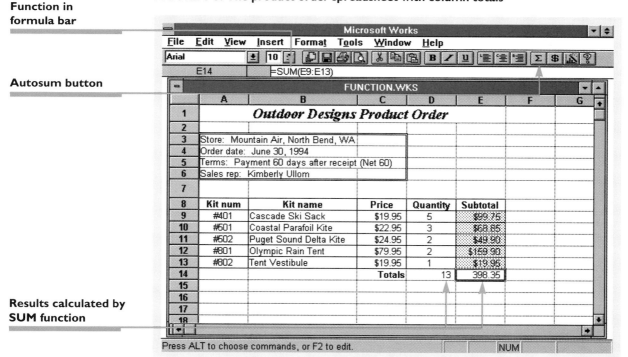

FIGURE 6-3: The product order spreadsheet with column totals

Function in formula bar

Autosum button

Results calculated by SUM function

QUICK **TIP**

[Ctrl][M] is the keyboard equivalent of clicking the Autosum button.

Using date and time functions

The Works date and time functions let you display the current date and time in your spreadsheet, and can help you calculate the time between important events. The date and time functions are listed in Table 6-2, along with their respective arguments and a brief description of each. In the following steps you'll use the NOW function to enter the current date into the spreadsheet, then use the Number command to format the style of the date. You'll also enter a formula that uses the current date to calculate when the payment is due from the Mountain Supplies store.

STEPS

1   Click **cell A16**, type **Ship date:**, then press **[→]**
The label *Ship date:* is entered into cell A16, and cell B16 highlights.

2   Type **=NOW( )** and press **[Enter]**
The NOW function is entered into the spreadsheet, and a serial number representing the current date and time appears in cell B16. Since NOW doesn't require any arguments, it is easier to type the function than to insert it with the Function command. Works uses a special number called a **serial number** to store dates and times internally. To change the serial number into a date humans can understand, you need to format it with the Number command.

3   Click the **Format menu,** then click **Number**
The Number dialog box displays.

4   Click the **Date option button**
Today's date is displayed in seven different formats in the Options list box. You can convert the serial format to any of these formats.

5   Double-click the **fourth date format in the list**
The Number dialog box closes and today's date appears in cell B16. The fourth date format is *July 05, 1994* in this example, but your date will be different. Now calculate the day when full payment is due from the store, assuming a 60-day payment grace period.

6   Click **cell A17**, type **Pmt due:**, then press **[→]**
The label *Pmt due:* is entered into cell A17, and cell B17 highlights.

7   Type **=** and press **[↑]** to highlight cell B16, type **+60**, then press **[Enter]**
The formula *=B16+60* displays in the formula bar, and a date serial number displays in cell B17. Now format the serial number with the same date format you used in cell B16.

8   Click **Format**, click **Number**, click the **Date option button**, then double-click the **fourth date format**
The payment due date displays in cell B17, as shown in Figure 6-4. The payment due date is determined by adding 60 days (net 60) to the current date. Works takes into consideration the number of days in each month as it makes its calculation.

9   Click 🖫 to save your additions to the spreadsheet

FIGURE 6-4: The product order spreadsheet after data calculations

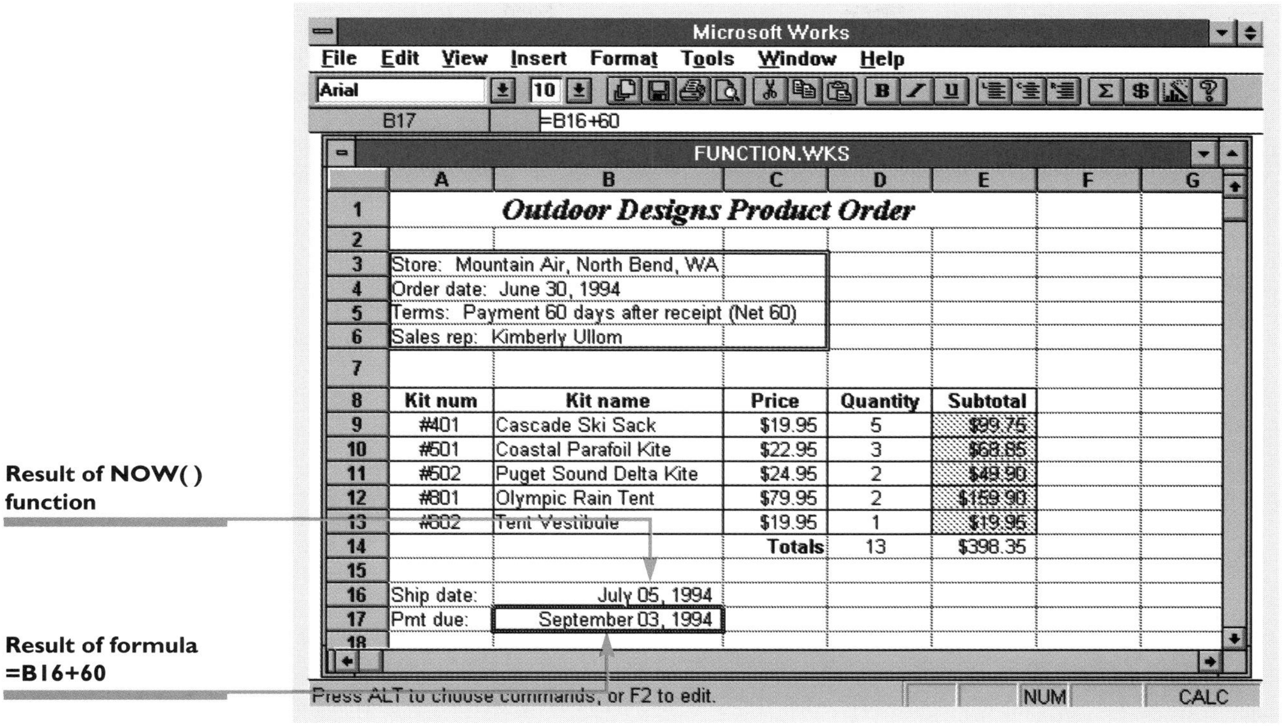

**Result of NOW( )
function**

**Result of formula
=B16+60**

	A	**B**	**C**	**D**	**E**	**F**	**G**
1		*Outdoor Designs Product Order*					
2							
3	Store: Mountain Air, North Bend, WA						
4	Order date: June 30, 1994						
5	Terms: Payment 60 days after receipt (Net 60)						
6	Sales rep: Kimberly Ullom						
7							
8	Kit num	Kit name	Price	Quantity	Subtotal		
9	#401	Cascade Ski Sack	$19.95	5	$99.75		
10	#501	Coastal Parafoil Kite	$22.95	3	$68.85		
11	#502	Puget Sound Delta Kite	$24.95	2	$49.90		
12	#801	Olympic Rain Tent	$79.95	2	$159.90		
13	#802	Tent Vestibule	$19.95	1	$19.95		
14				Totals	13	$398.35	
15							
16	Ship date:	July 05, 1994					
17	Pmt due:	September 03, 1994					
18							

Cell B17 = B16+60

TABLE 6-2: The Works date
and time functions

FUNCTION	DISPLAYS
NOW( )	Serial number for the current date and time
DATE(*Year,Month,Day*)	Serial number of the specified date
DAY(*SerialNumber*)	Day of the month using the specified serial number
MONTH(*SerialNumber*)	Month using the specified serial number
YEAR(*SerialNumber*)	Year using the specified serial number
TIME(*Hour,Minute,Second*)	Serial number of the specified time
SECOND(*SerialNumber*)	Seconds using the specified serial number
MINUTE(*SerialNumber*)	Minutes using the specified serial number
HOUR(*SerialNumber*)	Hour using the specified serial number

QUICK **TIP**

The valid range for
dates in Works 3.0
is January 1, 1900
through
February 6, 2040.

Using statistical functions

The Works statistical functions let you assemble, classify, and tabulate numeric data in your spreadsheet. The statistical functions are listed in Table 6-3 with their respective arguments and a brief description of each. In the following steps you'll use the AVG function to determine the average dollar value of the product orders, then format the cell for currency.

STEPS

1   Click **cell A19**, type **Ave order:** and press **[→]**
The label *Ave order:* is entered into cell A19, and cell B19 is highlighted.

2   Click **Insert**, then click **Function**
The Insert Function dialog box displays.

3   Click the **Statistical option button**, then double-click the **AVG function template**
The Insert Function dialog box closes and the AVG function template appears in the formula bar. AVG determines the average of all the arguments included between the parentheses. You can specify numbers, cell names, or cell ranges.

4   Select the arguments **RangeRef0,RangeRef1,...** inside the parentheses and press **[Del]**
The template part of the AVG function is deleted.

5   Select **cells E9 through E13** in the spreadsheet, then press **[Enter]**
The range *E9:E13* is entered as an argument in the AVG function in the formula bar. When you press [Enter], Works enters the formula into the spreadsheet, calculates the average of cells E9 through E13, and displays the number 79.67 in cell B19.

6   Click the **Currency button** 💲 to format the cell with currency format
The cell is formatted for currency, as shown in Figure 6-5.

TABLE 6-3: The Works statistical functions

7   Click 💾 to save your changes

FUNCTION	RESULT DISPLAYED
AVG(*RangeRef0,RangeRef1,...*)	The average of the specified arguments
COUNT(*RangeRef0,RangeRef1,...*)	The number of arguments in the list
MAX(*RangeRef0,RangeRef1,...*)	The largest number in the list
MIN(*RangeRef0,RangeRef1,...*)	The smallest number in the list
STD(*RangeRef0,RangeRef1,...*)	The standard deviation of the arguments
SUM(*RangeRef0,RangeRef1,...*)	The total of the arguments
VAR(*RangeRef0,RangeRef1,...*)	The variance of the arguments

FIGURE 6-5: The product order spreadsheet with the AVG function

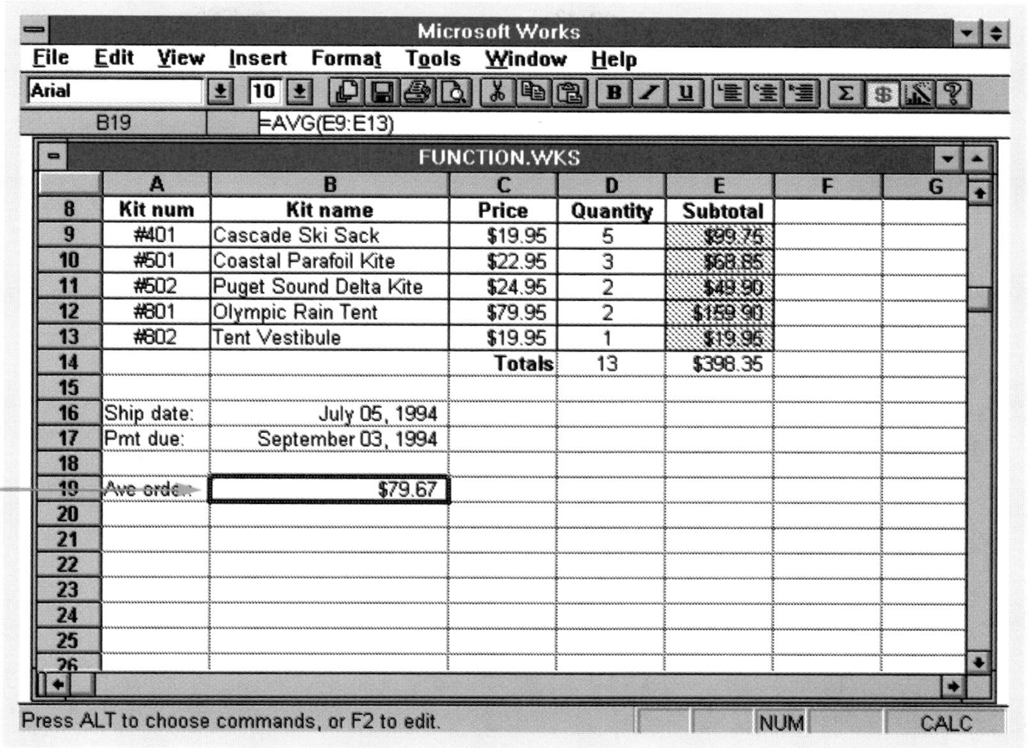

Result of AVG function

The mathematical functions

Another useful category of functions that produce numbers as results are the mathematical functions. The **mathematical functions** perform many of the mathematical and trigonometric calculations found on a standard scientific calculator, including ABS (absolute value), COS (cosine), LOG (logarithm), and SQRT (square root). Most of the mathematical functions take a single number as an argument, and produce a single number as a result. For more information about using the mathematical functions in the Spreadsheet, search for "math functions" in the Works on-line help.

QUICK **TIP**

You can include one function as an argument in another function if the result is compatible. For example, the formula =SUM(5, SQRT(9)) adds together the number 5 and the square root of 9, then displays the result (8).■

Using financial functions

The Works financial functions help you calculate loan payments, appreciation, and depreciation using spreadsheet data. The most useful financial functions are listed in Table 6-4 with their respective arguments and a brief description of each. Outdoor Designs extends credit to approved wholesale customers who want to pay off their purchases over a two-year period. In the following steps you'll use the PMT function to determine what the monthly payment would be for the Mountain Air store if they chose to finance their outstanding balance.

1 Click **cell A20**, type **24 pmts:**, and press **[→]**
The label *24 pmts:* is entered into cell A20, and cell B20 highlights.

2 Click **Insert**, then click **Function**
The Insert Function dialog box displays.

3 Click the **Financial option button**, then double-click the **PMT function template**
The Insert Function dialog box closes and the PMT function template appears in the formula bar. PMT determines the periodic payment for a loan based on the principal loan amount, the interest rate charged, and the payment term (number of payments). The function arguments can be specified as numbers or cell references.

4 Select **Principal,Rate,Term** inside the parentheses and press **[Del]**
The template arguments of the PMT function are deleted.

5 Click **cell E14**, then type a **comma (,)**
The cell reference E14 (representing the amount financed) is entered as the Principal argument in the formula bar. Next you'll specify the *Rate* and *Term* arguments.

6 Type **19%/12,24** and press **[Enter]**
A 19% interest rate (divided by 12 months) and a 24-month payment term are entered as arguments, then Works calculates the monthly payment. A result of 20.08027266 displays in cell B20.

7 Click the **Currency button** 💲 to format the cell with currency format
A monthly payment of $20.08 appears in the cell, as shown in Figure 6-6. This is the amount Mountain Air would pay monthly for two years if they chose to finance their purchase.

8 Click 💾 to save your changes

TABLE 6-4:
Useful financial functions

FUNCTION	RESULT DISPLAYED
PMT(*Principal,Rate,Term*)	Periodic payment of an investment
FV(*Payment,Rate,Term*)	Future value of an investment
RATE(*FutureValue,PresentValue,Term*)	Growth of an investment
SLN(*Cost,Salvage,Life*)	Depreciation for an item using the straight-line method
SYD(*Cost,Salvage,Life,Period*)	Depreciation for an item using the sum-of-the-year's-digits method

FIGURE 6-6:
The product order spreadsheet with the PMT function

Result of PTM function

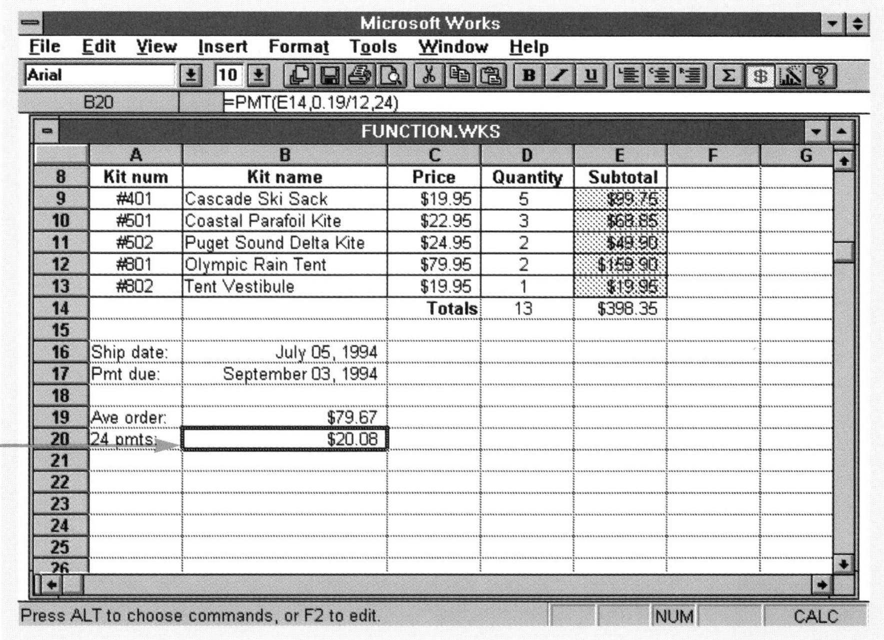

Using the Mortgage and Loan Analysis Template

The PMT function can also be used to help you calculate the principal and interest payments for home and auto loans. Works includes a Mortgage and Loan Analysis template to simplify these calculations, as shown in Figure 6-7. To use the template, choose the **Templates command** from the File menu to display the template categories in the Startup dialog box. Click **AutoStart Personal** in the template group list box, click **Personal Finances** in the category list box, then double-click **Mortgage and Loan Analysis** in the template list box. The Mortgage and Loan Analysis template opens with a CueCards window that explains how the template works. When you've finished using the template, save your calculations to disk with the Save As command.

Enter your loan data in these four cells

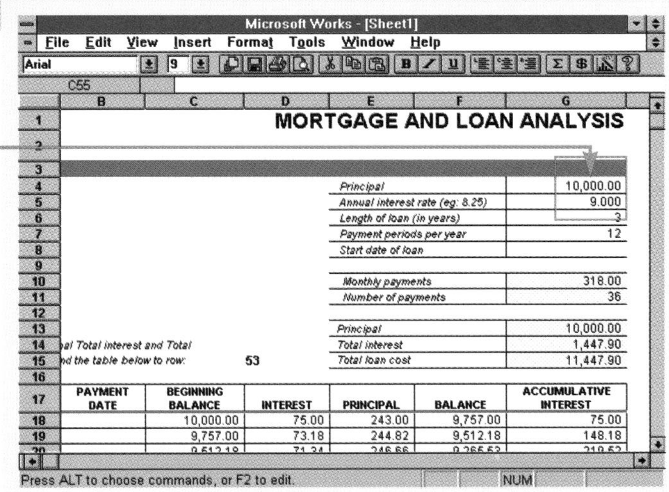

FIGURE 6-7:
The Mortgage and Loan Analysis template

QUICK **TIP**

To replicate a financial function in a spreadsheet, select the formula you want to copy and the cells you want to copy it to, then choose the **Fill Down** or **Fill Right command** on the Edit menu.■

Using text functions

The Works text functions let you compare, convert, and reformat the text in your spreadsheet. The most useful text functions are listed in Table 6-5 with their respective arguments and a brief description of each. In the following steps you'll use the REPEAT function to repeat a phrase at the bottom of the spreadsheet.

STEPS

1   Click **cell A22**

2   Click **Insert**, then click **Function**
The Insert Function dialog box displays.

3   Click the **Text option button**, then double-click the **REPEAT function template**
The Insert Function dialog box closes and the REPEAT function template appears in the formula bar. REPEAT replicates text in a cell the number of times you specify. REPEAT requires a *TextValue* argument, which can be a word enclosed in quotation marks or a cell reference, and a *Count* argument, the number of times you want the *TextValue* repeated.

4   Select **TextValue,Count** inside the parentheses and press **[Del]**
The template part of the REPEAT function is deleted.

5   Type **"Outdoor Designs * ",4** and press **[Enter]**
Be sure to type the quotation marks and comma exactly as shown, and type a space on either side of the asterisk. The text Outdoor Designs * is repeated four times in the spreadsheet, as shown in Figure 6-8.

6   Click 🖫 to save your changes

TABLE 6-5:
Useful text functions

FUNCTION	DESCRIPTION
REPEAT(*TextValue,Count*)	Repeats text the specified number of times
UPPER(*TextValue*)	Capitalizes every letter of the specified text
LOWER(*TextValue*)	Makes every letter of the specified text lowercase
PROPER(*TextValue*)	Capitalizes the first letter of each word in the specified text
TRIM(*TextValue*)	Removes blank spaces from the specified text
VALUE(*TextValue*)	Converts the specified label to a numbers
LENGTH(*TextValue*)	Displays the number of characters in the specified text
MID(*TextValue,Offset,Length*)	Extracts one or more characters from *TextValue*

FIGURE 6-8: The product order spreadsheet with the REPEAT function

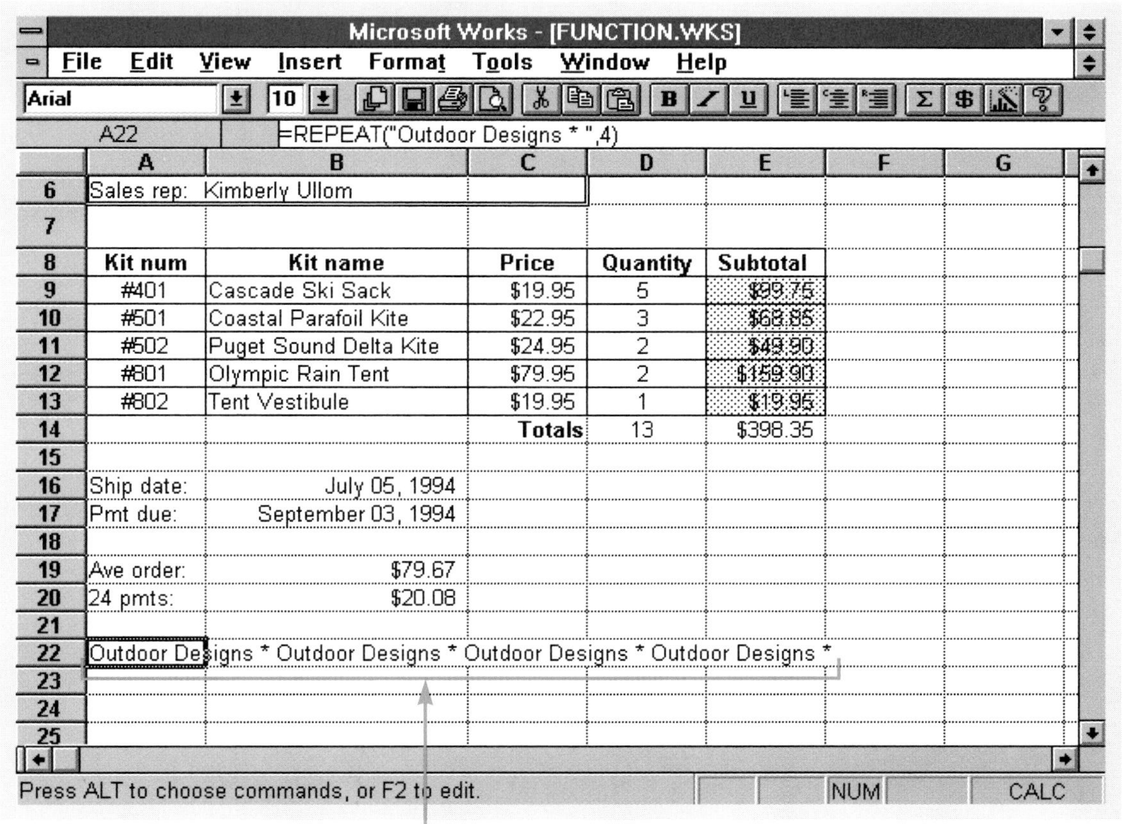

	Microsoft Works - [FUNCTION.WKS]						

File Edit View Insert Format Tools Window Help

Arial | 10 | B I U | Σ $

A22 | =REPEAT("Outdoor Designs * ",4)

	A	B	C	D	E	F	G
6	Sales rep:	Kimberly Ullom					
7							
8	**Kit num**	**Kit name**	**Price**	**Quantity**	**Subtotal**		
9	#401	Cascade Ski Sack	$19.95	5	$99.75		
10	#501	Coastal Parafoil Kite	$22.95	3	$68.85		
11	#502	Puget Sound Delta Kite	$24.95	2	$49.90		
12	#801	Olympic Rain Tent	$79.95	2	$159.90		
13	#802	Tent Vestibule	$19.95	1	$19.95		
14			**Totals**	13	$398.35		
15							
16	Ship date:	July 05, 1994					
17	Pmt due:	September 03, 1994					
18							
19	Ave order:	$79.67					
20	24 pmts:	$20.08					
21							
22	Outdoor Designs * Outdoor Designs * Outdoor Designs * Outdoor Designs *						
23							
24							
25							

Press ALT to choose commands, or F2 to edit. | NUM | CALC

Result of the REPEAT function

QUICK **TIP**

The UPPER, LOWER, and PROPER functions can help you standardize the look of your spreadsheet, and are especially useful for formatting arguments in other functions.

Sorting rows and printing

You've added all the requested functions to the product order spreadsheet. Before you print a final copy, use the Sort Rows command to sort the product order information by kit price. This command sorts rows in the spreadsheet by comparing values in one or more columns. Rows can be sorted alphabetically or numerically, and in ascending or descending order. In the following steps, you'll sort rows 9 through 13 using the price column.

1 Select **rows 9 through 13** with the mouse
Rows 9 through 13 appear highlighted in the spreadsheet.

2 Click the **Tools menu,** then click **Sort Rows**
The Sort Rows dialog box displays. It contains 1st Column, 2nd Column, and 3rd Column text boxes, with Ascend and Descend option buttons under each column. You indicate the column you want to use as the criterion for the sort by placing the column number in the 1st Column text box. The 2nd Column and 3rd Column text boxes are used to direct the sort if there are duplicate items in the 1st Column.

3 Move the dialog box to the bottom of the screen
To move a dialog box, you click the dialog box title bar and drag. With the dialog box out of the way, you can clearly see the selected rows.

4 Type **C** in the 1st Column text box, then press **[Tab]** twice
The letter C appears in the 1st Column text box, indicating you want to use the Price column to direct the sort. The cursor appears in the 2nd Column text box, as shown in Figure 6-9.

5 Type **D** and press **[Enter]**
The letter D appears in the 2nd Column text box, indicating you want to use the Quantity column to resolve any duplications in the first sort. The Sort Rows dialog box closes and rows 9 through 13 are sorted according to kit price, as shown in Figure 6-10. Notice that Kit #802 (Tent Vestibule) is now at the top of the list, followed by #401, #501, #502, and #801.

You can sort the rows in your spreadsheet any number of times, depending on the order in which you want to present your information. To undo the results of a sort, you would choose the Undo command from the Edit menu.

6 Click 🖫 to save your changes

7 Click the **Print button** 🖨 to print a final copy of the product order spreadsheet
Turn on your printer first, if necessary. After a few moments the final product order spreadsheet emerges from the printer, ready for the order processing department. Congratulations! You've completed another useful business document.

8 Click **File,** then click **Exit Works**
The FUNCTION.WKS document closes and the Works program exits. The Program Manager appears, with the Microsoft Works for Windows group highlighted.

FIGURE 6-9: The Sort Rows dialog box

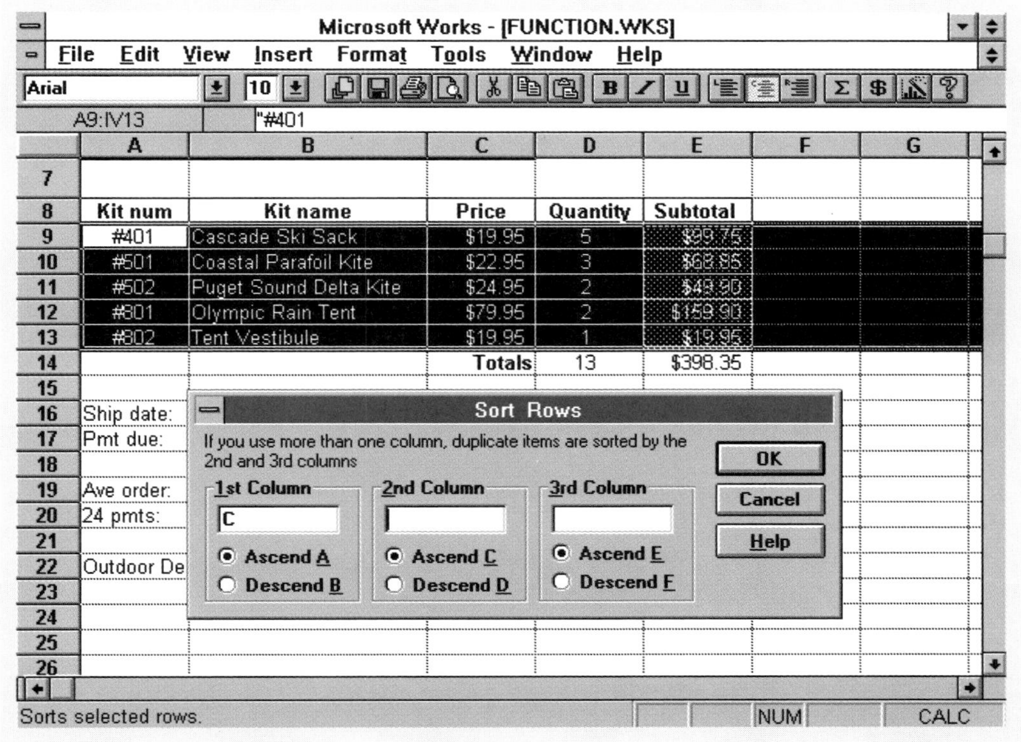

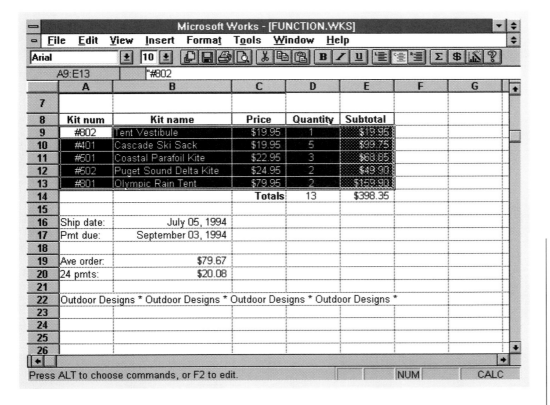

FIGURE 6-10: The order information sorted by kit price (column C)

QUICK **TIP**

Works cannot sort
your spreadsheet by
column, so be sure
to design your spread-
sheet so it can be
sorted by rows if
you want to reorder
the information.■

CONCEPTSREVIEW

**Match components of the formula
=SUM(5,SQRT(9)) with their descriptions.**

1 SUM

2 5

3 SQRT(9)

4 =

5 ,

a. Symbol used to separate arguments in function

b. Function name

c. Function used as argument in function

d. Number used as argument in function

e. Symbol indicating the following text is a formula

Select the best answer from the list of choices.

6 Which answer best describes a function argument?

a. A number, cell reference, or expression that helps a function make its calculation

b. The result of a function calculation

c. The abbreviated name of the function

d. The parentheses following the function name in the formula bar

7 Which answer best describes the purpose of the Statistical functions?

a. Functions used for loan payments, appreciation, and depreciation

b. Functions used for average, sum, variance, and standard deviation calculations

c. Functions used for mathematical and trigonometric calculations

d. Functions involving tables of date and time calculations

8 Many of the Spreadsheet functions can also be used in which Works application?

a. Communications

b. Word Processor

c. WordArt

d. Database

9 Which Spreadsheet function can be accessed through the toolbar?

a. SUM function

b. PMT function

c. AVG function

d. REPEAT function

10 Which command is used to enter functions into the formula bar?

a. Sort Rows command

b. Border command

c. Function command

d. Customize Toolbar command

11 What answer does Works calculate for the formula =SUM(5,3,1)?

a. 7

b. 8

c. 9

d. 10

12 What is a function serial number?

a. A special number used to identify the function a result comes from

b. A special number Works uses to store dates and time internally

c. The time difference between your time zone and Greenwich Mean Time

d. The column number of the highlighted cell

13 What type of argument is used in the NOW( ) function?

a. A text string

b. A cell reference

c. A cell range

d. The NOW( ) function doesn't have arguments.

14 How are date and time serial numbers formatted so humans can understand them?

a. With the Number command

b. With the NOW( ) function

c. With the Alignment command

d. With the SUM button on the toolbar

15 What does E9:E12 represent in the formula =SUM(E9:E12)?

a. A range of five cells

b. A range of four cells

c. Two cell references

d. The average of cells E9 and E12

16 Which of the following functions would you use to display the largest number in a cell range?

a. The AVG function

b. The STD function

c. The MAX function

d. The MIN function

17 How would Works evaluate the formula =SUM(2,SQRT(16))?

a. 2

b. 4

c. 6

d. 8

18 What does the argument RATE represent in the PMT function?

a. The interest charged

b. The principal loan amount

c. The number of payments

d. The monthly payment

19 What does the formula =REPEAT("**", 2) display?

a. **

b. ***

c. ** **

d. ****

20 Which of the following is *not* an element in the Sort Rows dialog box?

a. 1st Column text box

b. Ascend option button

c. Descend option button

d. 1st Row text box

APPLICATIONS REVIEW

1 Start Works and open the file UNIT_06.WKS on your Student Disk.

a. Start Works.

b. In the Startup dialog box, click the Open an Existing Document button. Double-click the filename UNIT_06.WKS.

c. Use the Save As command to save the file as func2.

2 Use the SUM function to total the Quantity and Subtotal columns.

a. Enter the label **Totals** in cell C14, then right-align the label and make it bold.

b. Click cell D14, then type **=**

c. Click the Function command on the Insert menu, then click the Statistical option and double-click the SUM function template.

d. Delete the arguments between the parentheses, select cells D9 through D13, then press [Enter].

e. Click cell E14, click the Autosum button on the toolbar, then select cells E9 through E13 and press [Enter].

f. Format cells D14 and E14 to match the formatting in the cells above them, then click the Save button to save your changes.

3 Enter today's date in cell A16, then calculate the payment date considering a 45-day payment grace period.

a. Enter the label **Ship date:** in cell A16 and the label Pmt due: in cell A17.

b. Enter the formula **=NOW( )** in cell B16.

c. Enter the formula **=B16+45** in cell B17.

d. Format cells B16 and B17 with long date format with the Number command.

4 Use the AVG function to determine the average of the numbers in the Quantity column.

a. Enter the label **Q average:** into cell A19.

b. Enter the formula **=AVG(D9:D13)** into cell B19.

5 Use the PMT function to determine the monthly payment for the order total, using a 14% annual interest rate and a term of 36 months.

a. Enter the label **36 pmts:** into cell A20.

b. Enter the formula **=PMT(E14,14%/12,36)** into cell B20.

c. Click cell B20, then click the currency button to add currency formatting.

6 Use the REPEAT function to repeat the phrase BUY YOUR KITS NOW... four times in row 22.

a. Click cell A22.

b. Enter **=REPEAT("BUY YOUR KITS NOW... ",4)** into the cell.

7 Use the Sort Rows command to sort the order information using the Quantity column.

a. Select rows 9 through 13 with the mouse.

b. Click the Sort Rows command from the Tools menu.

c. Type **D** in the 1st Column text box, press [Tab] twice, then type **E** and press [Enter].

d. Click the Print button to print a copy of the final spreadsheet.

e. Save your changes and exit Works.

INDEPENDENT
CHALLENGE

A local travel agency, working with travel guides from Outdoor Designs, has been marketing guided outdoor adventures — including helicopter skiing, orienteering, hang gliding, ballooning, trail riding, and backpacking.

To perform this independent challenge, open the file UNIT_06C.WKS (which contains the number of trips sold for each sport by month for 1993) from your Student Disk and complete the following exercises. As you work through the following steps, consult the Works on-line help if you have questions about any of the functions.

1 To practice using statistical functions: Use the MAX function to identify the most popular trip. Then use the SUM function to find the total number of trips taken each month. Have Works enter the totals in cells B11 to M11 and in cells N5 to N10. Also enter a SUM function that calculates a grand total in cell N11.

2 To practice using text functions: Use the REPEAT function to enter the text "SUPER!!!" five times in row 1. Then use the REPLACE command to change SUPER!!! to THRILLING!!! and use REPEAT again to display the text six times.

3 In a blank cell, practice using financial functions: Use the TERM function to find how long it will take you to save $1,950 for a balloon vacation in France if you put $150 per month into a savings account earning 4 ½ percent interest compounded monthly. Use Works on-line help to learn about the TERM function. Then use the PMT function to find out what the monthly payment would be if you borrowed the $1,950 at 14 percent with 12 months to repay. Format the answer as currency.

4 Save the file as TRIPS93. You'll use this file in the independent challenge following Unit 7.

UNIT 7

OBJECTIVES

▶ Plan your chart

▶ Create a chart

▶ Change the chart type

▶ Add a subtitle and gridlines

▶ Change the fonts and colors

▶ Paste a spreadsheet table into the Word Processor

▶ Paste a chart into the Word Processor

Creating CHARTS WITH THE SPREADSHEET

In Unit 6 you learned how to manipulate information in the spreadsheet using built-in functions. In this unit you'll learn how to display spreadsheet information graphically using **charts**. You create a chart by selecting spreadsheet data, then plotting the data with one of the eight chart types in the Chart accessory. ▶ In this unit you will create a chart to graphically show the Outdoor Designs regional sales figures for the first and second quarters of 1994. First you'll learn how to plan your chart and select an appropriate chart type. Next you'll create your chart using the Spreadsheet file UNIT_07.WKS, save your chart to disk, and change the chart type, fonts, and title. Finally you'll learn how to paste the spreadsheet and the chart into the Word Processor, and print out a final copy. ▶

Planning your chart

Business, science, statistics, and other disciplines have used charts for years to graphically depict and compare information. The strength of a chart is that it transforms the data into a picture. If a picture is worth a thousand words, then a well-organized chart may be worth at least a thousand numbers. A chart can present the number of kite kits sold in a month or the amount of water consumed each summer, in a format that's easy to understand and remember. ▶ The Works chart accessory is designed to perform several different charting operations. Figure 7-1 shows the eight chart types available in Works and Table 7-1 describes the most popular use for each type of chart. ▶ Before you create a chart, you need to do some general planning. The steps given in this lesson show the kinds of questions you'll need to ask as you plan to create a chart for Outdoor Designs in this unit as well as for other charting projects in the future.

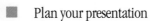

■ Plan your presentation

What data are you including in the spreadsheet? How will the data fit into the report or memo you're creating? What data would you like to highlight with a chart?

■ Determine the chart type

Consider the eight chart types described in Figure 7-1 and Table 7-1. What type of chart will best represent the data you want to include? Do you want to show one category of data or make comparisons between two categories?

■ Design the spreadsheet so Works will create the chart you want

Group your data into logical rows and columns. As you'll see in the next lesson, Works uses the Spreadsheet row and column labels to create labels and other identifiers for the chart.

■ Now you're ready to choose the type of chart you want, create the chart, and edit it

You'll start the Chart accessory and create your first chart in the next lesson.

FIGURE 7-1: The eight chart types in Works

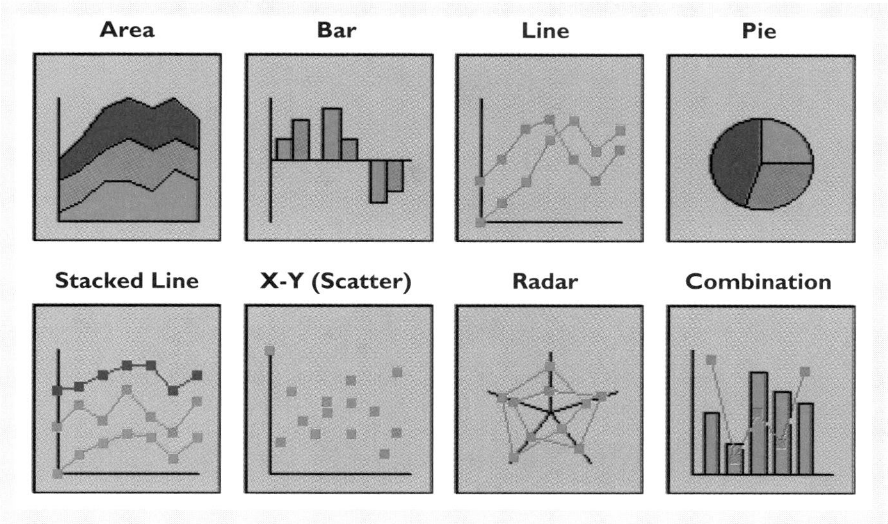

Area Bar Line Pie

Stacked Line X-Y (Scatter) Radar Combination

TABLE 7-1:
Chart types available in Works and common use of each

CHART TYPE	COMMON USE
Area	Shows relative importance of values over a period of time
Bar	Compares categories of data to each other
Line	Shows trends by category over a period of time
Pie	Describes relationship of the parts to the whole
Stacked line	Shows relationship of values in each category to total in that category
X-Y (scatter chart)	Shows relationship between two kinds of related data
Radar	Shows changes in data or data frequency relative to a center point
Combination	Includes both line and bar graphs in single chart

QUICK **TIP**

In addition to the eight chart types shown in Figure 7-1, Works provides 3-D versions of the area, bar, line, and pie charts.■

Creating a chart

Sue Ellen has placed the file UNIT_07.WKS on your Student Disk and has asked you to create a bar chart that graphically depicts the sales data in the file. UNIT_07.WKS contains sales figures for the past two quarters for the four sales territories in the United States: Northeast, South, Midwest, and West. The Outdoor Designs sales and marketing group will use your chart to evaluate how the business is growing and to determine which regions need special attention. You'll open the file, save it with a new name, and create a bar chart in this lesson.

1   Start Works from the Program Manager, then click the **Open an Existing Document button**
Works starts and the Open dialog box displays.

2   Open the spreadsheet UNIT_07.WKS on the Student Disk

3   Save the spreadsheet as **94SALES.WKS** in the MY_FILES directory on the Student Disk
Take a moment to review the sales data in the spreadsheet. In the next step you'll select data for the bar chart.

4   Select **cells A5 through C9**
The cell range A5:C9 highlights in the spreadsheet, as shown in Figure 7-2. This is the information that will be used to create the bar chart. Notice that you selected the row and column labels, but not the column totals.

5   Click the **New Chart button** 📊 on the toolbar
The New Chart dialog box displays. It lets you define how your chart will be created in the Chart accessory, and contains a preview window so you can experiment with different chart styles. The New Chart dialog box also asks you three questions about the data you have selected in the spreadsheet. In this case Works has supplied the correct answers to the questions, but if these assumptions were wrong you could correct them.

6   Press **[Tab]** and type **Outdoor Designs--Regional Sales 1994** in the Chart title text box, then click **OK**
The dialog box closes and a new window displays a sales data bar chart, as shown in Figure 7-3. The interface elements of the Chart accessory appear, including a new menu bar and toolbar, and the new chart is identified as Chart1 in the title bar. Notice that the region names from the spreadsheet appear on the x-axis of the chart and that the sales amounts from the spreadsheet appear on the y-axis of the chart. The sales data are displayed graphically in the chart with red and green bars corresponding to the first quarter and second quarter, respectively.

Take a moment to identify the elements of the Chart accessory and the sales data chart, referring to Figure 7-3 for a description of the elements.

7   Click 💾 on the Chart accessory toolbar
The bar chart is saved as part of the 94SALES.WKS file. (Charts are not saved separately, but as part of the spreadsheet file.)

FIGURE 7-2: Chart data selected in the sales data speadsheet

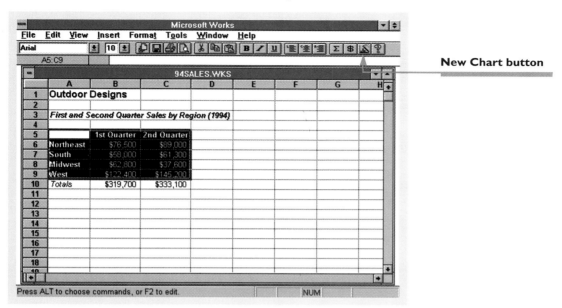

New Chart button

FIGURE 7-3: The Chart accessory and a bar chart in a window

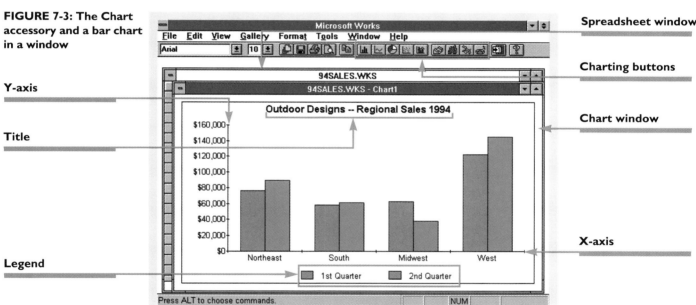

Spreadsheet window

Charting buttons

Chart window

Y-axis

Title

Legend

X-axis

TABLE 7-2: Summary of charting terms

TERM	DEFINITION
X-axis	The horizontal line in a chart containing a series of related values from the spreadsheet
Y-axis	The vertical line in a chart containing a series of related values from the spreadsheet
Labels	Text describing the data in the chart
Legend	A box explaining what the labels, colors, and patterns in the chart mean
Gridlines	Horizontal and vertical lines connecting to the x-axis and y-axis

QUICK **TIP**

Press **[F1]** for an on-line overview of the Chart accessory and the elements of the Chart accessory interface.

Changing the chart type

The chart interface contains nine charting buttons on the toolbar and a Gallery menu on the menu bar. You can change the chart type by clicking one of the charting buttons, or by clicking one of the charting commands on the Gallery menu. You can display each chart type in one of several styles, depending on how you want to present the information. Table 7-3 describes the different charting buttons on the toolbar. Use the 3-D Bar Chart button to change the way your chart is displayed in the following steps.

1   Click the **3-D Bar Chart button** 🏢 on the toolbar
The 3-D Bar dialog box displays, as shown in Figure 7-4. It contains six different 3-D Bar chart styles. Styles 1, 4, 5, and 6 depict each category as a separate bar in the chart, and styles 2 and 3 combine the categories into one divided bar. Try using style 2 in the next step.

2   Double-click **style 2** in the dialog box
The chart in the window is transformed into a 3D bar chart. Since you've chosen one of the combined styles, the sales numbers for the two quarters are stacked together in segmented bars. This chart highlights the fact that the West is the leading region in year-to-date sales, with a combined sales total between $250,000 and $300,000.

3   Click the **3-D Bar Chart button** 🏢 again, then double-click **style 1** in the dialog box
The chart in the window is transformed into a style 1 3D bar chart, as shown in Figure 7-5. Style 1 displays the first and second quarter sales figures as separate bars, so you can compare the results of each quarter as well as the overall results. This chart emphasizes that each of the regions experienced a growth in sales except the Midwest region, in which sales declined by approximately 40 percent. The sales and marketing group will probably be *very* interested in this trend.

4   Click 💾 to save your changes to the bar chart

TABLE 7-3:
Charting buttons on the Chart accessory toolbar

ICON	CREATES A	ICON	CREATES A
📊	Bar chart	🖎	3-D area chart
📈	Line chart	🏢	3-D bar chart
🥧	Pie chart	📉	3-D line chart
📊	Scatter chart	🥧	3-D pie chart
📊	Combination (Mixed) chart		

FIGURE 7-4: The 3-D Bar dialog box

3-D Bar Chart button

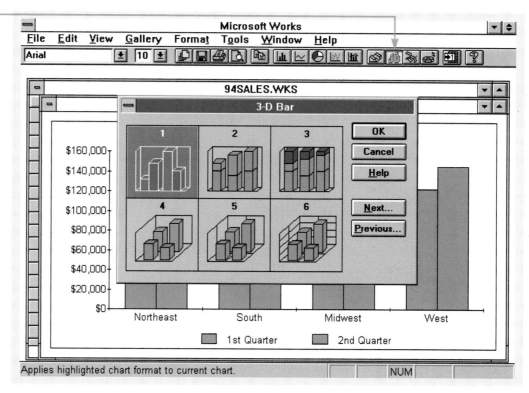

FIGURE 7-5: The sales chart

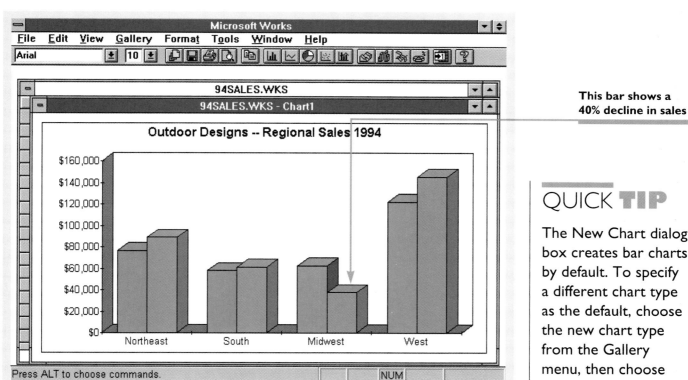

This bar shows a
40% decline in sales

QUICK TIP

The New Chart dialog
box creates bar charts
by default. To specify
a different chart type
as the default, choose
the new chart type
from the Gallery
menu, then choose
**Set Preferred
Chart** from the
Gallery menu.■

Adding a subtitle and gridlines

Now that you have created a chart in the spreadsheet, you can customize the chart to suit your needs. In this lesson you'll add a subtitle and gridlines to clarify the data you're presenting. In the next lesson you'll change the fonts and colors in the chart.

1   Click the **Edit menu,** then click the **Titles command**
The Titles dialog box displays. It contains text boxes for a chart title, a subtitle, a label for the x-axis, a label for the y-axis, and a label for the right vertical axis (not applicable in this situation). The chart title you entered earlier is currently highlighted in the Chart title text box.

2   Press **[Tab]**, type **First and Second Quarters** in the Subtitle text box, then click **OK**
The subtitle First and Second Quarters displays below the chart title. Next you'll add horizontal and vertical gridlines to the chart.

3   Click the **Format menu,** then click the **Horizontal (X) Axis command**
The Horizontal Axis dialog box displays. It contains a Show Gridlines check box, for displaying a gridline between items on the x-axis; a Show Droplines check box, available in area charts only; a No Horizontal Axis check box, for removing the horizontal axis from the chart; and a Label Frequency text box, for specifying which spreadsheet cells the axis labels should be taken from.

4   Click the **Show Gridlines check box,** then click **OK**
Gridlines appear between the four regions listed along the x-axis. If you're confused by vertical gridlines coming from the Horizontal (X) Axis command, you're probably not alone. To keep this straight, think about which axis the gridlines are *connected to*. Because the gridlines come from the x-axis, they are x-axis gridlines.

5   Click **Format,** then click the **Vertical (Y) Axis command**
The Vertical Axis dialog box displays. It lets you change the minimum, maximum, and interval of the numbers along the y-axis, and the style of chart displayed; it also lets you show gridlines, use a logarithmic scale, and remove the vertical axis.

6   Press **[Tab]** twice, then type **25000** in the Interval text box
The value 25000 appears in the Interval text box, indicating you want amounts listed in multiples of $25,000 on the y-axis.

7   Click the **Show Gridlines check box,** then click **OK**
Gridlines extend from the y-axis and amounts are listed in multiples of $25,000, as shown in Figure 7-6. The gridlines make it easier to read the sales totals represented by the bars in the chart.

8   Click 🖫 to save your changes

FIGURE 7-6: The sales chart with a subtitle and gridlines

Gridlines

Intervals on the
y-axis

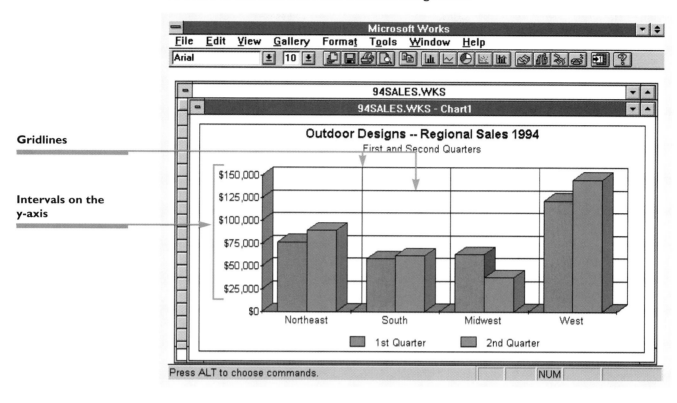

Changing the chart legend

The chart **legend** is the collection of boxes and labels beneath the chart that explain what the colors, patterns, and markers in the chart mean. The text in the legend comes from spreadsheet data. In the Outdoor Designs sales chart, the legend text comes from the column labels 1st Quarter and 2nd Quarter in cells B5 and C5, respectively. When you selected these labels in addition to the sales data, Works automatically used them to create a legend for the chart. To change the text in a legend, you would choose the Legend/Series Labels command from the Edit menu and specify different cells in the Legend/Series Labels dialog box (or type in your own text for legend labels). To remove the legend from the chart, you would choose the Add Legend command from the Format menu.

TROUBLE?

The Chart accessory doesn't have an Undo command, so be careful when you are formatting or deleting labels or titles in a chart. To fix your mistakes, you'll have to reformat or retype the information.■

Changing the fonts and colors

In this lesson you'll learn how to change the font and style of text in the chart, and the color and pattern of the bars in the chart. Changing the font and style in the Chart accessory is different than changing the font and style in the Spreadsheet or Word Processor. There are only two types of text in a chart: the title text and everything else. The subtitle, axis labels, and legend text are all linked together in the chart and must be in the same font and style. In the following steps you'll change the fonts and colors in the Outdoor Designs sales chart.

1 Click the **Format menu,** then click the **Font and Style command**
The Font and Style for Subtitle and Labels dialog box displays. The title of this dialog box changes depending on the text currently selected in the chart. By default, all text in the chart *except* the title is selected. The dialog box contains elements you can use to change the font, size, color, and style of the text. As in the Word Processor and Spreadsheet, a sample rectangle lets you preview font and style changes.

2 Scroll down in the Font list box until **Times New Roman** appears, then double-click it
The dialog box closes and the sales chart displays. The text in the subtitle, x- and y-axis, and legend changes to Times New Roman, which is listed as the active font in the Font Name drop-down list box on the toolbar. Next you'll select the title and change the title font.

3 Click the **Edit menu,** then click the **Select Title Text command**
The chart title highlights in the chart. (You can also select the chart title by clicking on it.)

4 Click the **Font Size drop-down list box** on the toolbar, click **14,** then press **[Ctrl][T]** to remove the highlight on the chart title
[Ctrl][T] is the same as choosing the Select Title Text command from the Edit menu. Next you'll change the color of the bars in the chart.

5 Click **Format,** then click the **Patterns and Colors command**
The Patterns and Colors dialog box displays. It lets you change the colors and patterns of the series (bars) in your chart. Because your chart only contains two series (1st Quarter and 2nd Quarter), option buttons representing the 3rd through 6th series appear dimmed in the dialog box. The Markers list box appears dimmed also, because it applies only to line charts.

6 Click **Blue** in the Colors list box and **Dense** in the Patterns list box, then click the **Format button**
The 1st quarter bars and the 1st quarter legend box change from solid red to a shaded blue pattern.

7 Click the **2nd Series option button,** click **Yellow** in the Colors list box, scroll down and click **Dark ** in the Patterns list box, then click **Format**
The 2nd Quarter bars and the 2nd Quarter legend box change from solid green to a striped yellow pattern.

8 Click the **Close button** to close the Patterns and Colors dialog box, then click
The completed chart is shown in Figure 7-7.

FIGURE 7-7: The sales chart with font and color changes

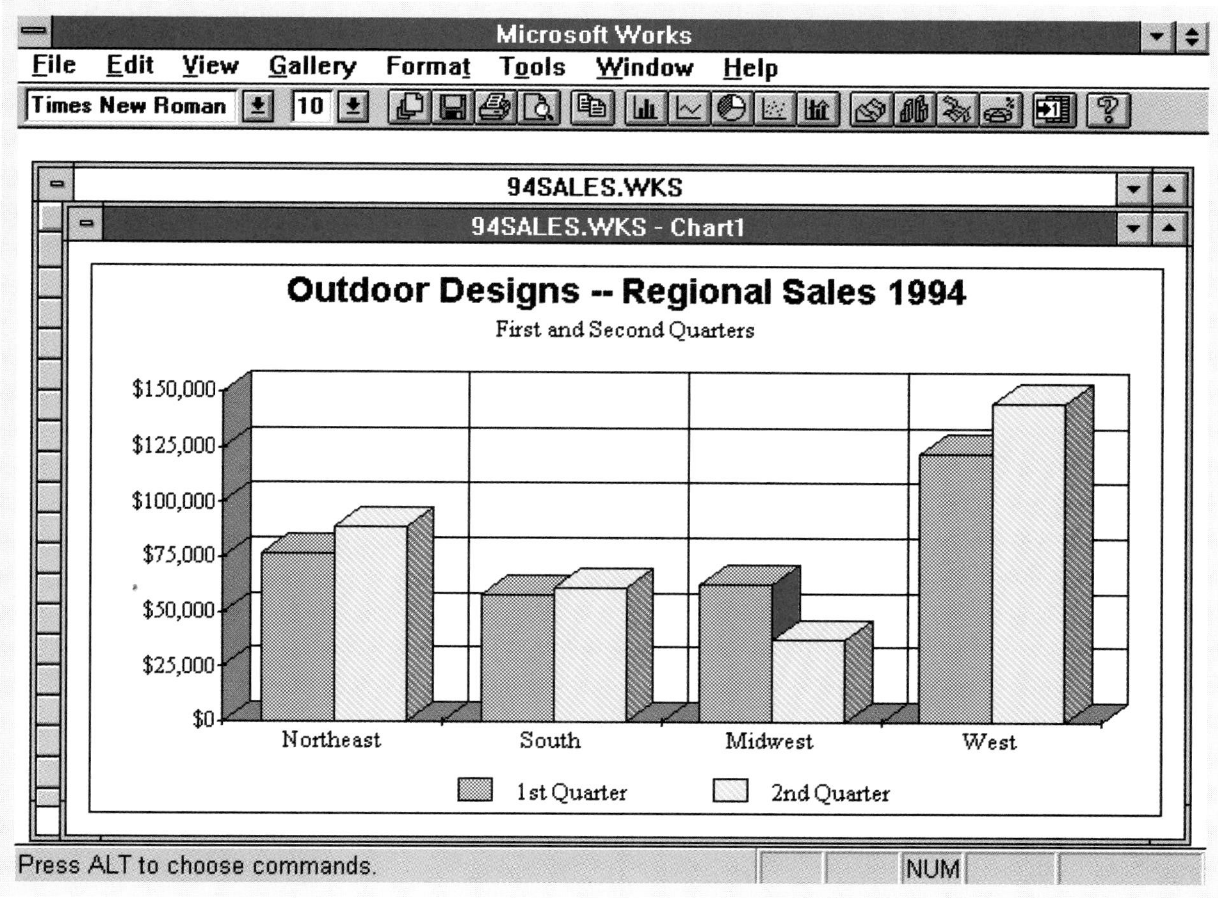

QUICK TIP

If you don't have a color printer attached to your computer, you won't see colors in your final printout. To see the chart as it will be printed, choose the **Display as Printed command** from the View menu.

Pasting a spreadsheet table into the Word Processor

Now that you have a completed spreadsheet and chart, you could print the two documents, staple them together with a quick note, and submit them to the Outdoor Designs sales and marketing staff. But wouldn't it look nicer if everything were neatly arranged on one page? Combining the output of different Works applications is easy, because all the tools were designed to be used together. In this lesson you'll learn how to paste part of the sales information spreadsheet into a memo in the Word Processor, and in the next lesson you'll add the sales chart to the same page.

1 Click the **Window menu**, then click **94SALES.WKS** (the first filename in the list at the bottom of the menu)
The 94SALES.WKS spreadsheet window moves in front of the chart window. Works can have several files open at once. The open files are listed at the bottom of the Window menu.

2 Select **cells A5 through C10** in the spreadsheet, then click 📋
The cell range A5:C10 highlights and is copied to the Windows clipboard. This is the spreadsheet data you'll paste into the Word Processor in the following steps.

3 Click 📋, then open the letterhead template UNIT_02.WPS on the Student Disk
UNIT_02.WPS is the Outdoor Designs letterhead file you used in Unit 2.

4 Save the document as REPSALES.WPS in the MY_FILES directory on the Student Disk
You'll type the contents of your memo beneath the letterhead.

5 Press **[Ctrl][End]** to move to the last line of the file, then type:
To: Sales and marketing staff [Enter]
Fm: Melissa Cavanaugh [Enter]
Date: July 12, 1994 [Enter]
Re: Sales figures are in [Enter]
[Enter] [Enter]
Here are the sales figures for the first two quarters of 1994:
[Enter]
[Enter]

6 Click the **Paste button** 📋 to insert the spreadsheet data
Cells A5 through C10 are pasted into the Word Processor, as shown in Figure 7-8. The cells appear as a **table** in the Word Processor, maintaining their row and column relationships.

7 Click 💾 to save your changes

FIGURE 7-8: A spreadsheet table in a Word Processor document

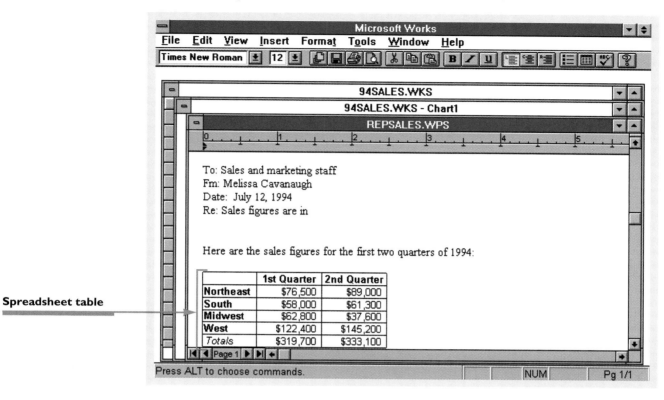

Spreadsheet table

Working with tables in the Word Processor

After you enter a spreadsheet table into a Word Processor document it becomes an **object**, which you can resize, edit, or delete. To resize a table, you would select the table, then drag one of its edges until the table is the shape you want. You could also drag the selected table to another location, change its alignment, or delete it by pressing [Del]. (In these ways the table object is just like any other selected item in the Word Processor.) To edit a table you would double-click it, which starts the Spreadsheet application and places a cursor in the table. You would then edit the table as you would any Works spreadsheet. After editing, you would return to the Word Processor by clicking anywhere in the document.

QUICK **TIP**

You can insert a new spreadsheet table into the Word Processor by choosing the Spreadsheet/ Table command from the Insert menu. You can select, resize, and edit a new table just like a table pasted in from a spreadsheet.■

Pasting a chart into the Word Processor

In this lesson you will paste the sales chart into the REPSALES.WPS document and print out the memo for the sales and marketing department. Pasting a chart into the Word Processor is similar to pasting a spreadsheet table. Because the chart contains color, however, you'll want to use Print Preview to examine the chart before you print the memo. If the chart shading is not to your liking, you can double-click the chart and change the patterns before you print.

1   Click the **Window menu,** then click **94SALES.WKS - Chart1**
The sales chart window displays in front of the spreadsheet and memo windows.

2   Click 🖺 on the toolbar
The chart is copied to the clipboard.

3   Click the **Window menu,** then click **REPSALES.WPS**
The memo window displays in front of the other windows.

4   Press **[Ctrl][End]** and press **[Enter]** three times
The cursor moves to the end of the document and two blank lines are inserted below the spreadsheet table.

5   Type the following text:
And here is the same information in visual form: [Enter] [Enter]

6   Click 🖺 to insert the chart
The sales chart is inserted into the Word Processor, as shown in Figure 7-9. The chart appears as an **object** in the Word Processor, and can be selected, resized, aligned, deleted, and edited just like the spreadsheet table. Congratulations! You've completed the sales memo. Next you'll examine it in Print Preview and print a final copy for distribution.

7   Click 🔍 on the toolbar
The memo displays in Print Preview. Use the **zoom pointer** to examine the spreadsheet table and the chart closely. If part of the spreadsheet or chart has been cut off or appears in the wrong size, you would return to Normal view, select the object, then resize it. If one of the chart bars doesn't look right in black and white, you would return to Normal view, double-click the chart object, then modify the bar with the Patterns and Colors command. When the memo looks just right, you're ready to print.

8   Click the **Print button** on the right side of the Print Preview window
Turn on your printer first if necessary. After a few moments, a final copy of the memo is printed.

9   Click 💾 to save your changes, click **File,** then click **Exit Works**
The Word Processor, Spreadsheet, and Chart windows close and the Works program exits.

FIGURE 7-9: The sales chart in the memo

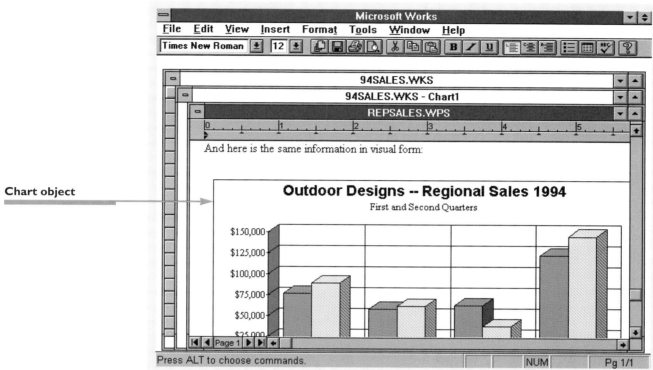

Chart object

Establishing a link between documents

The copy-and-paste technique you used in this unit to exchange information is called **embedding an object**. An embedded object "remembers" how to run the application that created it. Embedding lets you edit the spreadsheet table and the chart you pasted into the Word Processor by simply double-clicking the table or chart object.

Another type of information exchange is called **linking documents**. When documents are linked, any changes made to the original, or **source**, document are automatically included in the linked document. This is useful when you want to pass data from some key source document to one or more linked documents. To link data to a document in the Word Processor, you would select data from the source document, copy it to the clipboard, then start the Word Processor and choose Paste Special from the Edit menu. In the Paste Special dialog box, you would click the Paste Link button, then click OK. Works establishes a link between the two documents, and updates the linked document to include all changes made to the source document from that point on.

QUICK **TIP**

To display the sales chart the next time you open the 94SALES.WKS spreadsheet file, choose the **Chart command** from the View menu, then double-click **Chart1** in the Charts dialog box.

CONCEPTSREVIEW

Label each of the elements of the Chart accessory, as shown in Figure 7-10.

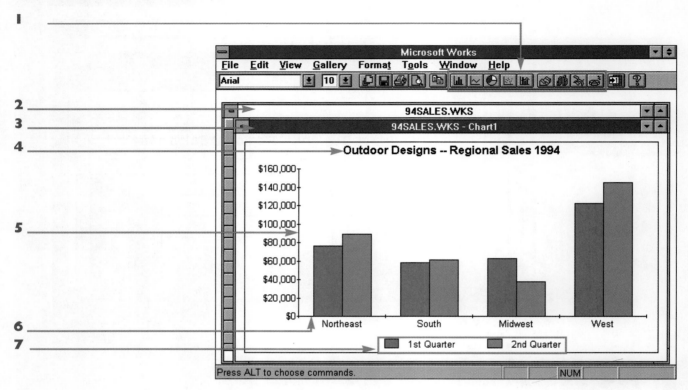

FIGURE 7-10

Match each charting button on the toolbar to the type of chart it creates.

8

9

10

11

12

13

14

15

16

a. 3-D Pie chart button

b. 3-D Line chart button

c. 3-D Bar chart button

d. 3-D Area chart button

e. Mixed chart button

f. Scatter chart button

g. Pie chart button

h. Line chart button

i. Bar chart button

Select the best answer from the list of choices.

17 Which of the following definitions best describes the x-axis in a works chart?

   a. The vertical line that contains a series of related spreadsheet values

   b. The horizontal line that contains a series of related spreadsheet values

   c. A box explaining what the labels, colors, and patterns in the chart mean

   d. Horizontal and vertical lines connecting to the x-axis and y-axis

18 Which steps do you follow to create a new chart in the Spreadsheet?

   a. Click the Chart icon in the Works Startup dialog box

   b. Click the New Chart button, then select the spreadsheet data you want to chart

c. Select the spreadsheet data you want to chart, then click the New Chart button

d. Click the Print Preview button, then click Zoom In

19 Which of the following is *not* a valid way to select the type of chart you want?

a. Select the chart type in the New Chart dialog box

b. Choose the chart type from the Gallery menu

c. Click one of the charting buttons on the toolbar

d. Select the chart type in the Patterns and Colors dialog box

20 Which of the following *cannot* be set with the Vertical (Y) Axis command?

a. The chart style

b. Labels on the y-axis

c. The interval between numbers on the y-axis

d. Gridlines

21 How do you change the color of a bar in a chart?

a. Choose a new color for the bar series in the Patterns and Colors dialog box

b. Choose a new color with the Color drop-down list box in the Font and Style command

c. Double-click the bar, then specify the new color

d. Choose the Display as Printed command from the View menu

22 What steps do you follow to copy a Spreadsheet table into the Word Processor?

a. Copy the data in the Spreadsheet, then paste it into the Word Processor

b. Copy the data in the Spreadsheet, then paste it into the Chart accessory

c. Double-click a range of cells in the Spreadsheet

d. Paste the data into the Word Processor, then copy it from the Spreadsheet

23 When a Spreadsheet table is inserted into the Word Processor, it becomes:

a. a table with entries separated by tabs

b. regular text that can be formatted

c. a chart that can be printed

d. an object that can be resized, edited, or deleted

24 How do you change the font size in a chart that has been inserted into the Word Processor?

a. Select the chart, then change the font size with the Font Size drop-down list box

b. Select the chart, choose Page Layout view, then press [F1]

c. Double-click the chart, then change the font size in the Chart accessory

d. Once the chart has been inserted, the font size cannot be changed

25 How does an embedded object differ from a linked object?

a. An embedded object is not updated automatically; a linked object is

b. A linked object is the only object that you can resize, edit, or delete

c. Embedded objects must be inserted into documents with the Paste Special command

d. The Word Processor can only accept linked objects

APPLICATIONSREVIEW

1 Open the file UNIT_07.WKS and create a pie chart for 1st quarter sales.

a. Start Works and open the file UNIT_07.WKS

b. Select the cell range A5:B9, then click the New Chart button.

c. Click Pie in the drop-down list box, type **1st Quarter 1994 Sales** in the Chart Title text box, then click OK.

2 Change the chart type to 3-D Pie chart (style 6).

a. Click the 3-D Pie Chart button.

b. Click style 6 in the 3-D Pie dialog box, then click OK.

3 Add a subtitle to the chart.

a. Click the Edit menu, then click the Titles command.

b. Press [Tab], type **Outdoor Designs Sales Reps** in the Subtitle text box, then click OK.

4 Change the chart font to Courier New, then explode the slice of the pie for the West region.

a. Click the Font drop-down list box, then click Courier New to change the font of the subtitle and labels to Courier New.

b. Click the chart title, then click the Font drop-down list box and click Courier New to change the font of the title to Courier New.

c. Click the Format menu, then click the Patterns and Colors command.

d. Click 4 in the Slices list box, click the Explode Slice check box, click the Format button, then click Close.

e. Click the Save button to save your changes.

5 Paste the 1st quarter sales data from the spreadsheet into the letterhead template file in the Word Processor.

a. Click the Window menu, then click 94SALES.WKS to display the sales spreadsheet.

b. Select the cell range A5:B10, click the Copy button, then click the Startup button on the toolbar.

c. Double-click the LETTERHD.WPS file in the Recently used files list box.

d. Save the file as QUARTER1.WPS.

e. Press [Ctrl][End], then type the following lines:

To: Sales and marketing staff [Enter]

Fm: Melissa Cavanaugh [Enter]

Date: July 14, 1994 [Enter]

Re: 1st quarter sales numbers [Enter]

[Enter] [Enter]

Here are the sales figures for the first quarter of 1994: [Enter]

[Enter]

f. Click the Paste button to insert the spreadsheet table as an object in the Word Processor.

6 Paste the 1st quarter sales chart into the Word Processor, then print the memo.

a. Click Window, then click 94SALES.WKS - Chart 2.

b. Select Copy from the Edit menu, click Window, then click QUARTER1.WPS.

c. Press [Ctrl][End], press [Enter] three times, then type the following text:

And here is the same information in visual form: [Enter]

[Enter]

d. Click the Paste button to insert the chart as an object in the Word Processor.

e. Click the Print Preview button and verify that everything looks right in the memo before you print it.

f. Click the Print button to print a final copy, click the Save button, then exit Works.

INDEPENDENT
CHALLENGES

In this unit you created bar charts and pie charts using the data in the 94SALES.WKS file. Spend some time now creating a few more charts with the Chart accessory. Open the 94SALES.WKS file, then open the bar chart you created (Chart1) with the Chart command on the View menu. Now try the Area, Line, Stacked Line, XY (Scatter), and Combination commands on the Gallery menu to see what the sales data looks like in each of those chart types. As you can see, you have quite a few options when it comes to presenting your data graphically. If you have any questions about any of these charts, consult the Works on-line help.

To continue your work with charts, open the file TRIPS93.WKS you created in the independent challenge for Unit 6, save the file as TRIPS93B.WKS, and perform the following exercises. (If you did not complete the Unit 6 Independent Challenge, go back and do it now.) As you examine each chart type, think about its strengths and weaknesses in communicating information. If you have any questions about any of these charts, consult the charting overview on the Works on-line help.

1 Highlight cells A4 to M10 and create a Bar chart showing the number of trips sold for each activity.

2 Copy row 5 of the data (the helicopter skiing) into a blank row somewhere beneath the data and copy row 8 of the data (ballooning trips) into the row beneath it. Highlight the two rows and create an Area chart of the data. Notice how clearly it shows the seasonality of each activity.

3 Create a Line chart of the same data, then create a Stacked Line chart. Try to explain the differences between the two graphs.

4 Highlight cells A4 to M5 and create a pie chart of the data. Which months are most popular for helicopter skiing? What is the problem with this type of chart? Try a radar chart instead. Does that show the data as clearly, without the confusion about the labels for the summer months? Is a Scatter chart equally dramatic? A 3-D Area chart? A 3-D Bar chart?

5 Highlight cells A4 to M10 again and choose the format you think shows the overall popularity and seasonality of each type of type. Call the chart Outdoor Adventure Trips - 1993. Examine the chart in Print Preview and print a copy of the chart. If you have a color printer, your printed version will resemble the screen. Otherwise, Works substitutes line patterns for the different colors.

UNIT 8

Building
A DATABASE

*I*n Units 2 through 7 you learned how to use the Works Word Processor and Spreadsheet. In this unit you'll learn about the Works **Database application**, a set of tools that will help you manage and manipulate customer information at Outdoor Designs. Think of a database as an organized collection of information stored electronically in a file. A database can contain information of any kind, from sales and financial records about your business, to a list of school friends and associates, to the compact discs in your music collection. Outdoor Designs uses a database to manage the names, addresses, and phone numbers of all its customers. ▶ In this unit you'll learn how to start the Database, create a database form, and enter information in database **fields** and **records**. Next you'll learn how to change the information stored in a database, add and delete database fields, and change the font and style of the text on forms. Finally, you'll learn how to print the records of the database. ▶

Starting the Database

You start the Database application from the Works Startup dialog box. The Database has a graphical interface that's similar to the Word Processor and Spreadsheet applications. If you worked through Units 2 to 7 you'll recognize many of the toolbar buttons and menu commands. Figure 8-2 identifies the unique elements of the Database interface, and Table 8-1 lists the buttons unique to the Database toolbar. You'll start Works and the Database application now.

1   Double-click the **Microsoft Works** program icon to start the Works program
    The Startup dialog box displays, as shown in Figure 8-1. The Startup dialog box contains buttons that start the Word Processor, Spreadsheet, Database, and Communications applications.

2   Click the **Database button** to start the Works Database application
    The Startup dialog box and the Database application opens in a window, as shown in Figure 8-2. A dialog box describing how database fields are created may also display in the window (this dialog box does not appear after you create your first database). The Database contains interface elements found in every Works application: a menu bar, toolbar, document window, scroll bars, toggle indicators, sizing buttons, and control menu boxes. Unique to the Database interface are a **cursor reference box** that shows the location of the cursor in the document window, a **record number indicator** that shows the number of the database record displayed in the document window, **record navigation buttons** that you can use to scroll to other records in the database, and a **formula bar** where you enter and edit items in the database.

3   Click **OK** to close the dialog box (if it is displayed)
    The dialog box closes. Next you'll name the database and save it to your Student Disk.

4   Click the **File menu**, then click the **Save As command**
    The Save As dialog box displays. It includes a File Name text box where you can enter a descriptive file name of eight characters or less, a Directories list box where you can choose the destination directory for the file, a Drives drop-down list box where you can choose a destination disk, a Save File as Type drop-down list box where you can identify the type of the file you are saving, and four command buttons. Put your Student Disk into drive A or drive B now if it is not there already. This time you'll specify drive A and the destination directory in the File Name text box.

5   Type **a:\my_files\custdata** and click **OK** or substitute b: if your Student Disk is in drive B
    The database file CUSTDATA.WDB is saved in the MY_FILES directory on the Student Disk.

FIGURE 8-1:
The Works Startup
dialog box

Database button

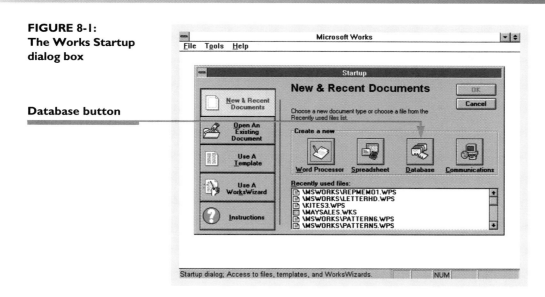

FIGURE 8-2: The Works Database with unique elements labeled

Menu bar

Cursor reference box

Formula bar

Record number
indicator

Record navigation
buttons

Sizing buttons

Toolbar

Scroll bars

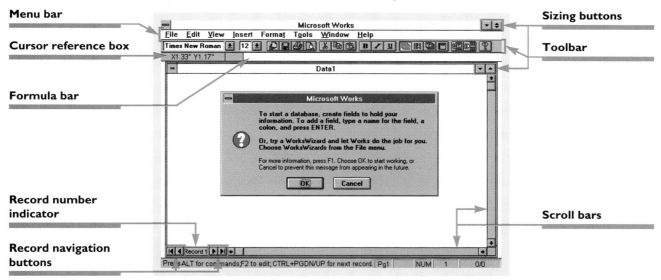

TABLE 8-1:
Toolbar buttons unique to the Database

BUTTON	FUNCTION
	Displays the database in form view
	Displays the database in list view
	Queries the database to display specific records
	Creates a report that summarizes database information
	Adds a field to a database form
	Inserts a new record into the database

QUICK **TIP**

To get on-line help
as you work in the
Database application,
choose **Cue Cards**
from the Help menu,
then click **I want help
from Cue Cards.**

Creating a form

In the Database application, the document window is called a form. A **form** is a space where database information is entered and displayed. The categories of information in a database form are called **fields**, as shown in Figure 8-3. A Works database can contain up to 256 fields representing items such as business names, addresses, or phone numbers. All the information about a business or other entity is known as a **record**. ▶ Sue Ellen has assigned you the task of creating a database to keep track of each Outdoor Designs customer. You'll start working on the database now by creating a label and several fields on the form and saving it to disk. In the next lesson you'll add records to the database for several of Outdoor Designs' customers.

STEPS

1 Press [↓], then type **Outdoor Designs Customer Database** and press **[Enter]**
   The text Outdoor Designs Customer Database is added to the form. This text is considered a **label** on the form, and is identified by a double quotation mark in the formula bar. Now enter the eight fields into the customer database, using Figure 8-3 as a guide.

2 Press [↓] three times, then type **Business:** and press **[Enter]**
   The colon tells Works that Business is the name of the field. A **Field Size** dialog box opens, prompting you for the width and height (in characters) of the field.

3 Type **35** and click **OK**
   A line 35 characters long displays on the form as part of the Business field.

4 Press [↓], then type **Address:** and press **[Enter]**
   The Address field is added to the form; then a Field Size dialog box opens, prompting you for the field size. Type **50** in the Width text box and click **OK**.

5 Press [↓], then type **City:** and press **[Enter]** twice
   The City field and a line 20 characters long (the default) are added to the form.

6 Press **[Shift][Tab]** to back up, press **[→]** twice, then type **State:** and press **[Enter]**
   The State field is added to the form. Type **6** in the Width text box and press **[Enter]**.

7 Press **[Shift][Tab]**, press **[→]** twice, then type **Zip:** and press **[Enter]**
   The Zip field is added to the form. Type **10** in the Width text box and press **[Enter]**.

8 Press **[Shift][Tab]**, press **[→]** twice, then type **Country:** and press **[Enter]** twice

9 Press **[Home]**, press [↓], then type **Phone:** and press **[Enter]** twice

10 Press **[Shift][Tab]**, press **[→]** twice, then type **Fax:** and press **[Enter]** twice
    The eighth and final field displays on the form, as shown in Figure 8-3.

11 Click 🖫 to save the form to disk

FIGURE 8-3: The Outdoor Designs Customer Database form

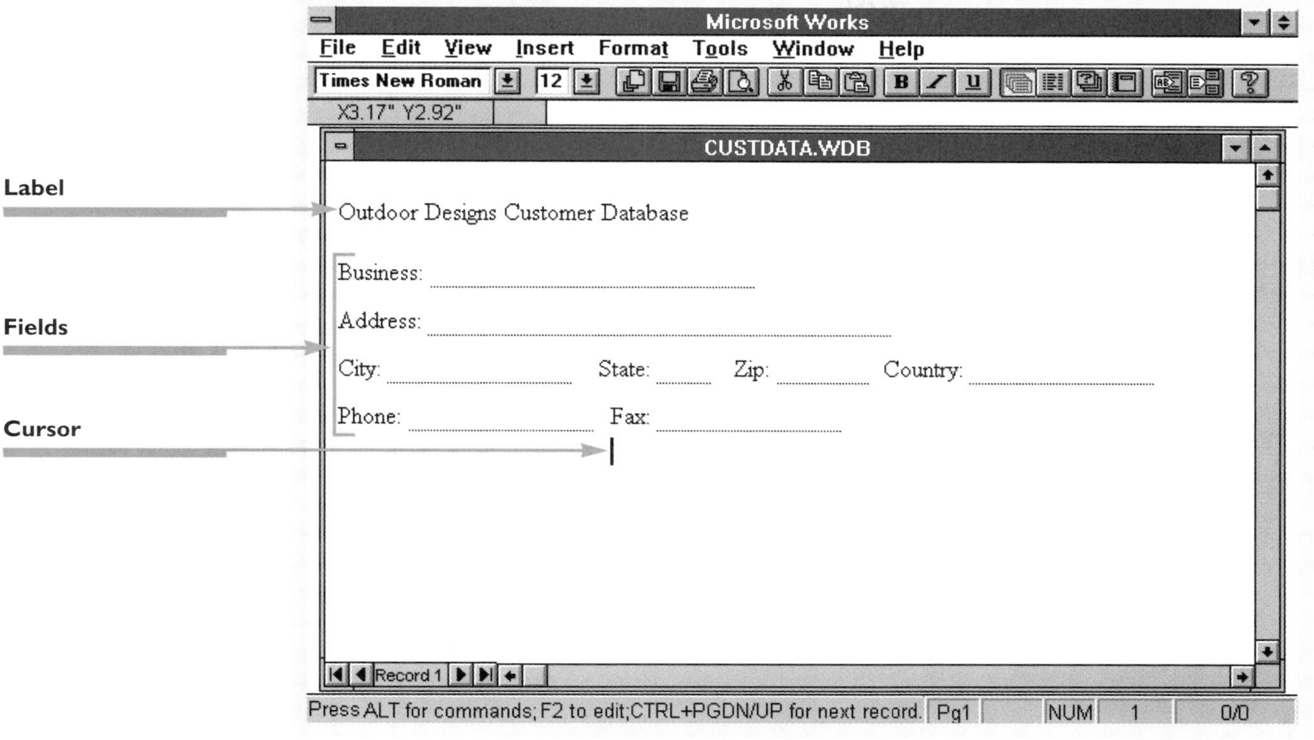

Label

Fields

Cursor

Planning your fields

Choosing the right fields for your database is an important task. Fields affect how data is entered into the database, as well as how the database will be sorted, searched, and reported later. It's usually better to be specific with your fields, using enough fields so that you can break out the important information, but not so many that it makes using the forms a burden. For example, it is usually better to use separate fields for the city, state, and zip code elements in the database, so later you can search for records from a particular city, state, or zip code individually. If you wish, you can design your form so that it precisely matches a printed form or looks like an invoice or statement that you want to mail to a customer later. When planning your fields you should also be sure to include descriptive labels to clarify what the fields do, and provide instructions for the people who will be using the database down the road.

QUICK TIP

You can also create a database form with the Quick Database WorksWizard. To use this WorksWizard, choose the **WorksWizard command** from the File menu, then double-click **Quick Database** in the WorksWizard list box.■

Entering data into fields

Now that you have created a database form for Outdoor Designs customers, you can enter information into it. To enter information into a field, you select the field, then type the data corresponding to the field name. You can enter text, numbers, or a formula in a field. Table 8-2 lists keys that are useful when working with fields. You'll enter a record into the database now for the company Cambridge Kite Supplies.

1   **Click the line after the Business field**
The data-entry portion of the Business field highlights. This part of the field is known as the **field value**. The first part of the field (the word Business and the colon) is known as the **field name**. See Figure 8-4.

2   **Type Cambridge Kite Supplies and press [Tab]**
Cambridge Kite Supplies is entered into the Business field and the Address field highlights.

3   **Type 1437 Wednesday Street and press [Tab]**
The company's address is entered into the Address field and the City field highlights.

4   **Type Cambridge and press [Tab], then type MA and press [Tab]**
The City and State fields are entered and the Zip field highlights.

5   **Type 02142 and press [Enter]**
The number 2142 is entered into the Zip field and the field remains highlighted. Note that Works automatically deleted the leading zero in the zip code. To put it back, you'll use the Number command on the Format menu.

6   **Click the Format menu, click Number, click Leading Zeros, type 5, then click OK**
The number 02142 displays in the Zip field. The Number command can be used to change the number format of any field in the database. When you have a Zip field in your database, you should always format the field with Leading Zeros and specify 5 in the Number of digits box.

7   **Press [Tab], then type USA and press [Tab]**
USA is entered into the Country field and the Phone field highlights.

8   **Type (617) 275-3333 and press [Tab], then type (617) 275-3344 and press [Enter]**
The Phone and Fax fields are entered into the database, as shown in Figure 8-4. Congratulations! You've completed your first entry or **record** in the Outdoor Designs database.

9   **Click 🖫 to save your first database record**

FIGURE 8-4: The Cambridge Kite Supplies record in the Customer Database

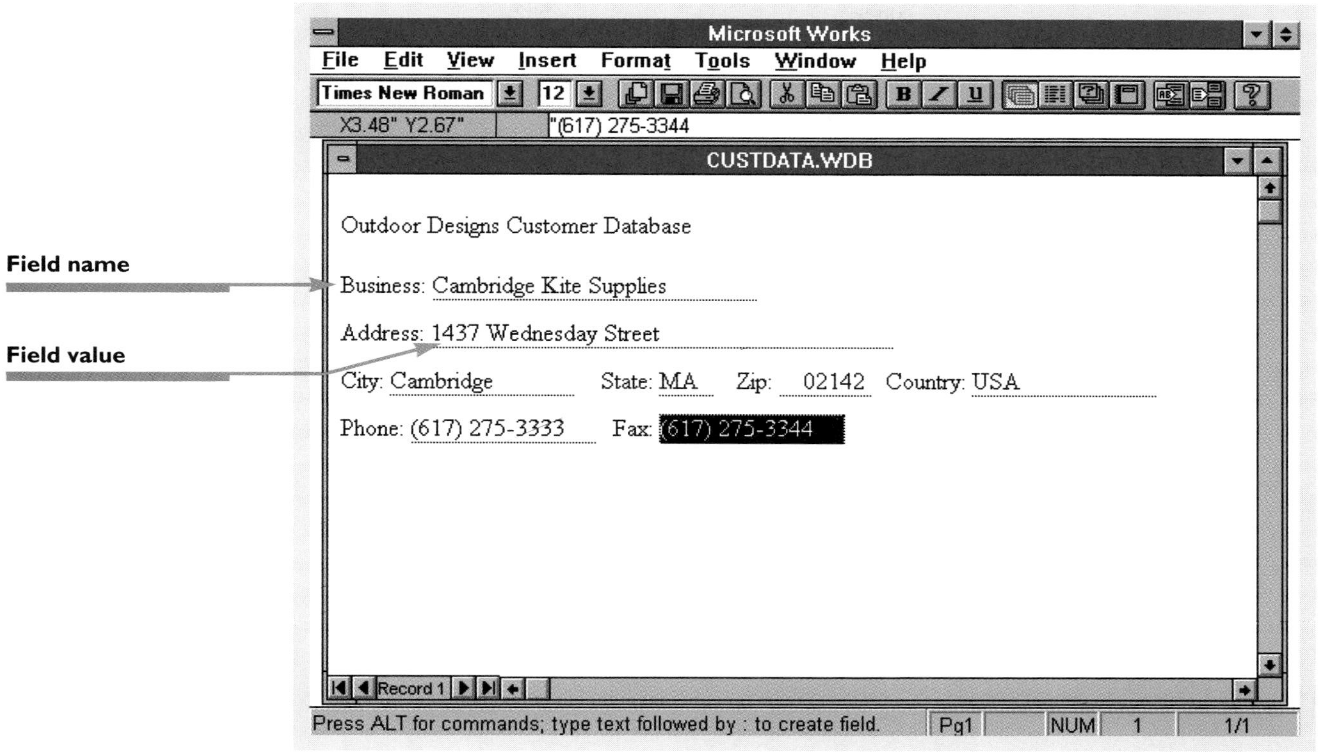

Field name

Field value

TABLE 8-2: Useful keys for working with database fields

KEY	FUNCTION
[Tab]	Highlights the next field in the database
[Shift][Tab]	Highlights the previous field in the database
[F2]	Lets you edit the highlighted field in the formula bar
[Del]	Deletes the contents of the highlighted field

QUICK **TIP**

A heavily used database can quickly grow to hundreds of records and can become an important asset to a person or a business. As your database grows, be careful to keep a backup copy in a safe place to avoid losing valuable information.■

Adding records to the database

In this lesson you'll learn to add new records to the database and to view the records in **list view**. To add a new record, you click the Insert Record button on the toolbar or press [Tab] when the last field in the last record is highlighted. The new, blank record appears on the form, and the previous record is hidden from view. The record number indicator is also updated. When there is more than one record you can use the record navigation buttons to scroll through the database. Try adding three more Outdoor Designs customer records in the following steps.

STEPS

1 Verify that the last field on the form is highlighted, as shown in Figure 8-4

2 Press **[Tab]**
A new, blank record is added to the database and the Cambridge Kite Supplies record is hidden from view. The Business field highlights and Record 2 displays in the record number indicator.

3 Type in the following customer data, pressing **[Tab]** between fields:
Mountain Air [Tab] **10 Blaine Street** [Tab] **North Bend** [Tab] **WA** [Tab] **98045** [Tab] **USA** [Tab] **(206) 888-1541** [Tab] **(206) 888-1532** [Enter]

4 Press **[Tab]** to add a new record, then type in the following customer data:
Ken's Outdoor Gear [Tab] **4545 64th Ave. SE** [Tab] **Olympia** [Tab] **WA** [Tab] **98503** [Tab] **USA** [Tab] **(206) 491-2222** [Tab] **(206) 491-2255** [Enter]

5 Click the **inside-left record navigation button** (see Figure 8-5) twice
The second and first records in the database display as you click. The inside navigation buttons let you scroll through the database one record at a time. The outside buttons move you to the first and last records of the database, respectively.

6 Click the **Insert Record button** 🖳 on the toolbar
A new, blank record displays at the beginning of the database, as shown in Figure 8-5. As you add records to the database you can add them to the end of the list, with the [Tab] key, or between existing records, with the Insert Record button. These two methods give you flexibility in how your database is organized. (You can also sort the database alphabetically. You'll learn about sorting in the next unit.)

7 Click the **Business field**, then type the following customer data:
The Essential Surfer [Tab] **100 Seawind Drive** [Tab] **Newport Beach** [Tab] **CA** [Tab] **92660** [Tab] **USA** [Tab] **(714) 837-4444** [Tab] **(714) 837-4436** [Enter]

8 Click 🖫 to save your new database records

FIGURE 8-5: A new record is inserted at the top of the database

Insert Record button

Inside-left navigation button

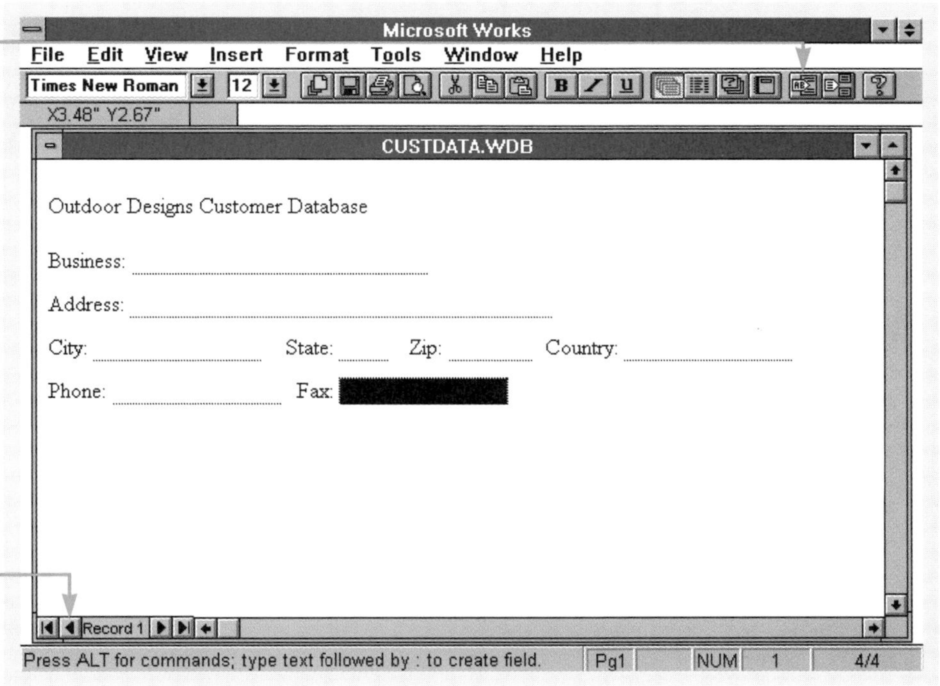

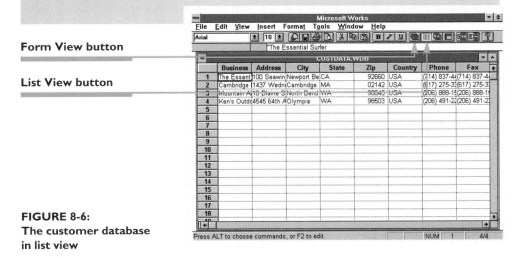

Viewing records in list view

You can display the records in the database in a table format of columns (records) and rows (fields) by clicking the **List View button** on the toolbar. When you click the List View button, the database appears in spreadsheet format, as shown in Figure 8-6. In this format you can compare the different database records for overall consistency, and quickly search for individual records. You can also add new records to the database and edit existing records. To widen a column of cells (so that you can read the entire contents of a field), click the title of the column you want to adjust, choose the **Field Width command** from the Format menu, and enter a larger field width. When you finish viewing your records in list view, return to form view by clicking the **Form View button** on the toolbar.

Form View button

List View button

FIGURE 8-6:
The customer database
in list view

QUICK **TIP**

In form view, [Ctrl][PgUp] and [Ctrl][PgDn] move you to the previous and next records in the database, respectively.∎

Editing data in fields

You can replace the information stored in a field by highlighting the field, typing the new entry, and pressing [Enter]. You can also edit a field value on the formula bar by highlighting the field and pressing [F2]. Table 8-3 lists several editing keys that are useful when editing text in the formula bar. In addition to these techniques, you can use the Cut, Copy, and Paste toolbar buttons to delete and replicate field entries in the database. You'll practice editing fields in the database now.

1 Return to form view, then click the **inside-right record navigation button** to scroll to Record 2 in the database
The customer record for Cambridge Kite Supplies appears.

2 Click the **Business field** and press **[F2]**
The text Cambridge Kite Supplies appears in the formula bar, along with a blinking cursor. Next you'll change the business name to Cambridge Kite Supply.

3 Press **[Backspace]** three times, then type **y** and press **[Enter]**
The revised business name is entered into the database.

4 Click the **inside-right record navigation button** twice to scroll to Record 4
The record for Ken's Outdoor Gear displays. Sue Ellen has informed you that this business is now receiving faxes on their voice line, so you should copy the value in the Phone field to the Fax field.

5 Click the **Fax field**, then click 🖊 on the toolbar
The old fax number is deleted from the record.

6 Click the **Phone field**, then click 🖺 on the toolbar
The value in the Phone field is copied to the Windows clipboard.

7 Click the **Fax field**, then click 🖺 on the toolbar
The phone number (206) 491-2222 is replicated in the Fax field, as shown in Figure 8-7. Note that the Cut, Copy, and Paste commands on the Edit menu are the menu command equivalents to the Cut, Copy, and Paste buttons. You can use any combination of these buttons and commands as you edit your database.

8 Click 🖫 to save your edits to disk

FIGURE 8-7: The record for Ken's Outdoor Gear after editing

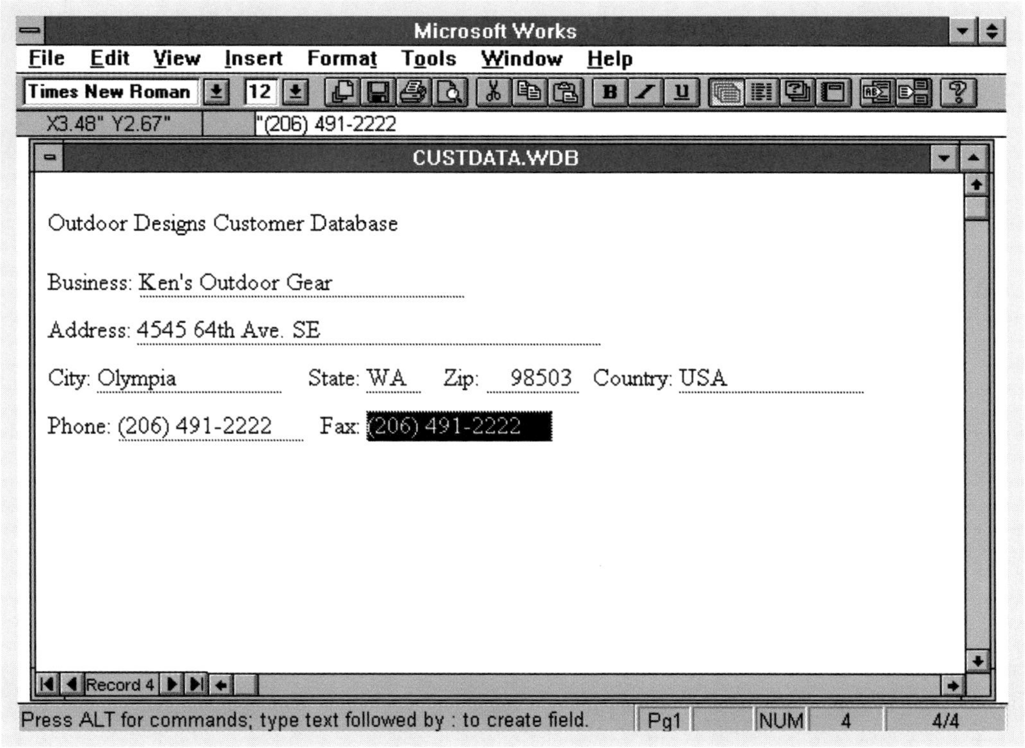

```
┌─────────────────────────────────────────────────────────────┐
│  ─                    Microsoft Works              ▼ ┆        │
│  File  Edit  View  Insert  Format  Tools  Window  Help        │
│  Times New Roman ± 12 ±  □□🖨️🔍 ✂️📋📋 B / U □📊📋📋 📊📋 ?     │
│  X3.48" Y2.67"        "(206) 491-2222                         │
│  ┌──────────────────── CUSTDATA.WDB ──────────────── ▼ ┆──┐  │
│  │                                                          │  │
│  │  Outdoor Designs Customer Database                       │  │
│  │                                                          │  │
│  │  Business: Ken's Outdoor Gear                            │  │
│  │                                                          │  │
│  │  Address: 4545 64th Ave. SE                              │  │
│  │                                                          │  │
│  │  City: Olympia        State: WA   Zip:   98503  Country: USA │  │
│  │                                                          │  │
│  │  Phone: (206) 491-2222    Fax:(206) 491-2222             │  │
│  │                                                          │  │
│  ├────────────────────────────────────────────────────────┤  │
│  │ |◀ ◀ Record 4 ▶ ▶| ◀                                    │  │
│  │ Press ALT for commands; type text followed by : to create field. │ Pg1 │ NUM │ 4 │ 4/4 │
└─────────────────────────────────────────────────────────────┘
```

TABLE 8-3: Useful keys for editing text on the formula bar

KEY	FUNCTION
[←]	Moves the cursor one character to the left
[→]	Moves the cursor one character to the right
[Home]	Moves the cursor to the beginning of the text
[End]	Moves the cursor to the end of the text
[Shift][←]	Selects the character to the left of the cursor
[Shift][→]	Selects the character to the right of the cursor
[Del]	Deletes the selected text

QUICK **TIP**

To reverse an editing change you made by mistake, press **[Ctrl][Z]** or choose the **Undo command** from the Edit menu.

Managing fields

You can add new fields or delete unwanted fields at any time. You can also move or resize existing fields to make them more appropriate for the information stored in the database. To practice managing fields in the Outdoor Designs customer database, delete the Country field, move the Fax field, and add a Comments field in the following steps.

1 Click the **Country field name** on the form
You can click the Country field in any record. However, be sure to click the field name (Country) and not the field value (USA). Sue Ellen has suggested that you delete the field, because Outdoor Designs has no active accounts outside the United States.

2 Press **[Del]**, then click **OK**
The Country field is deleted from the form and each record in the database. Next you'll move the Fax field below the Phone field.

3 Click the **Fax field name**, hold down the mouse button, drag the **Fax field** below the Phone field until the cursor reference box displays X1.33" Y3.00", then release the mouse button
The word Move appears beneath the mouse pointer when you drag the field. If you have trouble moving the field to the correct spot, choose the **Undo command** from the Edit menu and try again. Next you'll add a Comments field to the form.

4 Use the direction keys to position the cursor at location **X1.33" Y3.67"**
The [↑] and [↓] keys change the X coordinate of the cursor and the [→] and [←] keys change the Y coordinate of the cursor.

5 Click the **Insert Field button** 🔳 on the toolbar
The Insert Field dialog box displays.

6 Type **Comments**, press **[Tab]**, type **76**, press **[Tab]**, type **2**, then press **[Enter]**
A field named Comments that is 76 characters wide and two lines high is added to the form. Because there is still some room beneath the Comments field on the form, resize the field now so that it is three lines high.

7 Click the **Format menu**, then click the **Field Size command**
The Field Size dialog box displays. It contains the current dimensions of the Comments field.

8 Press **[Tab]**, type **3**, then press **[Enter]**
The height of the Comments field is extended to three lines, as shown in Figure 8-8. Each of the changes you have made to the form in this lesson has been replicated in every record in the database.

9 Click 🔳 to save your changes

FIGURE 8-8: The database form after field changes

Insert Field button

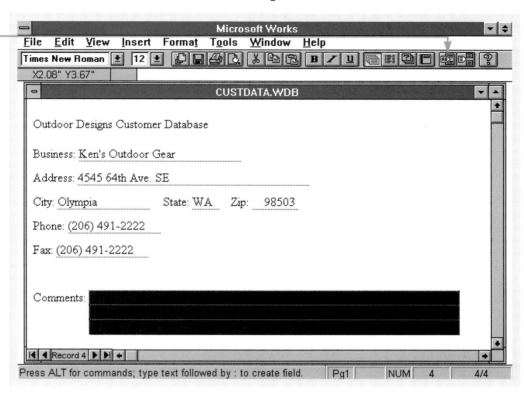

Changing the alignment in a field

You can change the alignment of a field value with the Alignment command on the Format menu. The Alignment options in form view are General, Left, Right, and Center. General alignment, the default, means that text is aligned to the left of the field and numbers are aligned to the right of the field. In the Outdoor Designs database, the style of the field entries would be more consistent if the Zip field were left-aligned. To left-align the Zip field you would click the line containing the zip code value, then choose the Alignment command from the Format menu. The Alignment dialog box would display, as shown in Figure 8-9. You would then click the Left option button and press Enter to left-align the field.

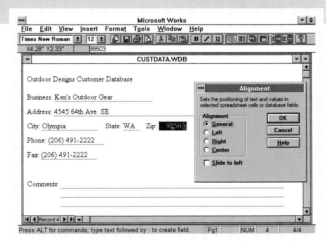

FIGURE 8-9:
Changing the alignment
of a field with the
Alignment command

TROUBLE?

Be careful when you delete fields from a form. Deleted fields are removed from every record in the database, and the deletion cannot be reversed with the Undo command.∎

Changing the font

You can change the font and style of the database labels and fields. You can also add borders and shading to make important information stand out. The font and style commands are identical to the commands in the Word Processor and Spreadsheet, and several of them are available as toolbar buttons. The Border and Patterns commands on the Format menu help you take advantage of the unique rectangular design of database fields, and can produce impressive formatting effects. You'll try working with the font command and other formatting commands now.

1   Click the label **Outdoor Designs Customer Database** at the top of the form
The label highlights.

2   Click **16** in the Font size drop-down list box and click **Arial** in the Font name drop-down list box
The size of the label changes to 16 points and the font changes from Times New Roman to Arial. Notice that the toolbar elements work exactly as they do in the Word Processor and Spreadsheet. You can also use the Font and Style command on the Format menu to accomplish these formatting changes.

3   Click **B** on the toolbar
The style of the label changes to boldface. Now you'll add color to both parts of the Business field.

4   Click the **Business field name**, then hold down **[Ctrl]** and click the **Business field value**
Business and Ken's Outdoor Gear highlight. (It doesn't matter which record is currently displayed, because font and style formatting applies to all records.) Holding down [Ctrl] lets you select more than one field at a time. After you have selected the fields, you can release [Ctrl].

5   Click the **Format menu,** then click the **Font and Style command**
The Font and Style dialog box displays.

6   Click the **Color drop-down list box,** then scroll down the list and click **Dark Blue**
Dark Blue is selected as the font color, and the text in the sample rectangle displays in dark blue.

7   Click **OK**
The Font and Style dialog box closes and the color of the highlighted text changes from white to yellow (the opposite of blue on the color wheel).

8   Click the **Address field** (or anywhere else on the form)
Now the Business field displays in dark blue, as shown in Figure 8-10. Formatting the Business field in a second color will draw attention to it in the database.

9   Click **[save]** to save your font changes

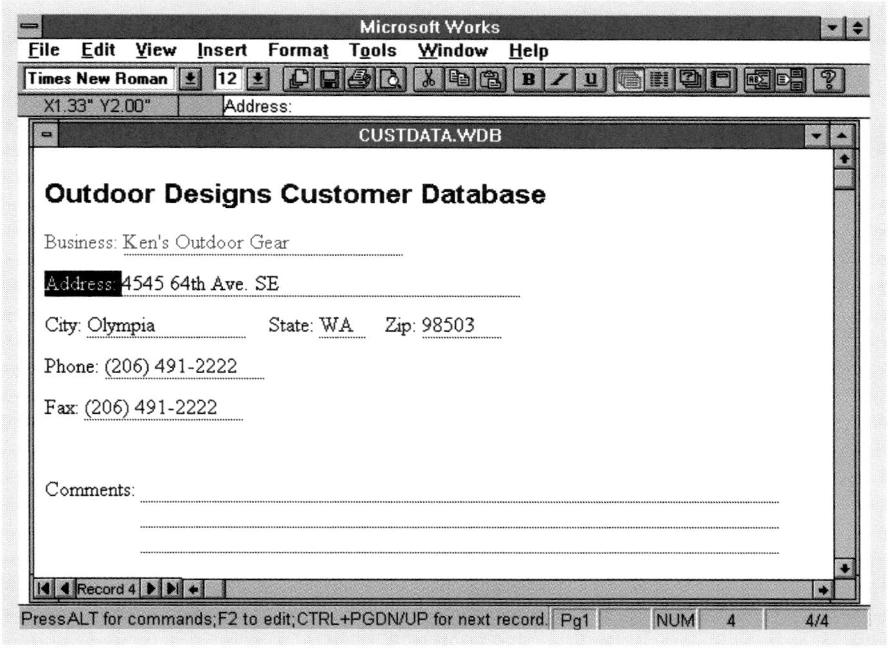

FIGURE 8-10:
The database after font and style changes

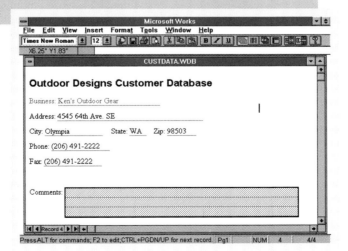

Adding shading and borders to fields

Another way to emphasize information in the database is to add shading or borders to fields. To add shading to a field, you click the field, then choose the **Patterns command** on the Format menu. When you click the Patterns command, a dialog box displays Pattern, Foreground, and Background drop-down list boxes. The Pattern drop-down list box contains 14 different shading patterns, ranging from slight shading to solid black. The lightest shading patterns usually work best when you're trying to emphasize a field with text in it. To outline a field with a border, you click the field, then choose the **Border command** from the Format menu. When you click the Border command, a dialog box displays Outline, Color, and Line Style elements. To add a thin border you would click the Outline button and click OK. Figure 8-11 shows the customer database after light shading and a thin border have been added to the Comments field.

FIGURE 8-11:
The Comments field with shading and a border

QUICK **TIP**

If you worked through Unit 4 in this book you learned how to add WordArt to a word processing document. You can also add WordArt to a database form by choosing the WordArt command from the Insert menu. See Unit 4 for more information about WordArt.■

Printing the database

Databases are not printed as often as Word Processor or Spreadsheet documents. Because a database can contain hundreds or even thousands of records, it is often not practical to print the whole thing at once. As you'll see in the next two units, a computer database is extremely powerful because it can be searched, sorted, and modified in ways that printed documents cannot. In this lesson you'll learn how to examine a single record in Print Preview and print a copy for someone in the office who has requested the customer's address and phone number. After you have printed the record, you'll exit Works.

1 Click 🔍 on the toolbar
The Print Preview window opens and the first record in the database appears as it will print. (By default Works prints one record per page in landscape orientation.) Several command buttons that control the operation of the Print Preview window appear on the right side of the window.

2 Click the **Zoom In button**
The record enlarges to half-size in the Print Preview window, as shown in Figure 8-12.

3 Click the **Next button**
The second record (Cambridge Kite Supply) displays in the Print Preview window. You'll print this record and give it to Sue Ellen for an upcoming account call.

4 Click **Cancel** to cancel Print Preview
You can print from Print Preview, but that would print the entire database. The File menu Print command lets you select records for printing.

5 Click the **File menu**, then click the **Print command**
The Print dialog box displays. It lets you specify the number of copies you want to print, the printing page range (if the form is longer than one page), and whether all the records or only the current record should be printed.

Take a moment now to verify that your printer is on-line and properly connected to your computer. If you have any questions, ask your instructor or lab manager for help.

6 Click **Current record only**, then click **OK** to print the record
The Print dialog box closes. After a few moments the database record for Cambridge Kite Supply emerges from the printer. Now save any changes you have made and exit Works.

7 Click 💾 to save your changes

8 Click **File**, then click **Exit Works**
The CUSTDATA.WDB database closes and the Works program exits.

FIGURE 8-12:
The first database
record in Print Preview

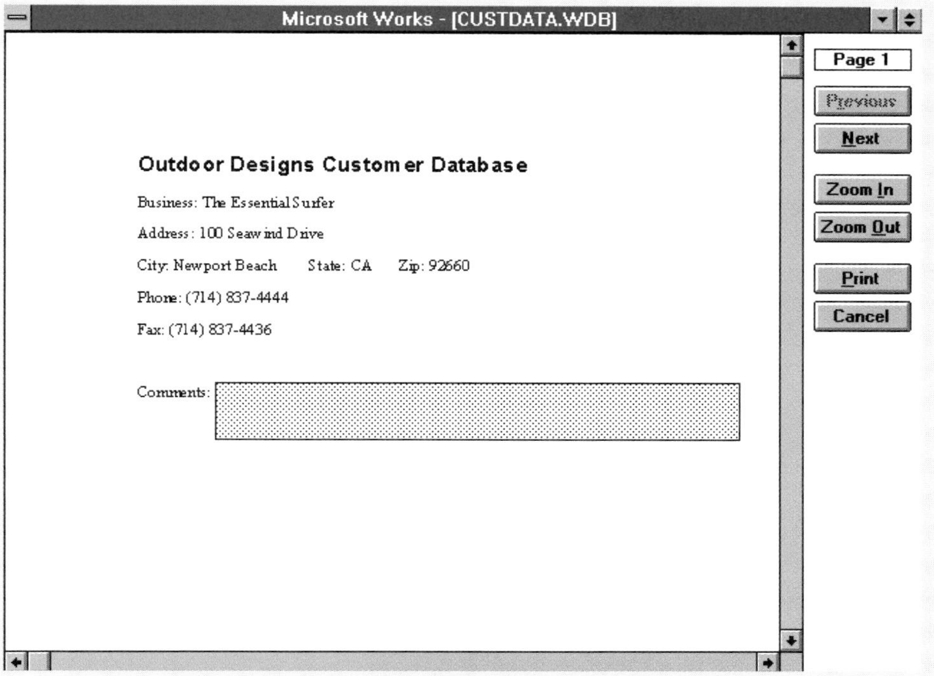

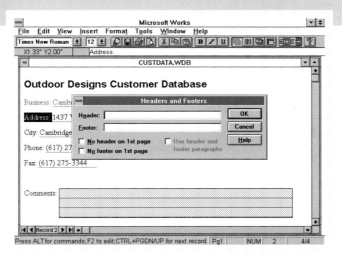

Adding headers and footers

When you print your records, you may want to add page numbers, the current date, or some other text to the top or the bottom of each page. You can add this information to your form with the Headers and Footers command on the View menu. The Headers and Footers dialog box is shown in Figure 8-13. A standard header or footer in Works is one line long and can contain one or several **header and footer codes**. The header and footer codes in the Database are identical to the header and footer codes in the Word Processor, listed in Table 3-3. Headers and footers don't display in form view, but you can examine them in Print Preview.

FIGURE 8-13: The Headers and Footers dialog box

QUICK **TIP**

You can print a table containing some or all of your database records by switching to list view before printing. This will save lots of paper if you're printing several records.■

CONCEPTSREVIEW

Label each of the elements of the Database application, as shown in Figure 8-14.

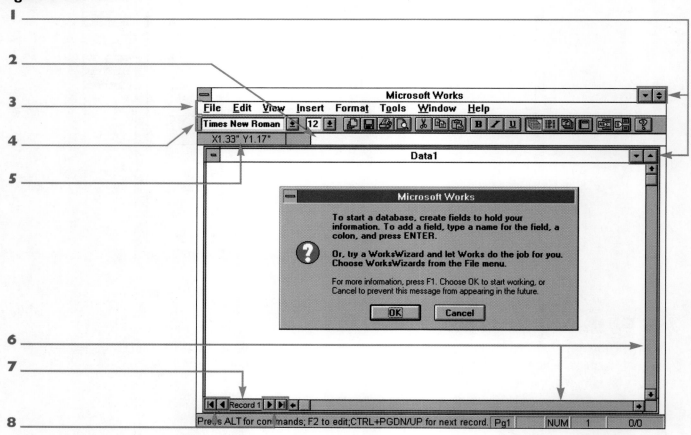

FIGURE 8-14

Match the buttons on the Database toolbar with their names.

9

10

11

12

13

14

a. Query View

b. List View

c. Report View

d. Insert Record

e. Form View

f. Insert Field

Select the best answer from the list of choices.

15 In the Database application, the document window is called a:

    a. Form

    b. Field

    c. Record

    d. Card

16 To add a database field to a form, you would:

    a. Type a double quotation mark followed by the field name, then press [Enter]

    b. Type the field name followed by a period, then press [Enter]

    c. Type the field name followed by a colon, then press [Enter]

    d. Press [Ctrl][PgDn]

17 Which key would you press to move between fields on a form?

a. [Enter]

b. [Tab]

c. [Esc]

d. [F1]

18 Which command would you use to add a leading zero to a zip code field?

a. Alignment command

b. Leading Zero command

c. Field Size command

d. Number command

19 Which key would you press to edit the contents of a field on the formula bar?

a. [Tab]

b. [F1]

c. [F2]

d. [Shift][Tab]

20 Which of the following techniques *cannot* be used to add a new record to the database?

a. Press [Tab] when the last field in the last record is highlighted

b. Click the Insert Record button on the toolbar

c. Choose the Record command from the Insert menu

d. Press [Ctrl][PgUp]

21 Which of the following is *not* a feature of list view?

a. List view lets you view more than one record at once

b. List view lets you compare different records in the database

c. List view lets you customize the look of your form

d. List view lets you print several records on one page

22 Which command would you use to resize a field on your form?

a. The Field Size command

b. The Font and Style command

c. The Alignment command

d. The Number command

23 How do you select more than one field at a time on a form?

a. Hold down the [Alt] key, then click on the fields

b. Hold down the [Ctrl] key, then click on the fields

c. Drag the mouse across the fields

d. Press [F8] twice

24 Which command would you use to change the color of a label on a form?

a. Font and Style command

b. Patterns command

c. Border command

d. Headers and Footers command

25 Which option in the Print dialog box lets you print the database record that is currently displayed on the screen?

a. The Number of Copies text box

b. The Print Range text box

c. The All Records option button

d. The Current Record Only option button

APPLICATIONS
REVIEW

1 Start the Database application and identify the elements of the interface.

a. Double-click the Microsoft Works icon in the Program Manager.

b. Click the Database button.

c. Identify the elements of the Database interface, referring to Figure 8-2 and Table 8-1 to identify the elements.

d. Save the database to your Student Disk under the name CUSTDAT2.WDB with the Save As command.

2 Create a database form with one label and eight fields as shown in Figure 8-3. Refer to the steps in the lesson "Creating a form" if you need help.

3 Add three customer records to the database.

   a. Click the Business field value (the line after the field name).

   b. Type in the customer records that follow, pressing [Tab] between fields:

     Queen Anne Kits [Tab] **500 Queen Anne Avenue** [Tab] **Seattle** [Tab] **WA** [Tab] **98109** [Tab] **USA** [Tab] **(206) 284-2222** [Tab] **(206) 284-2233** [Tab]

     Seaside Wind Runners [Tab] **100 Marion Street** [Tab] **Seaside** [Tab] **OR** [Tab] **97138** [Tab] **USA** [Tab] **(503) 738-7777** [Tab] **(503) 738-7788** [Tab]

     Mountain Family Company [Tab] **67 Highview Drive** [Tab] **Coeur D'Alene** [Tab] **ID** [Tab] **83814** [Tab] **USA** [Tab] **(208) 664-9999** [Tab] **(208) 664-9933** [Enter]

   c. Click the Save button to save the database on your Student Disk.

4 Edit the address in the first record and the phone number in the second record.

   a. Scroll to the first record in the database.

   b. Change the number in the Address field to **1275**.

   c. Scroll to the second record.

   d. Delete the phone number in the Fax field.

   e. Copy the number in the Phone field to the Fax field.

5 Delete the Country field and add a Contact field below the Phone field.

   a. Remove the Country field.

   b. Move the cursor to location X1.33" Y3.67".

   c. Insert a field named Contact that is 40 characters wide.

6 Change the color of the label and the font style of the Phone field.

   a. Change the color of the label Outdoor Designs Customer Database to dark green.

   b. Change the style of the Phone field value to boldface.

7 Print the Mountain Family Company record on the printer.

   a. Examine the record in Print Preview.

   b. Print the record.

   c. Save the database, then exit Works.

INDEPENDENT
CHALLENGES

Outdoor Designs is encouraging its employees to take part in a 20-mile Bread Walk to benefit the hungry. Robin Truefoot, Manager of Human Relations, has asked you to create a simple database that lists the employees involved, as well as the names of the donors who have pledged to support them, the amount per mile, the miles completed, and the date paid.

1 On a blank sheet of paper, create a design sketch to plan the layout of the records. This is a bit tricky, because each sponsor needs to have a field for name, amount pledged, and amount paid.

2 Start the database by entering the walker's name, as well as each sponsor's name and the amount/mile pledged.

3 Enter the records Robin has given you so far:

Robin Truefoot, sponsored by: Jane Xander ($0.25/mile); Ardis Levitt ($0.50/mile); Antos Triantophyllou ($1.00/mile); Rachel Truefoot, ($1.00/mile)

Ken Martinez, sponsored by: Alvin Chipper ($0.50/mile); Frances Erhardt ($0.50/mile); Max Torres ($1.00/mile); Alicia Rotstein ($1.00/mile)

Olivia Martinez, sponsored by: John Kelley ($0.25/mile); Alwyn Hayes ($1.00/mile)

Sue Ellen Martin, sponsored by: Babette Smith ($1.00/mile); Andres Martin, ($1.00/mile); Elinor Sherwood ($1.00/mile)

Melissa Cavanaugh, sponsored by: Ellen Freeman ($0.50/mile); Aline Remarque ($1.00/mile); Marion Redstone ($1.50/mile); Rachel Singer ($5.00/mile)

Frasier Steele, sponsored by: Ernest Frohlich ($0.50/mile) Edward Grace ($0.50/mile): Amy Bennett ($1.00/mile); Lou Innes ($1.00/mile); Nuri Eren ($1.00/mile)

4 Enter the data for each record. Can you think of any shortcuts that speed up data entry?

5 When you have finished, look at the records in Print Preview to make sure they are easy to read.

6 After you finish your calculations, print a copy of each walker's record. Save the database as BREAD94.

As the database grows in size, it will become an important asset to the employees at Outdoor Designs. Practice creating a backup copy of the database now using the Windows File Manager. Use File Manager to format a new, blank disk, then use the File Manager Copy command to copy the database from your Student Disk to the backup disk. When you finish, label the disk Database Backup and put it away in a safe place. If you modify your database regularly, it's a good idea to make a backup copy every week or so to protect the information. If you have any questions about using File Manager, review the File Manager lesson in the Working with Windows section at the beginning of the book. You can also use the File Manager on-line help.

UNIT 9

Working
WITH EXISTING DATABASES

I n Unit 8 you learned how to use the basic features of the Database application to create the Outdoor Designs customer database. In this unit you'll add more information to the database and will start working with the information in creative ways. ▶ First you'll add ClipArt to the database form and learn how to use field entries in calculations. Then you'll learn to sort records in the database, query the database for specific information, and protect the contents of the database from accidental tampering. Finally, you'll learn how to print mailing addresses on envelopes from the database. ▶

Opening an existing database

Sue Ellen has asked you to add ClipArt to the database and insert two new fields to record monthly sales and commissions. She and Frasier will use this information to evaluate how the Outdoor Designs products are selling in each of the stores, and to calculate the sales reps' compensation. In the steps that follow, you'll open the Outdoor Designs customer database (UNIT_09.WDB) from your Student Disk, save a copy under the name CUSTDAT3.WDB, and prepare to work with the database.

1 Start Works from the Program Manager
The Startup dialog box displays.

2 Put your Student Disk in drive A, then click the **Open an Existing Document button**
The Open dialog box appears, as shown in Figure 9-1. If you put the Student Disk in drive B, substitute drive B for drive A in step 4 below.

3 Click the **Drives drop-down list box**
The disk drives on your system display in the list box.

4 Click **a:** in the Drives list box
The File Name list box shows the Works files in the root directory of drive A.

5 Double-click **unit_09.wdb** to open the file in the Database
The dialog box closes. After a moment the Outdoor Designs customer database opens in a window, as shown in Figure 9-2. This file is identical to the file you created in Unit 8. Before you start to modify the database, save the file on your Student Disk with a different name to protect the original.

6 Click the **File menu**, then click the **Save As command**
The Save As dialog box displays.

7 Type **custdat3** in the File Name text box

8 Double-click the **my_files directory** in the Directory list box, then click **OK**
A dialog box displays, asking if you want to save the file to a different disk.

9 Click **No**
Works saves the file CUSTDAT3.WDB in the MY_FILES directory on the Student Disk.

FIGURE 9-1:
The Works Open
dialog box

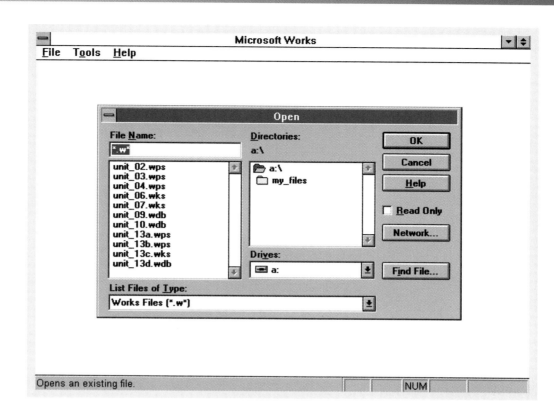

FIGURE 9-2: The Outdoor Designs customer database

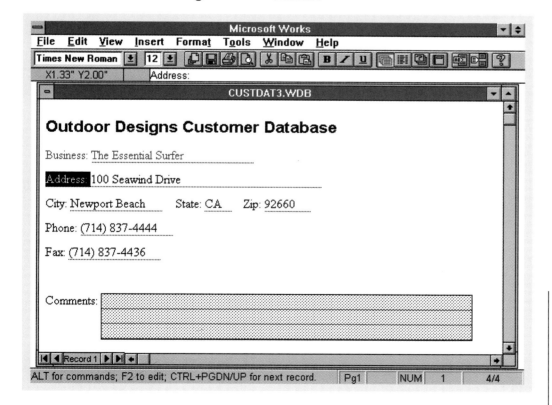

QUICK **TIP**

When you open an existing database, Works displays the record that was open when the file was last saved to disk.

Adding art to a database form

Works lets you add artwork and other types of information to your database with several commands on the Insert menu. In this lesson you'll add ClipArt to your form to make it more fun to use. You'll insert the sun ClipArt, an image similar to the one you added to the Outdoor Designs letterhead in Unit 1. Try adding ClipArt to your form now.

1   Use the direction keys to position the cursor at location **X5.42" Y1.25"**
As you move the cursor its position displays in the cursor reference box. X5.42" Y1.25" is just to the right of the label Outdoor Designs Customer Database.

2   Click the **Insert menu,** then click **ClipArt**
The ClipArt Gallery appears, as shown in Figure 9-3. The ClipArt Gallery gives you access to all the ClipArt images stored in the \msworks\clipart directory on your hard disk. Works normally includes 36 images in the ClipArt Gallery, accessible through the ClipArt list box. By default the images in all subject categories are displayed, but you can narrow the selection by clicking a different category in the Category list box. You'll select the sun ClipArt in the ClipArt Gallery. (The sun ClipArt is orange and yellow and is located at the bottom of the ClipArt Gallery.)

3   Click the **down arrow** on the ClipArt list box scroll bar six times
The ClipArt list box scrolls to the bottom of the window and the sun appears second from the left.

4   Double-click the **sun ClipArt**
The ClipArt Gallery closes and the sun ClipArt (Splat) displays in the form. The image appears in the upper-right corner of the form (where the cursor was), and is currently selected. (Works selects ClipArt when you insert it so you can move it or resize it if you want.) When the ClipArt is printed it will appear in black and gray, unless you have a color printer.

5   Click the **Business field** to remove the selection rectangle from the ClipArt
The Business field selects and the ClipArt displays in its final form, as shown in Figure 9-4. The sun will now appear in each record in the database, just like the label and fields.

6   Click 🖫 to save the ClipArt in the database

FIGURE 9-3: The ClipArt Gallery

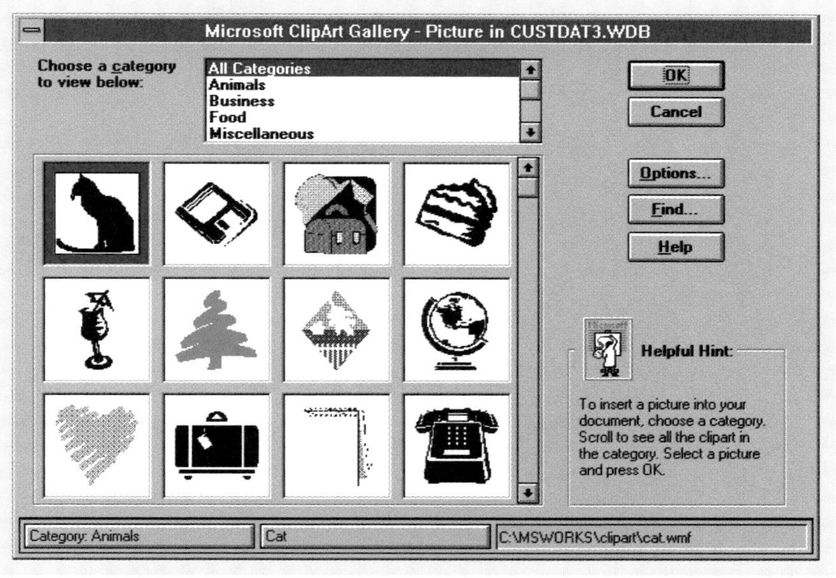

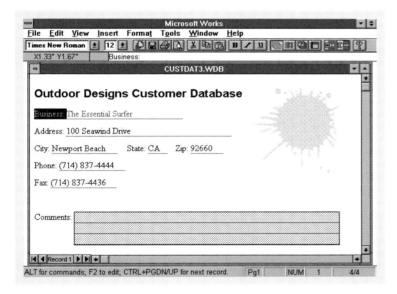

FIGURE 9-4: The sun ClipArt in the database form

Working with ClipArt objects

ClipArt images are called **objects** in the Database. ClipArt objects can be selected, moved, copied, pasted, and deleted like any other element on the database form. You can use menu commands, keyboard keys, or the toolbar to perform these basic operations. In addition, you can resize a ClipArt object by clicking the image, then dragging the right or left edge of the ClipArt frame with the sizing pointer.

QUICK **TIP**

You can add a pop-up note to your form with the **Note-It command** on the Insert menu. This is a useful way to include instructions or messages in your database. For more information about the Note-It accessory, consult the on-line help.■

Using field entries in formulas

To perform a calculation in the Database, you enter a formula in a field. As you learned in Unit 5, a formula is an equation that calculates a new value from existing values. In the Database, formulas can contain numbers, mathematical operators, field names, and functions. Table 9-1 lists some of the mathematical operators that can be used in a formula. You'll add two new fields to the form now, and use a formula to calculate a total based on one of the field entries.

STEPS

1   Use the direction keys to position the cursor at location **X3.42" Y2.67"**, then click [icon] on the toolbar
    The Insert Field dialog box displays.

2   Type **YTD Sales**, press **[Tab]**, type **16**, then press **[Enter]**
    A field named YTD Sales that is 16 characters wide is added to the form.

3   Position the cursor at location **X3.42" Y3.00"**, click [icon], then type **Commission**, press **[Tab]**, type **15**, and press **[Enter]**
    A field named Commission that is 15 characters wide is added to the form. Next you'll enter a formula that calculates the commission for the Outdoor Designs sales reps.

4   Type **=YTD Sales*0.15** and press **[Enter]**
    The equals sign (=) lets Works know you're about to enter a formula in the field. The formula multiplies the value in the YTD Sales field by the 15% sales commission rate. When you press [Enter], a zero (0) appears in the field, because no sales totals have been entered on the form yet. Now you'll add sales information to each of the records in the database.

5   Scroll to the **first record** (The Essential Surfer) in the database, click the **YTD Sales field**, type **5500**, then press **[Enter]**
    5500 appears in the YTD Sales field and 825 appears in the Commission field.

6   Enter **8230** as YTD Sales for the second record (Cambridge Kite Supply), **1600** for the third record (Mountain Air), and **2450** for the fourth record (Ken's Outdoor Gear)
    Now add currency formatting to the YTD Sales and Commission fields.

7   Click the **YTD Sales field value** (if it is not already selected), hold down **[Ctrl]**, then click the **Commission field value**

8   Click **Format**, click **Number**, click the **Currency option button**, then click **OK**
    The YTD Sales and Commission fields display with currency formatting, as shown in Figure 9-5.

9   Click [icon] to save the formula to disk

FIGURE 9-5: A formula in the Commission field calculates sales rep compensation

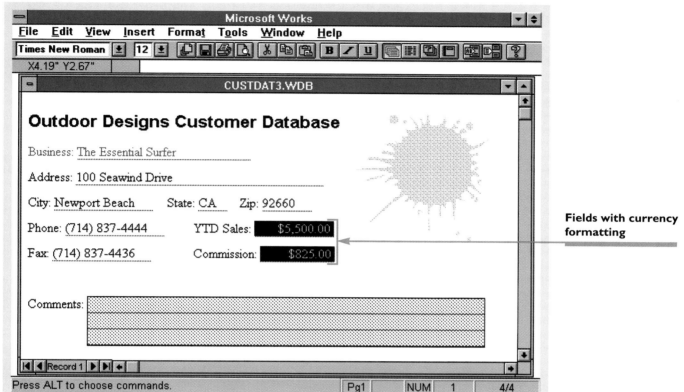

Fields with currency
formatting

TABLE 9-1:
Useful mathematical operators (in order of evaluation)

OPERATOR	DESCRIPTION	EXAMPLE	RESULT
( )	Parentheses	(3+6)*3	27
^	Exponential	10^2	100
*	Multiplication	7*5	35
/	Division	20/4	5
+	Addition	5+5	10
-	Subtraction	12-8	4

QUICK **TIP**

You can also use
Works functions in
Database formulas.
For more information
about working with
functions, see Unit 6.

Sorting database records

Works lets you sort the records in your database in alphabetical or numerical order. When you sort your database, you need to specify a key field for the sort. For example, in the Outdoor Designs customer database you could sort the records by the Business, Zip, or YTD Sales fields. In the following steps you'll sort the customer database by business name.

1 Click the **Business field value** on the database form, then click the **List View button** 📰 on the toolbar
The database displays in list view, and Works places the cursor in the Business field. The first eight fields of the database appear in columns across the screen. (The remaining fields can be viewed by clicking the right scroll arrow.) Because the default column width in list view is only 10 characters, several of the field entries are only partially visible. Before you sort the database, you'll adjust the column width of each field with the Field Width command.

2 Click the **Select All rectangle** above the first row and to the left of the Business column
The entire database highlights.

3 Click **Format**, click **Field Width**, click the **Best Fit check box**, then click **OK**
The column width of each field in the database adjusts to fit the data. (Note that this command affects list view only.) Now you'll sort the four records in the database alphabetically by business name.

4 Click **The Essential Surfer**, click the **Tools menu**, then click the **Sort Records command**
The Sort Records dialog box displays, as shown in Figure 9-6. It contains drop-down list boxes for the first, second, and third field names you want to use to sort the database with, respectively. The 1st Field drop-down list box contains the name of the Business field already, because you chose it before the sort. You'll specify a second field name in the 2nd Field drop-down list box next, to resolve any ties (identical company names in the database) that come up during the sort.

5 Click the **2nd Field drop-down list box**, then click the **City field**
The City field appears in the 2nd Field drop-down list box.

6 Click **OK** to sort the records
Works sorts the records and the result appears in the list view window, as shown in Figure 9-7. Cambridge Kite Supply is now the first record in the database.

7 Click the **Form View button** 📑 to return to form view

8 Click 💾 to save your changes

FIGURE 9-6: The Sort Records dialog box

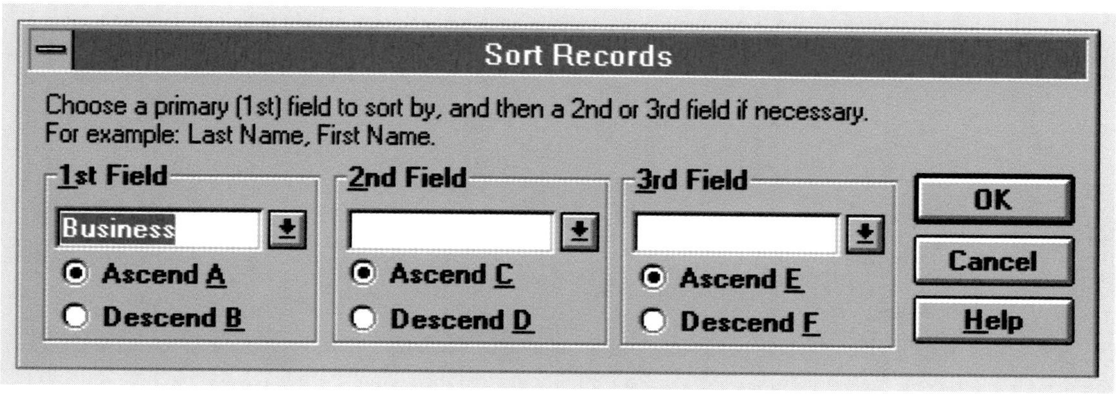

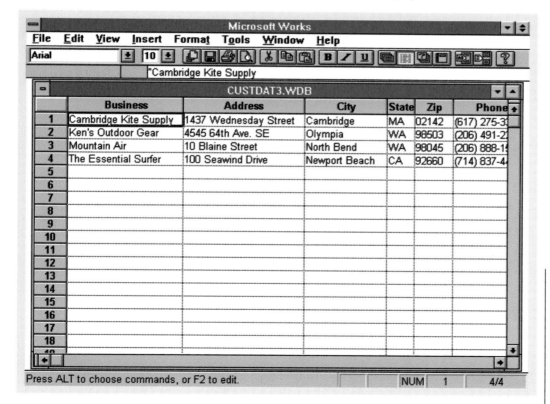

FIGURE 9-7: The customer database in list view, sorted alphabetically by business

QUICK TIP

To sort database records in descending order, click the **Descend option button** under each field list box you use in the Sort Records dialog box.∎

Querying the database

You can use the Find command on the Edit menu to search for a specific item in the database. However, you'll often find that you want to locate a group of records that match a certain criterion, such as all businesses in the state of California, or all addresses with the zip code 98503. In these instances you'll want to use a database query. A **query** is a question that compares one or more fields in the database with one or more values. You specify a query using the New Query dialog box. Practice using a query in the Outdoor Designs customer database now.

I   Click 🖿 on the toolbar

The customer database displays in list view. This is the best place to see the results of a query.

2   Click the **Tools menu,** then click the **Create New Query command**

The New Query dialog box displays, as shown in Figure 9-8. It contains a text box, where you name the query; a Choose a field to compare drop-down list box, where you specify which field you want to use in the query; a How to compare the field drop-down list box; and a Value to compare the field to text box, where you type a value to compare.

Now you'll compose a query to identify all businesses that have purchased at least $5000 worth of products from Outdoor Designs this year.

3   Press **[Shift][Tab]**, type **$5000 in sales**, then press **[Tab]**

$5000 in sales is entered as the name of the query in the name text box.

4   Click the **Choose a field to compare drop-down list box**, scroll to the bottom of the list, and click the **YTD Sales field**

YTD Sales is selected as the field for the query.

5   Click the **How to compare the field drop-down list box**, then click **is greater than or equal to**

Is greater than or equal to is selected as the comparison operator for the query.

6   Press **[Tab]**, type **$5000** as the comparison value, then click **Apply Now**

Works runs the query, and the two businesses with sales greater than or equal to $5000 display in the window, as shown in Figure 9-9.

7   Click the **Query View button** 🖳 on the toolbar

The query displays in the Business field, expressed as a Database formula. **Query view** is a special view you can use to see how Works stores a query internally. You can edit a query in this view by pressing [F2], then editing the query on the formula bar.

8   Click 🖳, click the **View menu,** then click **Show All Records**

The Show All Records command cancels the $5000 in sales query. Even though the query has been removed from the screen, it still exists in the computer's memory. If you want to keep it, be sure to save it to disk.

9   Click 🖫 to save the query to disk

FIGURE 9-8: The New Query dialog box

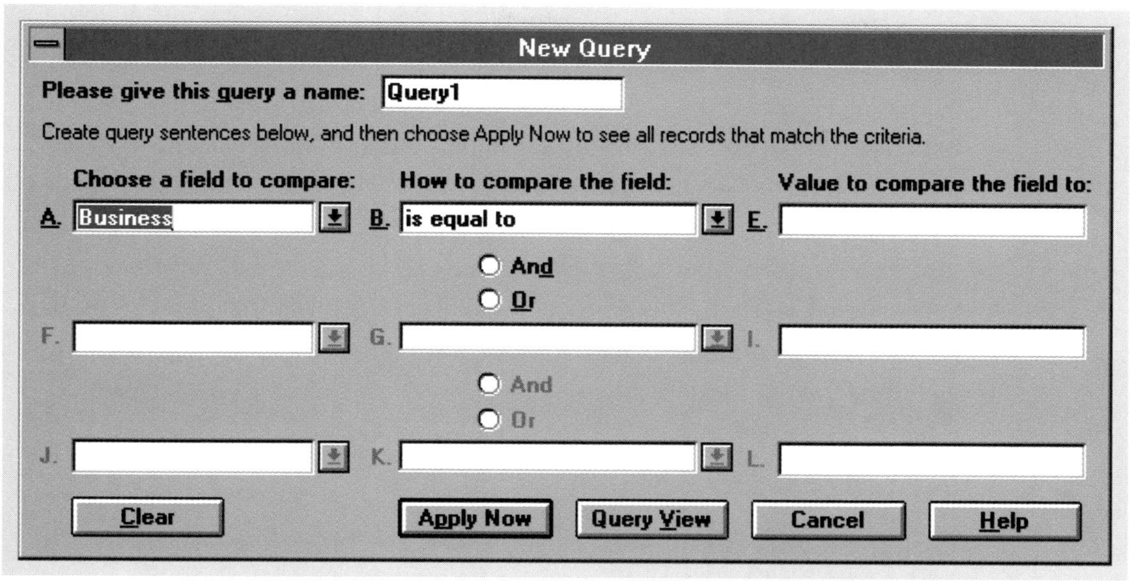

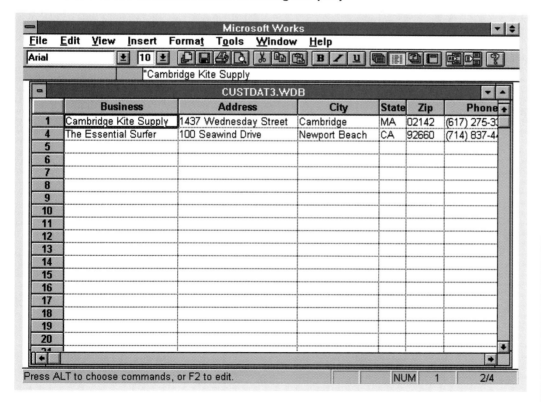

```
─                          New Query
Please give this query a name:  [Query1                ]
Create query sentences below, and then choose Apply Now to see all records that match the criteria.

     Choose a field to compare:   How to compare the field:    Value to compare the field to:
A. [Business          ] ▼     B. [is equal to        ] ▼  E. [                        ]
                              ○ And
                              ○ Or
F. [                  ] ▼     G. [                   ] ▼  I. [                        ]
                              ○ And
                              ○ Or
J. [                  ] ▼     K. [                   ] ▼  L. [                        ]

    [ Clear ]          [ Apply Now ] [ Query View ]  [ Cancel ]    [ Help ]
```

FIGURE 9-9: The two customer records matching the query

```
─                    Microsoft Works                     ▼ ◆
File  Edit  View  Insert  Format  Tools  Window  Help
[Arial     ] ▼ [10] ▼ ...icons...
              "Cambridge Kite Supply
─                    CUSTDAT3.WDB                        ▼ ▲
        Business          Address          City     State Zip    Phone
 1  Cambridge Kite Supply 1437 Wednesday Street Cambridge  MA  02142 (617) 275-3
 4  The Essential Surfer  100 Seawind Drive  Newport Beach CA  92660 (714) 837-4
 5
 6
 7
 8
 9
10
11
12
13
14
15
16
17
18
19
20
Press ALT to choose commands, or F2 to edit.          NUM  1   2/4
```

QUICK **TIP**

To run the $5000 in sales query again later, you would choose the Apply Query command from the View menu, then double-click $5000 in sales in the Apply Query dialog box.■

Using advanced queries

In the last lesson you learned how to enter a query with the New Query dialog box. In this lesson you'll use the New Query dialog box to enter a query with more than one comparison. Queries with multiple comparisons are linked together with the **And** or **Or conjunctions**. You use the And conjunction when you want both comparisons to be true in the query for a record to be selected. You use the Or conjunction when either comparison can be true in the query for a record to be selected. ▶ In the following steps you'll enter a query that searches for businesses that have purchased at least $5000 worth of products this year *and* who are located in California.

1 Click 📖 on the toolbar

2 Click the **Tools menu,** then click the **Create New Query command**
   The New Query dialog box displays.

3 Press **[Shift][Tab]**, type **$5000 in CA**, then press **[Tab]**
   $5000 in CA is entered as the name of the query in the name text box.

4 Click **YTD Sales** in the Choose a field to compare list box, click **is greater than or equal to** in the How to compare the field list box, press **[Tab]**, then type **$5000**

5 Click the **And option button** below the How to compare the field list box
   The And option button is the conjunction that links together the query on the first line with the query on the second line. Now you'll fill in the options for the second query.

6 Click **State** in the Choose a field to compare list box, click **is equal to** in the How to compare the field list box, press **[Tab]**, then type **CA**
   The completed query displays in the dialog box, as shown in Figure 9-10.

7 Click **Apply Now** to run the query
   Works displays the results of the query in the window, as shown in Figure 9-11. The Essential Surfer, with sales of $5,500, is the only record to match the query.

8 Click 📄, click the **View menu,** then click **Show All Records**
   The Show All Records command cancels the $5000 in CA query. Even though the query has been removed from the screen, it still exists in the computer's memory. If you want to keep it, be sure to save it to disk.

9 Click 💾 to save the query to disk

FIGURE 9-10: The New Query dialog box with two queries

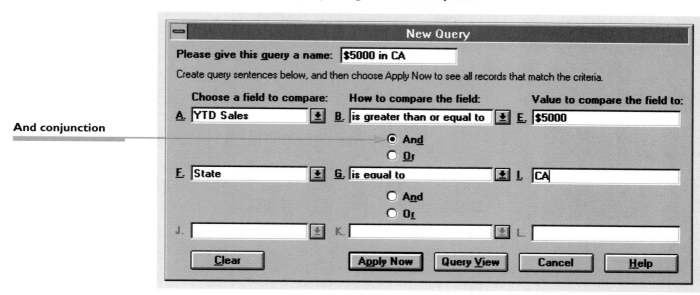

And conjunction

FIGURE 9-11: The customer record matching the combined query

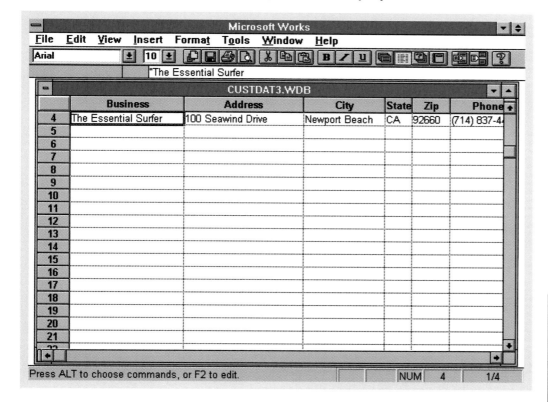

QUICK TIP

To delete a query from the database, choose the **Delete Query command** from the Tools menu, then select the query in the Delete Query dialog box and click **Delete.**

Protecting the database

Now that you have completed the Outdoor Designs customer form and entered information into the database, you should protect both the form and the data from accidental changes or deletion. Works lets you protect part or all of the database with the Protection command. In the following steps you'll protect the customer form and several field values in the database.

1   Click the **Format menu**, then click the **Protection command**
The Protection dialog box displays, as shown in Figure 9-12. (Be sure you are in form view before you click this command.)

2   Click the **Protect Form check box**, then click **OK**
The dialog box closes and Works protects the labels, fields, and ClipArt on the form from modification or deletion. To unlock the form later (so you can make changes), you would remove the x from the Protect Form check box.

Note that form protection does not prevent the data in the fields from being changed. Sue Ellen has asked you to protect all the fields in the database except the Comments field, so that the important fields are protected but employees are still able to include notes about customers. In the following steps you'll unlock the Comments field and protect the data in the rest of the fields.

3   Click the **Comments field value** on the form, click **Format**, then click **Protection**
The Protection dialog box displays.

4   Click the **Locked check box**, then click **OK**
The Comments field is unlocked. Now you'll protect the rest of the field entries.

5   Click **Format**, then click **Protection**

6   Click the **Protect Data check box**, then click **OK**
Works protects every field in the database, except Comments. To unlock the fields later (so you can change the data), you would remove the x from the Protect Data check box. Now enter some text into the unprotected Comments field.

7   Type **Account started by Jud Keim on 5/7/92** and press **[Enter]**
The text displays in the Comments field, as shown in Figure 9-13.

8   Click 🖫 to save the form and data protection to disk

9   Click the **File menu**, then click **Close** to close the customer database
The Database closes and the Startup dialog box displays.

FIGURE 9-12: The Protection dialog box

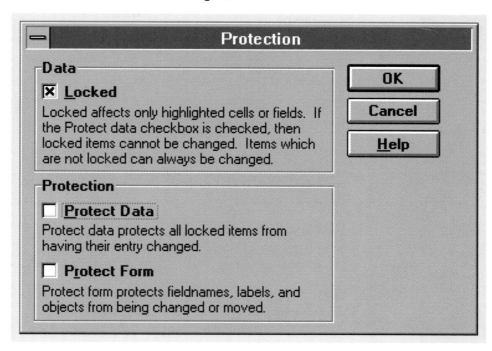

FIGURE 9-13: Typing text in the unprotected Comments field

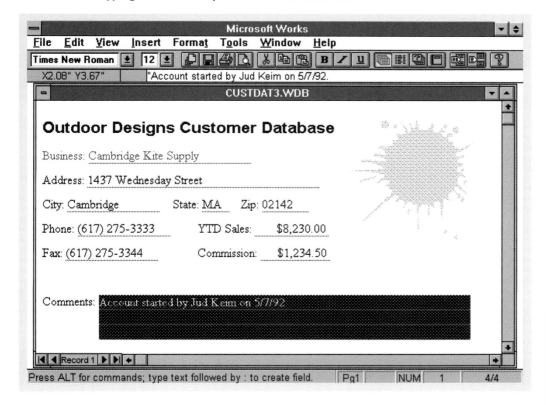

QUICK **TIP**

Press **[Tab]** to move to the next unprotected field in the database.■

Printing envelopes from the database

In this lesson you'll learn to print envelopes for customers in the Outdoor Designs database. You'll design the envelope in the Word Processor, then use the Fields button to import the necessary fields from the CUSTDAT3.WDB database. Complete this lesson even if your lab printer can't print envelopes (just skip step 9). You'll learn some valuable information about how Works inserts database fields into the Word Processor.

STEPS

1 Click the **Word Processor button** in the Works Startup dialog box
The Word Processor opens in a window.

2 Click the **Tool menu,** click the **Envelopes and Labels command,** then click the **Fields button**
The Envelopes tab displays, and the Fields button expands the dialog box to full size.

3 Click the **Database button,** click the **Use another file button,** then double-click **CUSTDAT3.WDB** in the list box
The CUSTDAT3.WDB database opens and its fields display in the database list box, as shown in Figure 9-14. You'll add some of these fields to your envelope in the following steps.

4 Click the **Business field** in the database list box, then click **Insert**
The Business field is inserted into the Address text box and surrounded by chevrons. The chevrons tell Works to insert field values from the database into the Word Processor when you print the envelopes.

5 Press **[Enter]**, click the **Address field** in the database list box, then click **Insert** and press **[Enter]**

6 Click **City**, click **Insert**, type a **comma (,)**, press **[Spacebar]**, click **State**, click **Insert**, press **[Spacebar]** twice, click **Zip**, then click **Insert**
The Address, City, State, and Zip fields are entered into the Address list box with proper spaces and punctuation.

7 Press **[Tab]**, then type the following address in the Return address list box:
Outdoor Designs
1820 Big Timber Drive
Seattle, WA 98555

8 Click the **Create Envelope button** to create the envelope, then save the file to your Student Disk under the name **CUSTENV.WPS**
The envelope displays in the Word Processor, as shown in Figure 9-15. If you have access to a printer that prints envelopes, print envelopes for the four records in the customer database now.

9 Click ▣ to print the envelopes, then click **OK** when you are asked to choose the CUSTDAT3.WDB database and when you are asked to merge all records

10 When the envelopes finish printing, exit Works

FIGURE 9-14: The Envelopes tab of the Envelopes and Labels dialog box

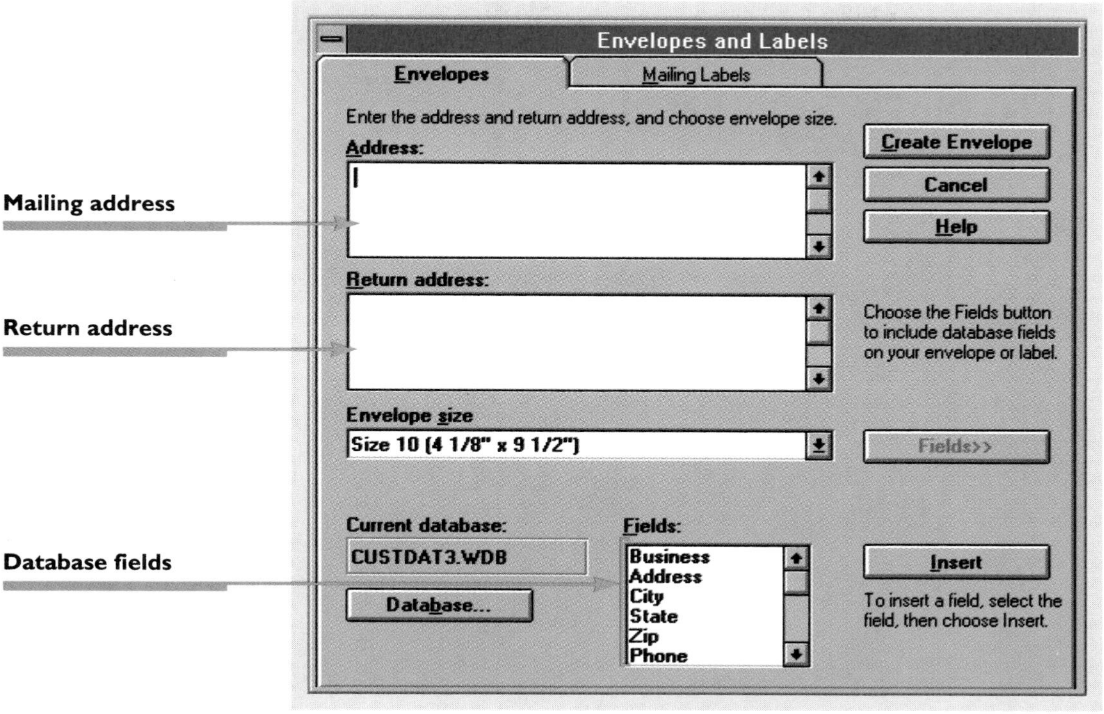

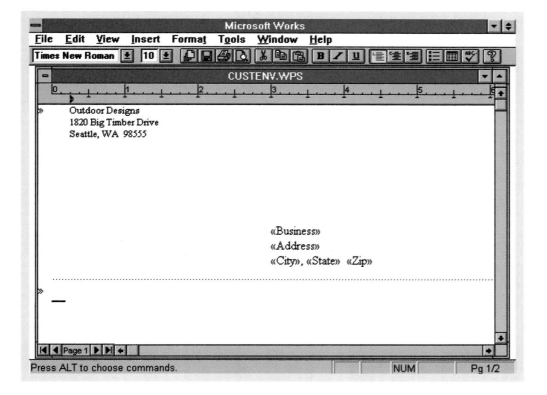

Mailing address

Return address

Database fields

FIGURE 9-15: The completed envelope in the Word Processor

QUICK **TIP**

In Print Preview, you can review each envelope as it will appear when printed. Click the **Next button** to move from one envelope to the next.

CONCEPTSREVIEW

Select the best answer from the list of choices.

1 When you open an existing database, Works displays:

   a. The record that was last modified

   b. The record that was visible when the database was closed

   c. The first record in the database

   d. The last record in the database

2 Which of the following techniques would *not* work to delete a piece of ClipArt from a form?

   a. Select the ClipArt and press [Del]

   b. Select the ClipArt and click 🔧

   c. Select the ClipArt and click 📋

   d. Select the ClipArt, then choose the Cut command from the Edit menu

3 What character would you use to begin a formula in a field?

   a. The equals sign (=)

   b. The plus (+) sign

   c. A dash (-)

   d. A parenthesis

4 What command would you use to format a field for currency?

   a. The Number command

   b. The Field Width command

   c. The Alignment command

   d. The Currency command

5 In the formula =YTD Sales*0.15, which item in the formula is a field reference?

   a. The equals sign (=)

   b. YTD Sales

   c. The asterisk (*)

   d. 0.15

6 Which mathematical operator is evaluated before the exponential operator (^)?

   a. Multiplication (*)

   b. Division (/)

   c. Addition (+)

   d. Parenthesis ( )

7 Which database view is most useful when you are sorting records?

   a. Form view

   b. List view

   c. Query view

   d. Report view

8 What command would you use to change the column width of database fields in list view?

   a. Field Width

   b. Record Height

   c. Protection

   d. Alignment

9 What is the maximum number of fields you can use in a sort?

   a. 1

   b. 2

   c. 3

   d. 4

10 What is the limitation of the Find command in the Database?

   a. It makes comparisons with mathematical operators.

   b. It can only search the next record in the database.

   c. It always searches through every record in the database.

   d. It can only display one record at a time.

11 Which of the following is not a valid comparison operator in a query?

   a. Is equal to

   b. Is greater than or equal to

   c. Contains

   d. Is a multiple of

12 What toolbar button would you press to see how a Query is stored internally by Works?

   a. 📊

   b. 🔍

   c. 📑

   d. 📇

13 Which conjunction would you use to link together two queries that *both* need to be true to select records in the database?

a. And

b. But

c. Or

d. =

14 Which check box would you click in the Protection dialog box to protect the database form from being modified?

a. Locked

b. Protect Form

c. Protect Data

d. Lock Form

15 What Works application would you use to print envelopes from the customer database?

a. Word Processor

b. Spreadsheet

c. Database

d. Communications

APPLICATIONSREVIEW

1 Open the UNIT_09.WDB database from the Student Disk and save a copy as CUSTDAT4.WDB.

a. Start Works and click the Open an Existing Document button.

b. Click a: in the Drives drop-down list box, then click a:\ in the Directories list box.

c. Double-click unit_09.wdb to open the file in the Database.

d. Save the file to the MY_FILES directory of the Student Disk under the name CUSTDAT4.WDB.

2 Add the tree ClipArt to the form at location X5.42" Y1.25".

a. Use the direction keys to position the cursor at location X5.42" Y1.25".

b. Click the Insert menu, then click ClipArt.

c. Double-click the tree ClipArt to insert the image on the form.

3 Add YTD Sales and Sales Tax fields to the form.

a Insert the YTD Sales field at location X3.42" Y2.67". Make the field 16 characters wide.

b. Insert the Sales Tax field at location X3.42" Y3.00". Make the field 15 characters wide.

c. Type **=YTD Sales*8.2%** in the Sales Tax field and press [Enter].

d. Enter **6000** as YTD Sales for The Essential Surfer record, **9500** for Cambridge Kite Supply, **2300** for Mountain Air, and **12400** for Ken's Outdoor Gear.

e. Format the YTD Sales and Sales Tax fields for currency with the Number command.

4 Sort the database records by zip code in list view.

a. Click the List View button.

b. Click the Tools menu, then click the Sort Records command.

c. Click the 1st Field drop-down list box, then click the Zip field.

d. Click the 2nd Field drop-down list box, then click the Business field.

e. Click OK to sort the records.

5 Query the database to find all businesses that have paid at least $800 in sales tax this year and are located in the state of Washington.

a. Click the Tools menu, then click the Create New Query command.

b. Press [Shift][Tab], type **$800 in WA tax**, then press [Tab].

c. Click Sales Tax in the first Choose a field to compare list box, click is greater than or equal to in the How to compare the field list box, press [Tab], then type **$800**.

d. Click the And option button.

e. Click State in the second Choose a field to compare list box, click is equal to in the second How to compare the field list box, press [Tab], then type **WA**.

f. Click Apply Now to run the query.

g. Click the Form View button, click View, then click Show all Records to cancel the query.

6 Protect the database form and all fields but Comments, Phone, and Fax.

a. Click the Format menu, then click the Protection command.

b. Click the Protect Form check box, then click OK.

c. Click the Comments field value, click Format, then click Protection.

d. Click the Locked check box, then click OK.

e. Repeat steps c and d for the Phone and Fax fields.

f. Click Format, click Protection, click the Protect Data check box, then click OK.

7 Create envelopes in the Word Processor that contain address fields from the database.

   a. Start the Word Processor, click the Tools menu, then click the Envelopes and Labels command.

   b. Use the dialog box to create addresses in the Address and Return address text boxes. Use the CUSTDAT4.WDB database to supply the necessary database fields.

   c. Click the Create Envelope button to create the envelope, then save the file to your Student Disk under the name CUSTENV2.WPS.

   d. Print the envelopes on your printer if you are able to do so. When you finish printing, exit Works.

INDEPENDENT
CHALLENGES

The Database application includes a Spelling Checker that you can use to check the spelling of words on your form and words in the database. You start the Spelling Checker by clicking the Tools menu, then clicking the Spelling command. Practice using the Spelling Checker now to check the spelling in the CUSTDAT3.WDB database. (If your form and data are still protected, remove form protection and data protection before you use the Spelling Checker.) You'll find the Spelling Checker useful for checking the words on your form, but rather tedious for checking the names and addresses in the database fields. For this reason, the Spelling Checker is not used as often in the Database application as it is in the Word Processor or Spreadsheet. If you have any questions about using the Spelling Checker, click the Help button in the Spelling dialog box.

Describe how each of the following items could be considered a database. On a sheet of paper, create a sample record and include the fields you would be likely to find in each database.

   a. Shopping list

   b. Mail-order catalog

   c. List of party invitations

   d. Cookbook

   e. Household inventory

   f. Telephone book

   g. Teacher's grade book

   h. Take-out menu

The weather was splendid last Sunday, and all walkers easily completed the Bread Walk. (You created this database in the first Independent Challenge for Unit 8. If you didn't complete that Independent Challenge, go back and do it now.) Now you'll update the records to reflect the money collected. In this challenge, you'll enter data telling how much each walker earned and discover who collected the most money for the hungry.

1 Open the database BREAD94.WDB you created in the independent challenge for Unit 8 and add a new field called Miles Completed.

2 Enter 20 miles in the Miles Completed field for each record in BREAD94 and enter the amount paid by each sponsor.

3 Insert a new field called Total Sponsors and enter the total number of sponsors listed for that walker.

4 Insert a new field called Total Paid and enter the total collected by each employee.

5 Sort the records in descending order so that the employees who collected the most money are at the top of the list.

6 Look at the database in list view and adjust the column widths so all the information is visible on the screen. Look at the database in Print Preview and print a copy for your records.

OBJECTIVES

▶ Create a new report

▶ Add report statistics

▶ View the report in Print Preview

▶ Format the report

▶ Name the report and print

Creating
DATABASE REPORTS

I n Unit 9 you learned how to sort and query a Works database and how to print envelopes containing database fields. In this unit you'll learn to organize the fields of a database in reports. A **report** is a summary of database information specifically designed for printing. A report can include one or more database fields, field statistics, and descriptive labels.

▶ In this unit you'll create a sales and commission report from the Outdoor Designs customer database. You'll create the report, add statistics to it, examine it in Print Preview, and format it for printing. Then you'll name the report and print a copy for distribution to Sue Ellen and the Outdoor Designs sales staff. ▶

Creating a new report

In this lesson you'll open the Outdoor Designs customer database and create a new report with the Create New Report command. To create a report you choose the database fields you want to include in the report, listing them in the order you want them to appear. In the following steps you'll create a report containing the Business, City, YTD Sales, and Commission fields from the Outdoor Designs customer database.

STEPS

1 Put your Student Disk in drive A, then start Works

2 Open **UNIT_10.WDB** on your Student Disk, then save it as **DBREPORT.WDB** in the MY_FILES directory
The Outdoor Designs customer database (the database you created in Unit 9) displays in a window. Now you'll create the report by extracting fields from the database.

3 Click the **Tools menu**, then click the **Create New Report command**
The New Report dialog box displays, as shown in Figure 10-1. It contains a text field where you type the title of your report, a Field list box where you highlight the fields included in the report, and a Fields in Report list box that displays the fields as you choose them. (The order in which you choose the fields affects their order in the report.)

4 Type **Outdoor Designs -- 1994 Sales and Commission Report**
The text appears in the Report Title text box. This is the heading that will appear at the top of the printed report. Now you'll add fields to the report.

5 Click the **Add button** to add the Business field to the report
The field appears in the Fields in Report list box.

6 Click the **City field**, click **Add**, click the **YTD Sales field**, click **Add**, then click **Add** to insert the Commission field
The four fields display in the Fields in Report list box, as shown in Figure 10-2. To delete a field you added by mistake, you would click the incorrect field in the list box, then click the Remove button.

Now you're ready to include statistics in the report. You'll do that in the next lesson.

FIGURE 10-1: The New Report dialog box

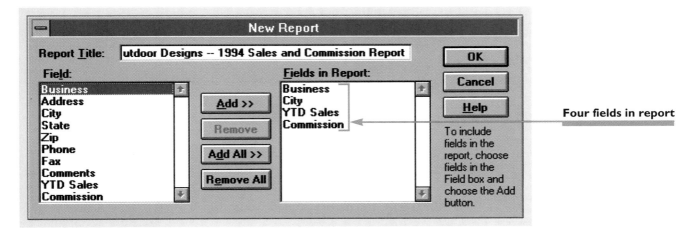

Report Title text field

Add button

Database fields

Fields in Report
list box

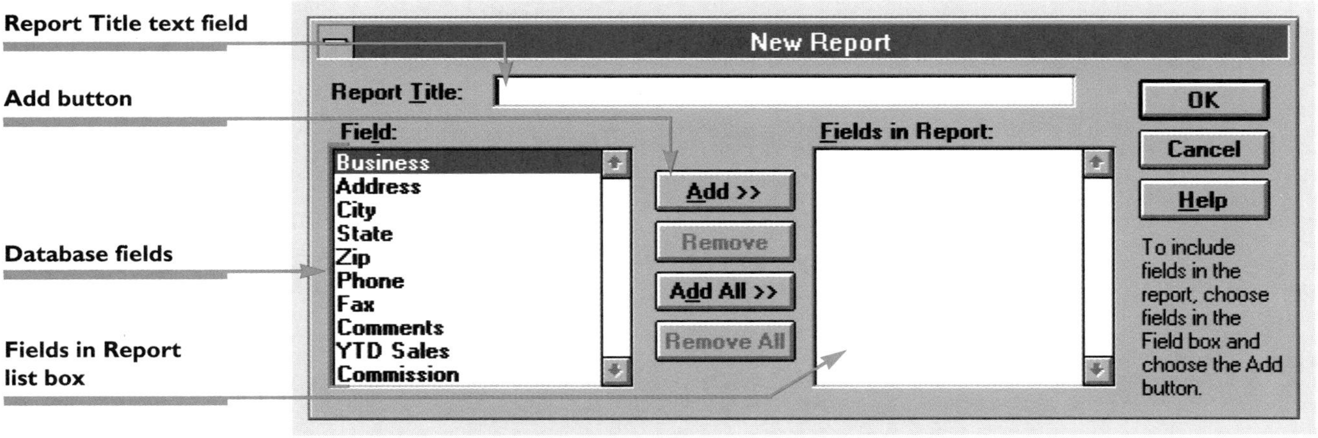

FIGURE 10-2: The New Report dialog box with a header and four fields

Four fields in report

QUICK **TIP**

You can also click
the Report View
button 🔲 on the
toolbar to create a
new report. It is the
toolbar equivalent
of the Create New
Report command.■

Adding report statistics

In the last lesson you added fields to the sales and commission report with the New Report dialog box. Now you'll add statistics to the fields you created. **Statistics** are descriptive calculations, such as a sum, average, or count, that operate on database fields. Table 10-1 lists the statistical operations you can use in Database reports. When you finish entering statistics, the completed report displays in **report view**, where you can format it for printing. You'll finish creating the report you started in the last lesson now.

1   Click the **OK button** in the New Report dialog box
The Report Statistics dialog box displays, as shown in Figure 10-3. It contains a list box where you select fields in the report and seven Statistics check boxes where you specify the statistics you want.

2   Click the **YTD Sales field,** then click the **Sum** and **Average** check boxes
An x displays in the Sum and Average check boxes, telling Works to calculate the sum and average of all the YTD Sales fields in the database, then to place them in rows in the report.

3   Click the **Commission field,** then click the **Sum check box**
An x displays in the Sum check box, telling Works to calculate the sum of all the Commission fields in the database, then to place it in a row in the report.

4   Click **OK** to create the report
Works creates the report and displays it in report view. A dialog box announces that the report instructions or **definitions** are complete. When you print, Works translates these instructions into an orderly report.

5   Click **OK** to close the dialog box
The report appears unobstructed in report view, as shown in Figure 10-4. Report view is a special view in the Database that lets you work with existing reports. It is similar to list view in the Database, but contains a few different menu commands. In this case it contains the rows Title, Headings, Record, and Summary on the left side of the window, which correspond to the report elements you created with the Create New Report command. Take a moment now to study the elements in the report view window.

6   Click 🖫 to save your report
Works saves the report with the database in the file DBREPORT.WDB.

FIGURE 10-3:
The Report Statistics
dialog box

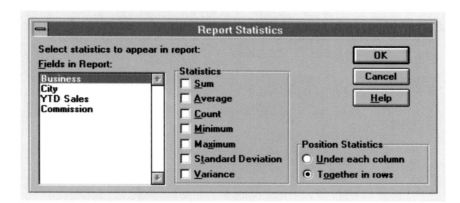

FIGURE 10-4:
The Sales and
Commission Report
displayed in report view

Title rows

Headings rows

Record row

Summary (statistics)
rows

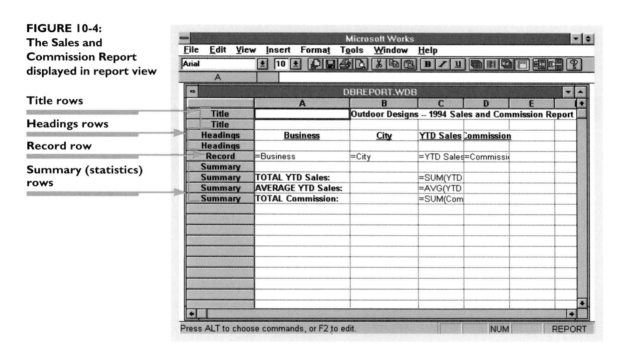

TABLE 10-1:
Statistical calculations available in Database reports

STATISTIC	CALCULATES
Sum	The total of all values in the field
Average	The average of values in the field
Count	The number of records in the database
Minimum	The smallest value in the field
Maximum	The largest value in the field
Standard deviation	The standard deviation of values in the field
Variance	The variance of values in the field

QUICK **TIP**

You can add more
field statistics to
your report at any
time by choosing
the Field Summary
command from the
Insert menu.■

Viewing the report in Print Preview

The report definition you created in the last lesson is not the report itself—it is an outline of the instructions to create the report. To view the report as it will be printed you need to use the Print Preview command. Print Preview displays the report with the title, headings, records, and statistics in place. Examining the report in Print Preview is an important step, because it lets you catch any formatting problems before you print. You'll examine the sales and commission report in Print Preview now.

1   Click the **File menu,** then click the **Print Preview command**
The sales and commission report displays in Print Preview, as shown in Figure 10-5. Print Preview shows the report on a simulated piece of paper exactly as it will be printed. Six buttons on the right side of the window control the operation of Print Preview. To zoom for a closer look at parts of the report, you can click the Zoom In button or click the report with the zoom pointer. The zoom pointer (a magnifying glass with the word *zoom* below it) appears whenever the mouse pointer is over the simulated page.

2   Click the **Zoom In button**
The top part of the report enlarges to half-size in the Print Preview window. At this magnification you can begin to see the information in the report, but a closer view would make it clearer.

3   Click between the **City** and **YTD Sales columns** with the **zoom pointer**
The report enlarges to full size in Print Preview, as shown in Figure 10-6. At this magnification the title, headings, records, and statistics in the report are clearly visible. Works has inserted the four database records into the report with their respective year-to-date sales and commission totals. Three statistics appear at the bottom of the report: Total YTD Sales, Average YTD Sales, and Total Commission. However, the characters ######## display in the Total YTD Sales row because the YTD Sales column in the report is not wide enough. The Commission heading is also partially obscured because the Commission column is not wide enough. You'll return to list view and fix these formatting problems in the next lesson.

4   Click the **Cancel button** to cancel Print Preview
The Print Preview window closes and the report definition appears in report view.

FIGURE 10-5: The Print Preview window

Zoom In button

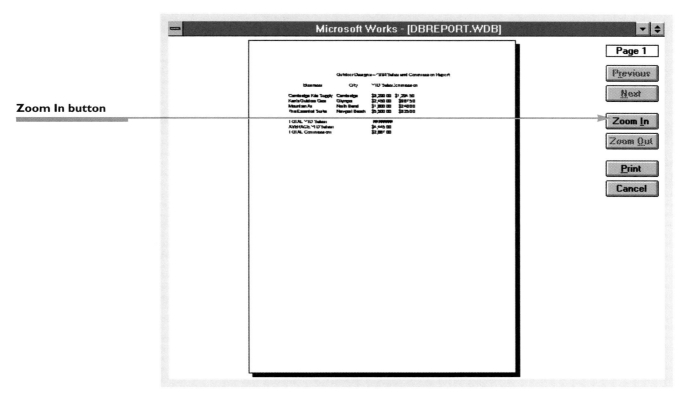

FIGURE 10-6: The Sales and Commission Report enlarged to full size

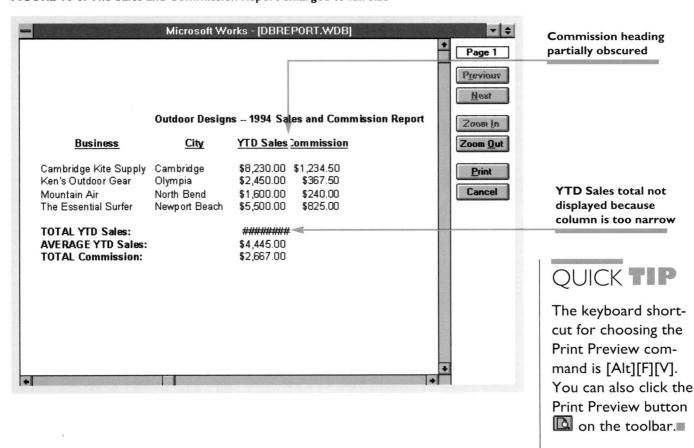

Commission heading partially obscured

YTD Sales total not displayed because column is too narrow

QUICK **TIP**

The keyboard short-cut for choosing the Print Preview com-mand is [Alt][F][V]. You can also click the Print Preview button on the toolbar.■

Formatting the report

In the last lesson you learned that the YTD Sales and Commission columns were not wide enough in the sales and commission report. You can fix these formatting problems in report view with the Column Width command on the Format menu. You can also insert blank lines and make font and style formatting changes to the report in report view. You'll format the report now and get it ready for printing.

STEPS

1 Click the **C** above the YTD Sales column to select column C of the report
   Column C highlights.

2 Hold down **[Shift]**, then click the **D** above the Commission column
   Columns C and D highlight. To select more than one column in report view, you hold down [Shift] between column clicks. Now you'll increase the column width in both columns to 12 characters.

3 Click the **Format menu,** then click the **Column Width command**
   The Column Width dialog box displays, as shown in Figure 10-7. It lets you specify the column width for the selected columns. The number is 10 highlighted in the dialog box. This is the current width of the selected columns.

4 Type **12,** then click **OK**
   The YTD Sales and Commission columns increase to 12 characters in width. Now you'll insert a blank line between the report title and the column headings.

5 Click the **second Title row** (the row name to the left of column A)
   To insert a blank line between the report title and the column heading, you need to insert an extra Title row.

6 Click the **Insert menu,** then click the **Row/Column command**
   The Insert Row dialog box displays. You use this dialog box to identify the type of row you want to insert.

7 Double-click **Title** in the list box
   A blank Title row is inserted into the report, as shown in Figure 10-8.

8 Click 🖫 to save your formatting changes

FIGURE 10-7: The Column Width dialog box and highlighted columns

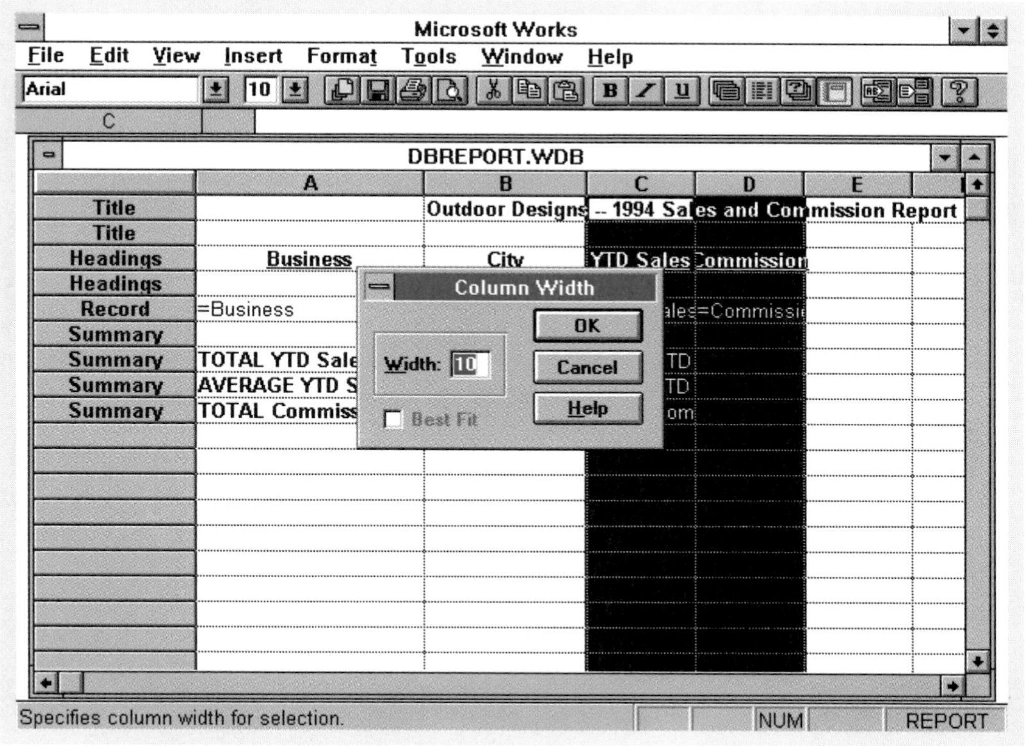

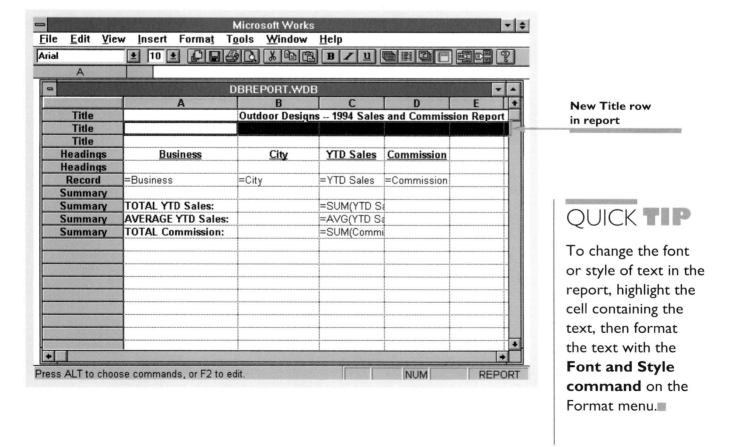

FIGURE 10-8: The Sales and Commission Report with formatting changes

New Title row
in report

QUICK **TIP**

To change the font
or style of text in the
report, highlight the
cell containing the
text, then format
the text with the
**Font and Style
command** on the
Format menu.

Naming the report and printing

Congratulations! The sales and commission report is finished, and you're ready to give it a name and print a copy for Sue Ellen and the Outdoor Designs sales staff. Naming the report will make it easy for you to recognize and open later. The Name Report command on the Tools menu allows you up to 15 characters to describe it. You'll name the report now and print a copy from Print Preview.

1 **Click the Tools menu, then click the Name Report command**
The Name Report dialog box displays, as shown in Figure 10-9. It lists the most recent reports that have been created from the database (up to eight) and lets you rename them. The sales and commission report appears in the list box as Report1.

2 **Press [Tab], type 1994 YTD Sales, then click the Rename button**
The sales and commission report is renamed 1994 YTD Sales.

3 **Click OK to close the Name Report dialog box**
Now you'll print the report from Print Preview.

4 **Click 🔍 on the toolbar**
The report displays in Print Preview. Before you print, use the **zoom pointer** to verify the formatting changes you made in the report.

5 **Click the report twice with the zoom pointer**
The report enlarges to full size in Print Preview, as shown in Figure 10-10. Because you changed the column widths in the report, the numbers and headers appear as they should on the page. The blank line you added between the title and the column headings also looks nice. The final report is ready to be printed.

6 **Verify that your printer is ready, then click the Print button**
Works sends the report to the printer. After a few moments the document emerges. Verify that it has printed correctly, and it is ready to give to Sue Ellen for distribution to the Outdoor Designs sales staff.

7 **Click 💾 to save your final report, then exit Works**

FIGURE 10-9:
The Name Report
dialog box

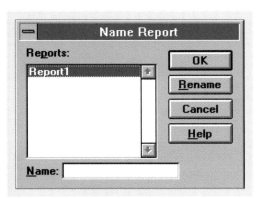

FIGURE 10-10:
The final report in
Print Preview

Report title

Column headings

Database records

Summary statistics

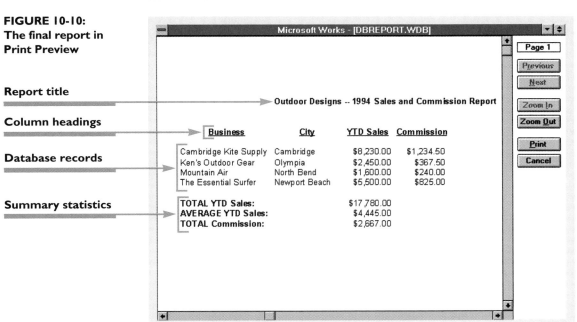

Opening the 1994 YTD Sales report later

Because Works saves your report with the database for which it was created, you can open an existing report any time the original database file is open. For example, to open the 1994 YTD Sales report you created in this unit, you would start Works and open the DBREPORT.WDB database, then choose the Report command from the View menu. The Reports dialog box would display, as shown in Figure 10-11. To open the 1994 YTD Sales report, you would simply double-click the report name in the list box.

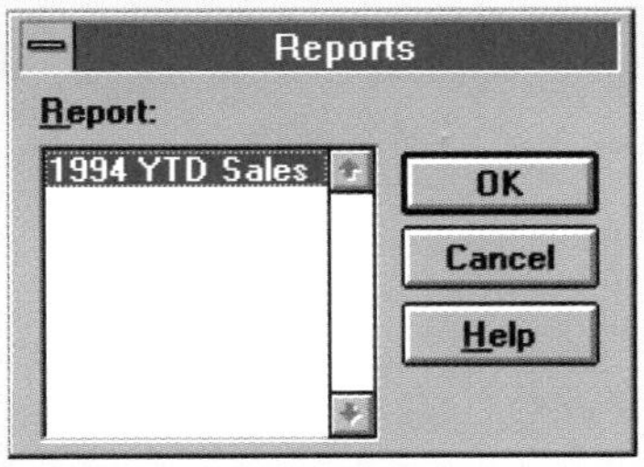

FIGURE 10-11:
The Reports dialog box

QUICK **TIP**

To print a report that includes only part of the records in the database, use a database query to select the records you want in the report before you print.■

CONCEPTSREVIEW

Label each of the database elements in the report view, as shown in Figure 10-12.

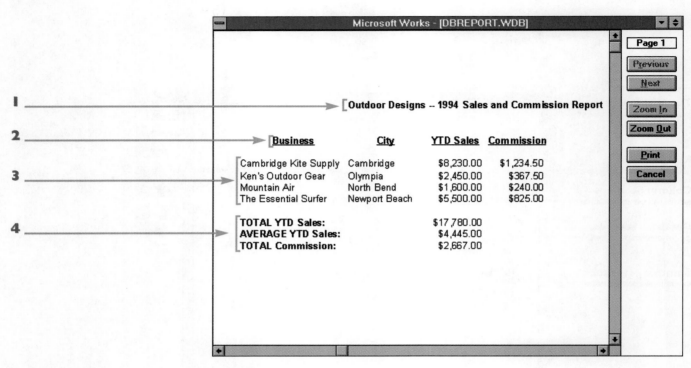

FIGURE 10-12

Match the statistical calculations with their descriptions.

5 Sum

6 Average

7 Cost

8 Minimum

9 Maximum

a. The largest value in the field

b. The total of all values in the field

c. The smallest value in the field

d. The number of records in the database

e. The average of all values in the field

Select the best answer from the list of choices.

10 A report is a summary of database information specifically designed for:

a. Sorting

b. Searching

c. Examining in form view

d. Printing

11 Which of the following elements *cannot* be included in a database report?

a. Fields

b. Statistics

c. ClipArt

d. Column headings

12 What button in the New Report dialog box would you use to add fields to a report?

a. Add

b. Insert

c. Remove

d. OK

13 Which of the following calculations is *not* available in the Report Statistics dialog box?

a. Sum

b. Net present value

c. Variance

d. Standard deviation

14 What is the name of the report instructions Works displays in the report view window?

a. The report definition

b. The database form

c. Print Preview

d. List view

15 Which of the following is *not* the name of a row label in the report definition?

a. Title

b. Subtitle

c. Record

d. Summary

16 What is the name of the mouse pointer when it is positioned over the report in Print Preview?

a. The Zoom In button

b. The magnification pointer

c. The zoom pointer

d. The enlargement pointer

17 What do the characters ######## mean if you see them in the report in Print Preview?

a. The selected field is not available in the database.

b. The selected field contains a negative number.

c. Works is busy calculating the statistic.

d. The column the characters are in is not wide enough in the report definition.

18 What is the keyboard shortcut for the Print Preview command?

a. [Alt][P][P]

b. [Alt][F][V]

c. [Ctrl][Ins]

d. [F9]

19 What command would you use to insert a blank row into the report definition?

a. Row/Column

b. Field Entry

c. Select Row

d. Column Width

20 What button would you click in the Name Report dialog box to name a report?

a. OK

b. Name

c. Rename

d. Add

APPLICATIONSREVIEW

1 Open the UNIT_10.WDB database, rename it, then use its fields to create a new report.

a. Open UNIT_10.WDB on the Student Disk, then save it as REPORT2.WDB in the MY_FILES directory.

b. Click the Tools menu, then click the Create New Report command.

c. Type **Outdoor Designs -- Commission Report** in the Report Title text box.

d. Use the Add button to add the Business, Phone, and Commission fields to the report, then click OK.

2 Specify the Sum, Average, Minimum, and Maximum statistics for the Commission field in the Report Statistics dialog box.

a. Click the Commission field, then click the Sum, Average, Minimum, and Maximum check boxes.

b. Click OK to create the report, then click OK to close the definitions dialog box.

c. Identify the elements of the report definition in the report view window.

3 Examine the report in Print Preview to spot any formatting problems.

a. Click the File menu, then click the Print Preview command.

b. Click the Zoom In button, then click the Phone field with the zoom pointer.

c. Check the column headings, records, and statistics for formatting problems.

d. Click the Cancel button to cancel Print Preview.

4 Increase the width of the Commission column to 12 characters and change the style of the report title to italic.

   a. Click the C above the Commission column to select column C in the report.

   b. Click the Format menu, then click the Column Width command.

   c. Type **12**, then click OK to increase the column width.

   d. Click the report title Outdoor Designs -- Commission Report, then click the Italic button on the toolbar.

   e. Click the Save button to save your changes.

5 Name the report then print it from Print Preview.

   a. Click the Tools menu, then click the Name Report command.

   b. Press [Tab], type **Commissions**, click the Rename button, then click OK.

   c. Click the Preview button on the toolbar, click the report twice with the zoom pointer, then check your formatting changes.

   d. Verify that your printer is ready, then click the Print button.

   e. Click the Save button to save your report, then exit Works.

INDEPENDENT
CHALLENGE

The Tools menu contains four commands you can use to manage the reports in your database: Create New Report, Name Report, Delete Report, and Duplicate Report. You used the Create New Report and Name Report commands in this unit to create the Outdoor Designs sales and commission report and name it in the database. The Delete Report command can be used to delete unwanted reports from the database. Because Works only allows you to have eight reports in the file, you'll eventually need to use Delete Report to delete older reports so you'll have room for new ones. The Duplicate Report command can be used to make a copy of an existing report so you can modify it in report view. Duplicating and editing a report can be a quick way to create a new report when the report you want is similar to one you already have.

Try working with the report commands in the following steps. If you have any questions about the commands, consult the Works on-line help.

1 Open the file BREAD94.WDB that you saved in the Unit 9 Independent Challenge. Create a report using the Total Paid field. Name the report BreadWalk Total and select the following statistics to appear in the report: Sum, Average, Minimum, and Maximum. Look at the report in Print Preview, then print a copy.

2 Create additional reports to find out how many walkers had three or more sponsors; four or more; five or more.

3 Create a report that helps you find the Maximum paid by any single sponsor. (You'll need to apply the Maximum statistic to more than one field.) Then find the Minimum paid. (You will need a Max and Min for each sponsor field; compare the Max and Min for each field to obtain the absolute Max and Min.) Print a copy of each report.

4 Create a report to list the total amount and the average collected by each participant in the Bread Walk. Print a copy of the report.

UNIT 11

OBJECTIVES

▶ Plan a telecommunication session

▶ Start the Communications application

▶ Set communications parameters

▶ Connect to a remote computer

▶ Search an on-line database

▶ Send e-mail on the Internet

▶ End your communications session

Exploring TELECOMMUNICATIONS

*I*n this unit you will learn how to use the Works Communications application to connect your computer to another computer using a modem and the phone lines in your school or home. Communicating with another computer over phone lines is called **telecommunicating**. Through telecommunication you can connect to the computers in your school or business, use sophisticated electronic services such as CompuServe or GEnie, or explore a global network of computers known as the **Internet**. ▶ In this unit you'll learn how to plan a telecommunication session, and how to connect to a remote computer using the Communications application. You'll learn to set communications parameters, search for books in an on-line library, send an electronic mail message over the Internet, and end a communications session. Because each telecommunication interface is different, not all the instructions in this unit will match your on-line service. Your instructor will provide customized instructions for your setting. ▶

Planning a telecommunication session

Before you start telecommunicating, you need to do some planning. Telecommunication requires a computer, a modem, and a phone line connecting your modem to the phone jack. In addition, you need to know the phone number of the computer or service you'll be connecting to and any necessary communication settings or **parameters**. Finally, you'll need a communications program, such as Microsoft Works, to connect the two computers and manage the telecommunication session. ▶ Figure 11-1 shows the hardware components in a typical telecommunication session. Use the guidelines below to plan your session. Ask your instructor for the phone number and parameters you'll be using to follow the steps in this unit.

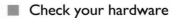

■ Check your hardware
Before you telecommunicate, you need to verify that your computer has the hardware necessary to link with another computer. A computer supports telecommunication through one of its **serial ports***. The actual work of telecommunication is done by a special peripheral called a* **modem** *that is fitted inside the computer or attached to one of the serial ports on the back of the computer. The modem is then connected to a standard phone jack with a phone line, as shown in Figure 11-1. If the computer you're using is in a lab, ask your instructor or lab manager if your computer has the necessary hardware to telecommunicate. If you're working on this unit at home, check with an experienced friend or your computer dealer to see if your computer has the necessary hardware to go on-line.*

■ Learn about the service you'll be using
After your computer has the necessary hardware, you need to determine what remote computer or service you'll be connecting to. There are dozens of options, some that are free of connect charges and some that will cost you money. You can connect to a comprehensive on-line service such as CompuServe, GEnie, or America On Line, or you can connect to a special-interest bulletin board, university computing facility, or electronic mail system. Several of these services will require that you sign up in advance, and will issue you a user name and password that you can use to access the system. Ask your instructor for details, then learn what you can about the service you'll be using.

■ Verify the phone number and communication parameters
Finally, get the phone number and the communication parameters for the service you'll be connecting to. Be sure to get a local phone number for the service, so you can avoid long distance phone charges. The communications parameters you need relate to how the data is transmitted by your modem, and include the baud rate, data bits, parity, stop bits, and terminal setting. (We'll discuss these terms later in the unit.) Your instructor will provide you with details. You can also find them in your telecommunication service documentation.

When you've checked your hardware and have the necessary details about your telecommunication service, you're ready to make the connection with the Works Communications application. You'll start the application in the next lesson.

FIGURE 11-1: The hardware components of a typical telecommunication session

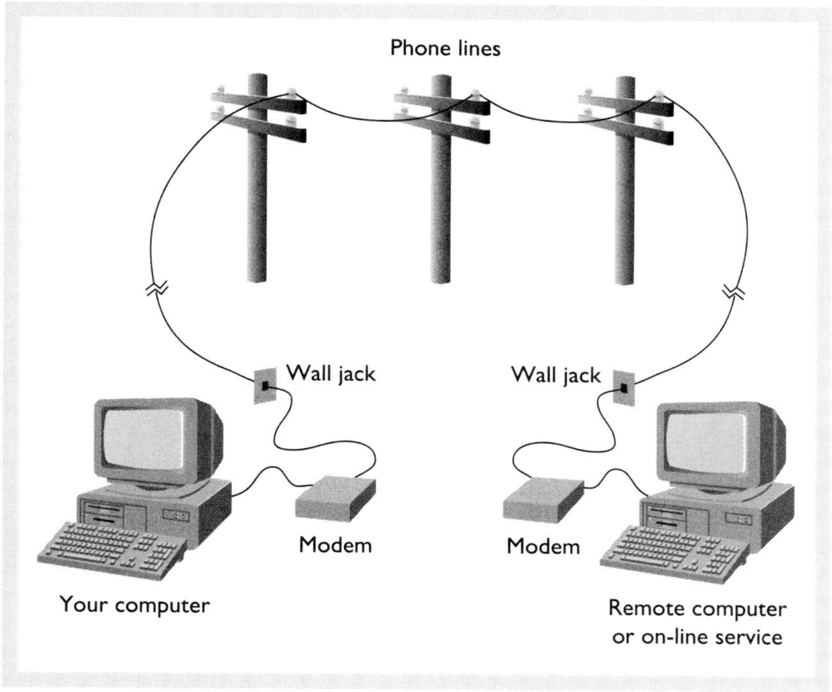

What is a modem?

A **modem** is a communications device that enables a computer to transmit information over a standard telephone line. Modem is short for modulator/demodulator, which means that a modem can convert the digital signals in your computer to the analog signals used in phone lines, and vice versa. When you telecommunicate, your modem converts the digital instructions from your computer and sends them over the phone lines to a remote computer's modem. The remote modem then converts the analog signals to digital signals and passes them on to the remote computer for processing.

TROUBLE?

If you have Call Waiting you should disable it before you telecommunicate. Incoming calls during a telecommunication session can break the phone link between computers or cause data loss.

Starting the Communications application

With the Works Communications application you can communicate with an on-line service, a university computing facility, or a computer belonging to a friend or colleague. The Communications application uses the modem to make the connection to the remote computer and handles the details of the telecommunication session. ▶ Figure 11-3 shows the elements of the Communications application, and Table 11-1 lists the most useful toolbar buttons. You'll start the Communications application now.

1   Double-click the Microsoft Works program icon
The Startup dialog box displays, as shown in Figure 11-2.

2   Click the Communications button
The Communications application opens in a window, as shown in Figure 11-3. An Easy Connect dialog box displays in the window, prompting you for the phone number and name of the service you'll be connecting to. (You may also see a Modem Setup dialog box if you haven't used your modem with Works before. If you do, ask your instructor how to fill out the dialog box.) The Communications application contains interface elements found in every Works application: a menu bar, a toolbar, a document window, scroll bars, toggle indicators, sizing buttons, and control menu boxes. Unique to the Communications interface are the **connect time box**, that displays the time you have been connected to a remote computer, and a **connection status box**, that displays messages relating to your telecommunication session.

3   Click Cancel to close the Easy Connect dialog box
In the future, you'll want to use the Easy Connect dialog box to connect to services you use regularly. However, because it is your first time telecommunicating, you'll specify the phone number and communications parameters with buttons on the toolbar.

TABLE 11-1:
Useful toolbar buttons

BUTTON	FUNCTION
	Change communications settings
	Change terminal settings
	Change phone settings
	Change file transfer settings
	Display Easy Connect dialog box
	Dial remote computer or (if a connection exists) hang up

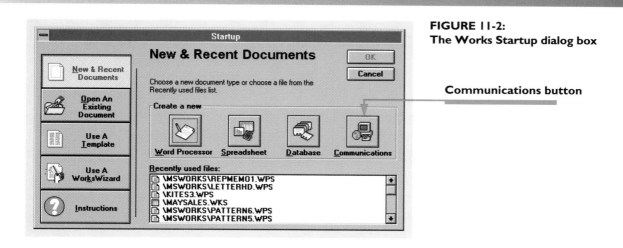

FIGURE 11-2:
The Works Startup dialog box

Communications button

Menu bar

Control menu boxes

Toolbar

Document (session) window

Sizing buttons

Scroll bars

Connection status box

Toggle indicators

Connect time box

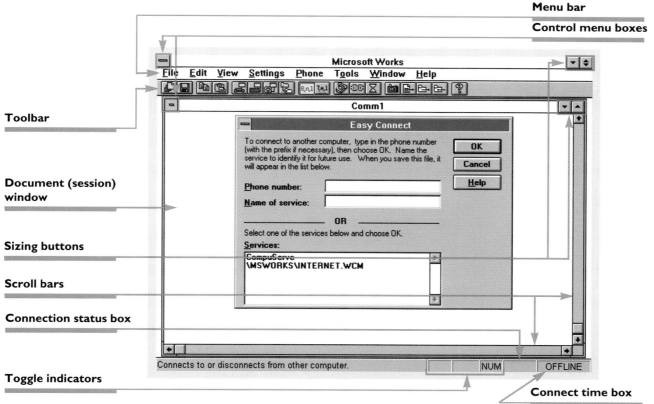

FIGURE 11-3: The Communications application with unique elements labeled

QUICK **TIP**

To save on connect charges, don't call an on-line service until you're ready to work. Many services charge by the minute.

Setting communications parameters

In this lesson you'll set the communication parameters for your telecommunication session. Sue Ellen has asked you to connect to the University of Washington computer facility and search for books relating to outdoor sports in the library database. When you find a suitable book, Sue Ellen has asked you to send an electronic mail message to a person at the university who can send you the book directly. Prepare for your telecommunication session now by setting the communication parameters for a service you can use to do similar work. Your instructor will give you the instructions for a similar facility.

1 Click the **Phone Settings button** 🖥 on the toolbar
The Settings dialog box displays, as shown in Figure 11-4. It contains a Phone number text box, where you type the phone number of the service you'll be using; a Name of service text box, where you type the name of the service you'll be using; and several elements related to the connection process. After you enter information in this dialog box and save it to disk, it appears in the Easy Connect dialog box when you start the Communications application. The dialog box also contains tabs for Communication, Terminal, and Transfer settings.

2 Type the number for the service you'll be using in the Phone number text box
This number will vary depending on your location and the service you're using. Ask your instructor for the proper information.

3 Press **[Tab]**, then type the name of the service you'll be using
The service name also will vary with your situation. Ask your instructor for help.

4 Click the **Communication tab** in the dialog box
The Communication tab displays, as shown in Figure 11-5. It contains settings for the computer communications port, the transmission baud rate, the parity, the data bits, the stop bits, and the handshake protocol. In most cases, you'll find that these settings are correct; the only one you may need to change is the baud rate. For example, the University of Washington dial-in service is limited to 2400 baud. The Works default is 9600.

5 Click the **Baud rate drop-down list box**, then click **2400** in the list box
The baud rate is set to 2400. (You may need to set a different baud rate.) Make any other changes now to match the settings your instructor gave you for your service.

6 Click the **Terminal tab** in the dialog box
The Terminal tab displays, as shown in Figure 11-6. It contains settings that control how your monitor and keyboard are configured (some services require a specific type of hardware configuration for the connection). Check with your instructor or telecommunication service manual for the proper settings in this dialog box tab. The University of Washington dial-in service is best suited for VT100 terminal emulation, listed third in the Terminal list box.

7 Click the **VT100 option** in the Terminal list box, then click **OK**
Congratulations! You've set your communication parameters. In the next lesson you'll make the connection.

FIGURE 11-4:
The Phone tab in the
Setting dialog box

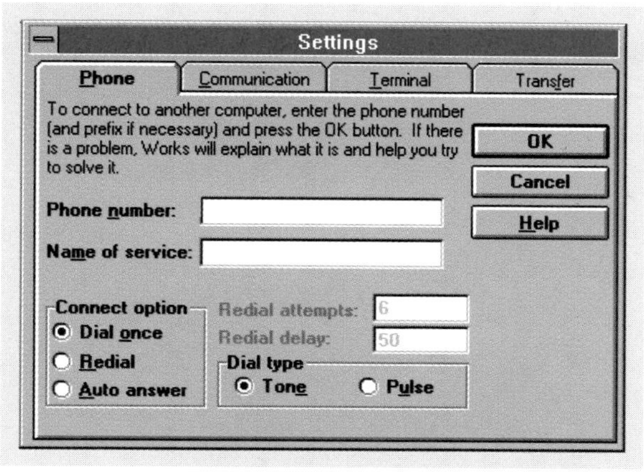

FIGURE 11-5: The Communications tab in the Settings dialog box

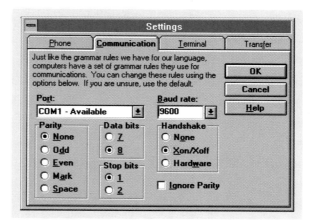

FIGURE 11-6: The Terminal tab in the Settings dialog box

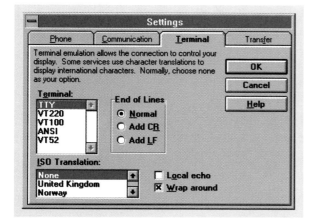

What is baud rate?

Baud rate is the rate at which data is transferred over the phone lines by your modem. Technically, it refers to the number of times a circuit can switch its electrical state each second. Typical baud rates are 1200, 2400, and 9600. The higher the baud rate, the faster the data transfer.

QUICK TIP

The Communication Settings button 🖫 and the Terminal Settings button 🖳 are the toolbar shortcuts for bringing up the Communication and Terminal tabs, respectively.■

Connecting to a remote computer

Now that you have set the communication parameters for your telecommunication session, you're ready to connect to the remote computer. To make the connection you click the Dial/Hangup button on the toolbar. Your modem will dial the remote computer and, if the computer is available, make the connection. The remote computer then prompts you through the **login** process, where you are validated as an authorized user of the system. Try making a connection to your remote computer or service now.

1 **Make sure you have the account information for your service handy**
This information will typically include a computer name, a user name, and a password. Ask your instructor for this information if you do not have it by your computer.

2 **Click the Dial/Hangup button** 🔲 **on the toolbar**
Works dials the phone number you specified in the Settings dialog box and attempts to connect with the remote computer. Some technical information displays on the screen as your modem and the remote modem interact. You are then prompted for your login information, as shown in Figure 11-7. Note that your screen and login information will be different. If the connection is not made for some reason, Works displays a message letting you know why (a common reason is that the line is busy).

3 **Enter your computer name, user name, and password as directed, pressing [Enter] after each item**
The remote computer validates your responses and, if you are an authorized user, admits you to the system. A welcome message displays, along with any instructions or announcements from the **system administrator**, the person in charge of the service. Figure 11-8 shows what the screen looks like for Melissa Cavanaugh after she has connected to the University of Washington computing facility.

Notice that the total connect time now displays in the connect time box. You can use this information to keep track of how long you are connected to the remote computer or service. If you need to disconnect from the remote computer for any reason, you can click the Dial/Hangup button on the toolbar to break the connection. However, you should always log out from the remote computer first, if possible. We'll cover this process later in the unit.

FIGURE 11-7: The remote computer prompts you for login information

Modem information

Computer name

User name

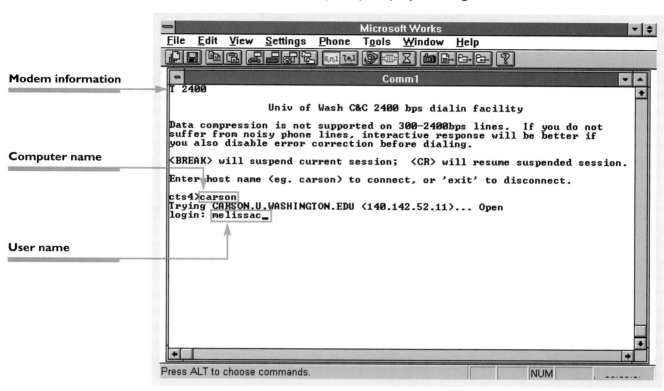

FIGURE 11-8: A typical telecommunication screen after the login process

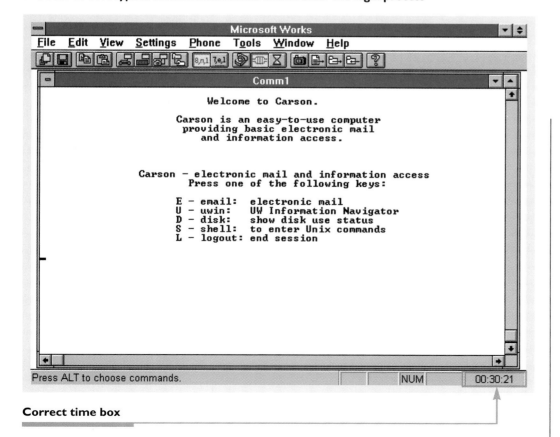

Correct time box

TROUBLE?

If you couldn't connect to the remote computer, or if you established a connection but found the screen cluttered with strange characters, you may need to adjust your communication or terminal settings. Ask your instructor for help or call a support person at your on-line service.■

Searching an on-line database

Now that you've connected to the remote computer, you can begin to access its resources. Sue Ellen has asked you to search for books relating to outdoor sports in the university library database. Follow along as Melissa searches for the books now in the University of Washington library database. If you can search for the books on your remote computer or service also, do it now. Most services provide this facility, but the commands you'll need to access your service database will probably be different.

1   Run the program that lets you access the library database
The command you type to run this program will vary from system to system. Ask your instructor or check your service documentation for details. Melissa types *uwin*, which runs the University of Washington Information Manager, a special program that helps students access University records and materials.

2   Run the search option in the library database
This option, which varies from system to system, displays a dialog box that helps you search for books in the database. The University of Washington search dialog box is shown in Figure 11-9. It contains Title Words, Author, and Subject Heading text boxes, and two Keywords text boxes.

3   Type outdoor sports in the Title Words text box (the name of your text box may be different)
The remote computer will use these words to search through its library database and retrieve the titles that match.

4   Press [Enter] to run the search (you may need to press a different key)
The remote computer searches the library database and displays a list of the titles that match. Spend a few minutes examining the books that would help the Outdoor Designs marketing staff with their upcoming fall promotion. A book that Melissa has picked out is shown in Figure 11-10.

5   Write down the citation for the book, then exit the library search program
The system menu reappears. (Melissa's system menu is shown in Figure 11-8.)

Next you'll send a student at the University of Washington some electronic mail and ask the student to send the book to you.

FIGURE 11-9: A typical library search dialog box

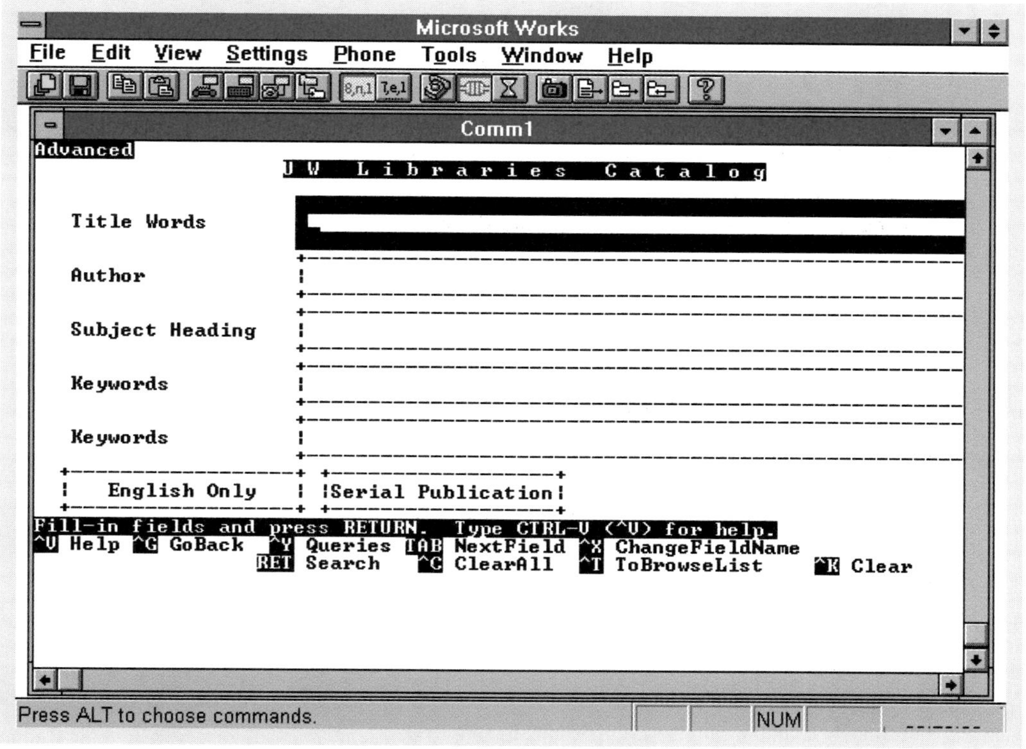

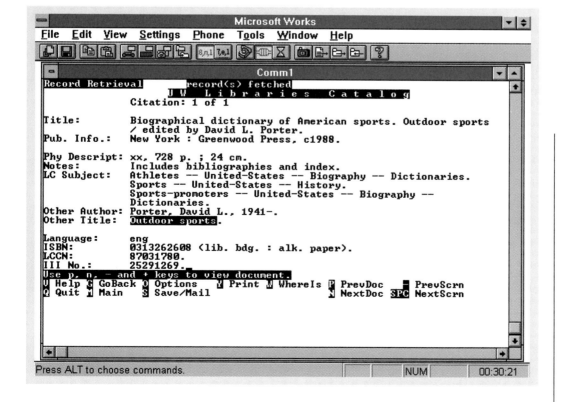

FIGURE 11-10: The on-line record for a book in the library

QUICK **TIP**

You can maximize the screen in the Communications application by clicking the Maximize button in the upper-right corner of the document window. This will make more room for the information displayed by the remote computer.■

Sending e-mail on the Internet

One of the best reasons for connecting to an on-line service is the ability to send electronic mail to another computer user. **Electronic mail**, or **e-mail**, is a computer-to-computer version of interoffice mail or the postal service. Each on-line service has its own program for controlling electronic mail, but often services are linked together in a network to exchange mail and other information. One such network is called the **Internet**. In this lesson, you'll send an electronic mail message to another student over the Internet. Ask your instructor how to use the electronic mail program in your on-line service, and for the e-mail name or **Internet address** of the student you'll be sending mail to.

1 Run the program in your service that lets you send **electronic mail**
   The commands you type to run this program will vary from system to system. Ask your instructor or check your service documentation for details. Melissa types *e*, which runs the Pine electronic mail program at the University of Washington, as shown in Figure 11-11.

2 Run the **compose message option** in the electronic mail program
   This option, which varies from system to system, displays a dialog box (see Figure 11-12) that lets you enter the contents of your electronic mail message. In most electronic mail programs, you press [Tab] to move from one prompt to the next.

3 Type a friend's **Internet address** after the To: prompt
   Every user with access to the Internet has a different address, depending on their location and the remote computer or service they receive mail from. Ask your instructor or system administrator for the Internet address of a user to whom you can send a test message. (If you don't want to bother anyone with a test message, you can send a test message to your own Internet address.)

4 Type **Looking for library book** after the Subject prompt highlights

5 Type the following in the message text area, pressing **[Enter]** as indicated (See Figure 11-12.)
   Can you send me the book Biographical Dictionary of American Sports, **[Enter]**
   edited by David L. Porter? I think it might be just the thing **[Enter]**
   for an upcoming promotion we're doing this fall at Outdoor Designs. **[Enter]**
   The book is in the Odegaard Undergraduate Library, and the call number **[Enter]**
   is GV697.A1 B49. **[Enter]**
   [Enter]
   Please use my student number for the checkout. **[Enter]**
   Thanks a million! **[Enter]**
   [Enter]
   Melissa

6 Type the command to send the message, then exit the e-mail program
   The mail program closes and the system menu reappears.

FIGURE 11-11: The electronic mail program at the University of Washington

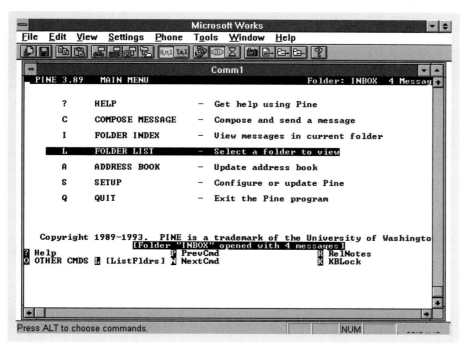

FIGURE 11-12: Composing an electronic mail message

Internet address

Subject

Message text

Electronic mail commands

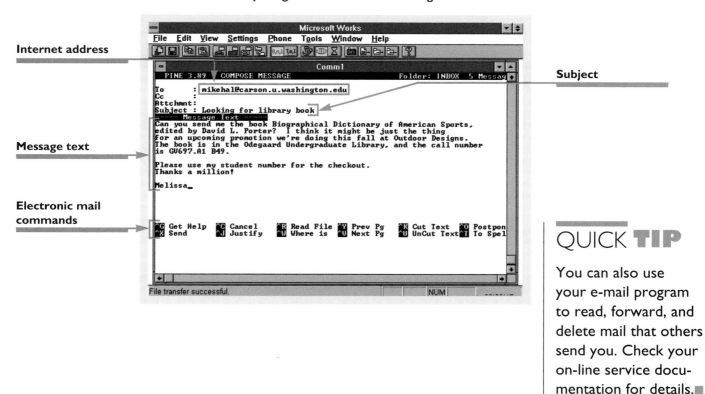

QUICK **TIP**

You can also use your e-mail program to read, forward, and delete mail that others send you. Check your on-line service documentation for details.

Ending your telecommunication session

When you've finished working with the remote computer you're ready to end your telecommunication session, or **log out**. Logging out entails two basic steps: first you log out from the remote computer, then you disconnect your phone connection. After you've logged out you can save your communication settings to a file on your Student Disk, so you won't have to enter them again the next time you telecommunicate. You'll log out from the remote computer now.

1 **Type the command to log out from your on-line service**
The command you type to log out will vary from system to system. Ask your instructor or check your service documentation for the exact command. Melissa types *l*, which logs her out of the carson computer, then she types *logout* to terminate the connection, as shown in Figure 11-13.

2 **Click the ▧ button on the toolbar**
Works displays a dialog box asking if you want to end the active session.

3 **Click OK to end the session**
Works instructs the modem to disconnect from the remote computer. Now save the communication settings to your Student Disk.

4 **Put your Student Disk in drive A, click the File menu, then click the Save As command**
The Save As dialog box displays.

5 **Type a:\my_files\telecom in the File Name text box, then click OK**
The communication settings are saved in the file TELECOM.WCM in the MY_FILES directory on your Student Disk. (WCM is the three-character extension for files created by the Communications application.) Notice that the filename also displays in the Communications title bar.

6 **Click the File menu, then click the Exit Works command to exit Works**

FIGURE 11-13:
Logging out from the
remote computer

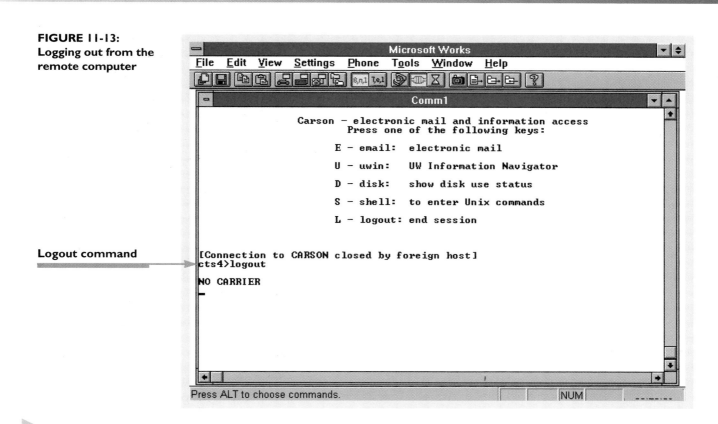

Logout command

Using the Easy Connect dialog box

The next time you start the Communications application, the name of the service you just used will appear in the Easy Connect dialog box, as shown in Figure 11-14. (Works gets the name of the service from the Phone tab in the Settings dialog box.) To connect to this service again, put your Student Disk in drive A, then double-click the name of the service in the dialog box. Works will load the settings from your Student Disk into Works automatically and dial the service. You only need to enter the communication settings for your service the first time. From that point on Works is able to load them directly from disk.

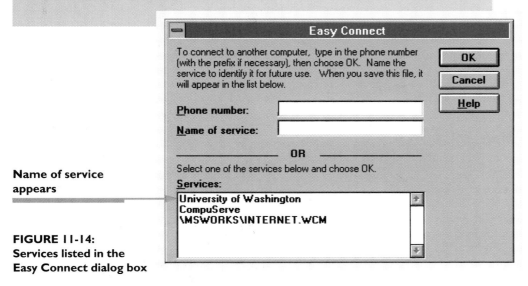

Name of service
appears

FIGURE 11-14:
Services listed in the
Easy Connect dialog box

TROUBLE?

Don't try to use your phone for calls while you are telecommunicating. Picking up the phone (even on another extension) may break your phone link with the remote computer.■

CONCEPTSREVIEW

Label each element of the Communications application, as shown in Figure 11-15.

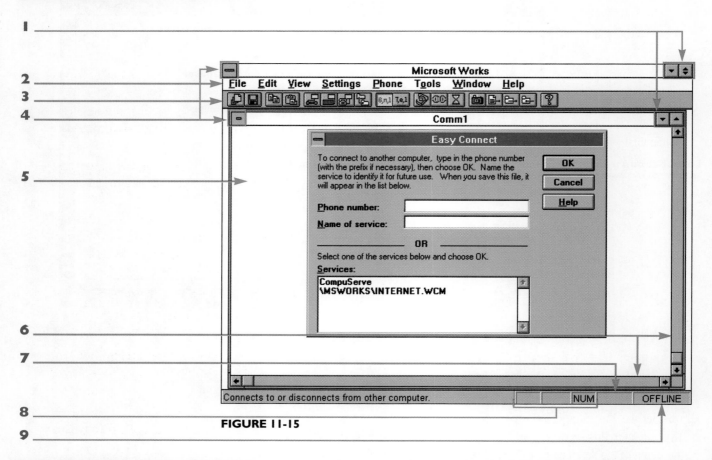

FIGURE 11-15

Match the toolbar buttons with their descriptions.

10
11
12
13
14

a. Dial remote computer or (if a connection exists) hang up
b. Display Easy Connect dialog box
c. Change communications settings
d. Change phone settings
e. Change terminal settings

Select the best answer from the list of choices.

15 Which of the following hardware components is not necessary for telecommunicating?

a. Modem
b. Phone line
c. Serial port
d. Mouse

16 Which of the following is usually required when you access an on-line service?

a. User name and password
b. Birth certificate
c. Photo identification
d. Spreadsheet

17 Which of the following is *not* a communication parameter?

a. Data bits
b. Modem
c. Parity
d. Stop bits

18 Modem is short for:

a. Motion Over Dense Electronic Media
b. Mode em frequency
c. Modulator/demodulator
d. University of Montana wireless experiment

19 What element in the Communications application displays the time you have been connected to a remote computer?

a. Connection status box

b. Toggle indicators

c. Connect time box

d. Document window

20 Which tab in the Settings dialog box would you click to change the communication baud rate?

a. Phone

b. Communication

c. Terminal

d. Transfer

21 Which tab in the Settings dialog box would you click to change the phone number?

a. Phone

b. Communication

c. Terminal

d. Transfer

22 Which button would you click to connect to a remote computer or service?

a.

b.

c.

d.

23 What is the Internet?

a. A library database that can be searched for books by title, author, or keyword

b. A university computing facility located in Seattle, Washington

c. A global network of computers that exchanges electronic mail and other information

d. An electronic mail program used by Melissa and the Outdoor Designs staff

24 Which of the following prompts does not appear in a typical electronic mail message?

a. To:

b. Subject:

c. Message Text:

d. Phone:

25 The process of disconnecting from a remote computer is called:

a. Rebooting

b. Logging out

c. Shutting down

d. Stopping

APPLICATIONS REVIEW

1 Start the Communications application and use the Easy Connect dialog box to connect to your telecommunication service again.

a. Verify that your hardware is ready to go and that you have the phone number, settings, and login information for your on-line service.

b. Start the Communications application, put your Student Disk in drive A, then double-click the service name in the Easy Connect dialog box to connect to the service.

c. Enter the computer name, user name, and password as required to gain admittance to the system.

2 Use the library database to search for books about climbing, then record the information.

a. Run the program that lets you access the library database.

b. Run the search option, then type **climbing** in the Title Words text box (the name of your text box may be different).

c. Review a few of the book descriptions found in the search, jot down their titles and author names, then exit the library search program.

3 Send an electronic mail message to a friend (or yourself) with the names of the books you found.

a. Run the program that lets you access electronic mail on your service.

b. Run the compose message option, then type an electronic mail message containing a subject and message text. Specify your friend's (or your own) Internet address after the To: prompt.

c. Send the message and exit the mail program.

4 Log out from the on-line service and disconnect from the remote computer.

a. Type the necessary commands to log out from the on-line service.

b. Click the Dial/Hangup button on the toolbar to end your session, then click OK in the Disconnect dialog box.

c. Save any settings changes you have made and exit Works.

INDEPENDENT
CHALLENGE

There are many different options open to you in the growing world of telecommunications. Through the Internet and a variety of on-line services you can explore financial topics, business, travel, games, simulations, music, news, special-interest forums, government services, the weather, and much more right from your home or classroom. There are on-line databases, bulletin boards and other types of electronic conferencing. Take some time to learn about the resources provided by the on-line services you have access to. You'll find them to be stimulating and an exciting place to meet new and interesting people.

By brainstorming with friends, checking with a librarian, looking at newspaper columns, listening to radio or television announcements, list at least five specific examples of e-mail applications you might use to obtain or share information rapidly using a computer and modem.

UNIT 12

OBJECTIVES

▶ Start Draw

▶ Work with the Draw tools

▶ Create a kite illustration

▶ Add text to the illustration

▶ Save and size the illustration

▶ Print the illustration

Creating
ILLUSTRATIONS WITH DRAW

*I*n Units 4 and 9 you learned how to add ClipArt to your Word Processor document and Database form with the ClipArt accessory. In this unit you'll learn how to create original illustrations and add them to your projects with the **Draw accessory**. You can use Draw to create company logos, decorative artwork, technical illustrations, and other useful drawings. Best of all, Draw contains several tools that create shapes automatically, so you don't have to be artistic to do useful work. ▶ In this unit you'll learn how to start the Draw accessory from the Word Processor and Database applications, and start working with the Draw tools and commands. You'll create a simple kite illustration for use in Outdoor Designs reports and brochures, and you'll learn how to format and size the illustration in the Word Processor. Finally, you'll learn how to save the illustration so you can use it later, and you'll print a copy for your colleagues. ▶

Starting Draw

In this lesson you'll start the Draw accessory from the Word Processor application. Draw has a graphical interface that is similar to the other Works applications and accessories you've used. In Draw the document window is known as the **canvas**. This is where you'll create your illustration. Along the left edge of the canvas are the **drawing tools**, which you'll use to create the lines, shapes, and text of your illustration. Near the bottom of the screen are the **Line** and **Fill palettes**, which let you change the colors of the lines and shapes in your illustration. Figure 12-2 identifies the unique elements of the Draw interface, and Table 12-1 describes the drawing tools. You'll start Works and the Draw accessory now.

1   Start Works from the Program Manager
The Startup dialog box displays.

2   Click the Word Processor button
The Word Processor application opens in a window.

3   Click the Insert menu, then click the Drawing command
The Draw accessory opens in a window, as shown in Figure 12-1. Notice that Works has shaded an area in the upper-left corner of the Word Processor window (you may have to move the Draw window to see the shaded area). This space is being reserved for the illustration you are about to create with Draw. When you finish your illustration and exit Draw, Works will put the drawing in this space. Now you'll maximize the Draw window so you can see all the elements of the Draw interface.

4   Click the Maximize button in the upper-right corner of the Draw window
The Draw accessory maximizes, as shown in Figure 12-2. Take a moment to identify the elements of the Draw accessory, referring to Table 12-1 to identify the drawing tools. You'll practice using the drawing tools in the next lesson.

TABLE 12-1: The drawing tools in the Draw accessory

TOOL	FUNCTION
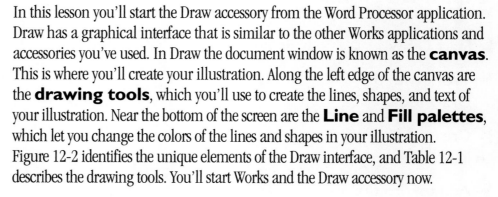	Selects objects in the illustration. Also used for moving objects.
	Enlarges part of the illustration for up-close viewing.
	Creates a straight line.
	Creates an ellipse. (Hold down [Shift] to create a circle.)
	Creates a rectangle with square edges. (Hold down [Shift] to create a square.)
	Creates a rectangle with rounded edges. (Hold down [Shift] to create a square with rounded edges.)
	Creates an arc or "pie slice."
	Creates polygons. (Hold down the mouse button to create freeform lines.)
	Inserts text (or labels) in the illustration.

FIGURE 12-1: The Draw accessory in the Word Processor

Draw accessory

Space reserved for illustration

Maximize button

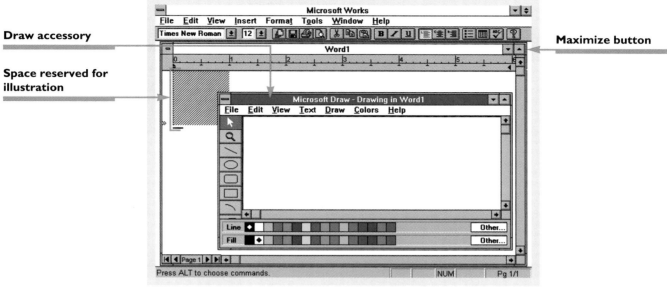

FIGURE 12-2: The Draw accessory interface

Menu bar

Drawing tools

Canvas

Line palette

Fill palette

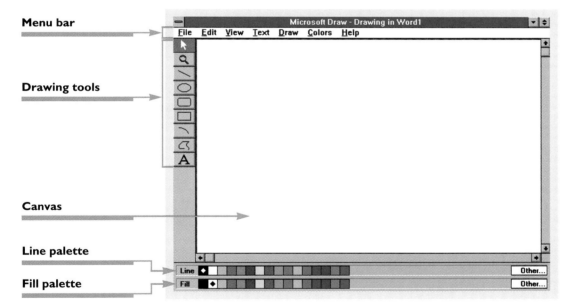

QUICK **TIP**

Draw illustrations can be added to Word Processor documents and Database forms only. For more information on the Draw accessory, press **[F1]** while Draw is running.

Working with the Draw tools

The drawing tools help you create your illustration or modify it when you want to change something later. Creating an illustration is easy, because Draw lets you build it one piece or **object** at a time. Each object retains its own identity and can be selected, moved, or deleted at any time. (That means one mistake can't ruin the whole thing.) In the following steps you'll practice using the drawing tools and the Fill palette to create an abstract face. Feel free to experiment, because you'll erase your creation at the end of the lesson.

1   Click the **Ellipse tool** 🔘
The Ellipse tool highlights and the mouse pointer changes to crosshairs. You'll try using the Ellipse tool to draw an ellipse on the left side of the canvas now.

2   Position the **Ellipse tool** on the canvas, hold down the mouse button, drag the crosshairs down and to the right, then release the mouse button
An ellipse appears on the canvas, surrounded by four selection rectangles. These rectangles, called **handles**, appear when an object is selected, and mean you can cut, copy, paste, or move it like any highlighted object in Works. Cut the ellipse object now.

3   Click the **Edit menu**, then click the **Cut command**
The object is removed from the canvas and placed in the Windows clipboard. Now you'll paste it with the Paste command.

4   Click the **Edit menu**, then click the **Paste command**
The object is pasted back on the canvas. Now move the object to the right.

5   Click the **Arrow tool** 🔼
The Arrow tool highlights and the mouse pointer changes to an arrow.

6   Click the **ellipse object** with the Arrow tool, hold down the mouse button, drag the object to the right, then release the mouse button
The object moves to the right. You can use the Arrow tool to drag any object on the canvas. Now fill the ellipse with dark green color.

7   Click the **dark green box** in the **Fill palette**
The ellipse fills with dark green color, as shown in Figure 12-3, and a check mark appears next to the dark green square on the palette. You can add color to any geometric shape with the Fill palette. To change the color of the lines in the object, you would click any color box in the Line palette.

8   Experiment with the Ellipse, Rectangle, Rounded Rectangle, and Arc tools on your own to create an abstract face similar to the one shown in Figure 12-4
See Table 12-1 for a description of the Rectangle, Rounded Rectangle, and Arc tools. (They work like the Ellipse tool.) If you want you can place one object on top of another. When you finish, you'll delete all the objects and clear the canvas.

9   Click the **Edit menu**, click the **Select All command**, then press **[Del]**
Draw deletes all the objects in the drawing.

FIGURE 12-3: An ellipse created with the Ellipse tool

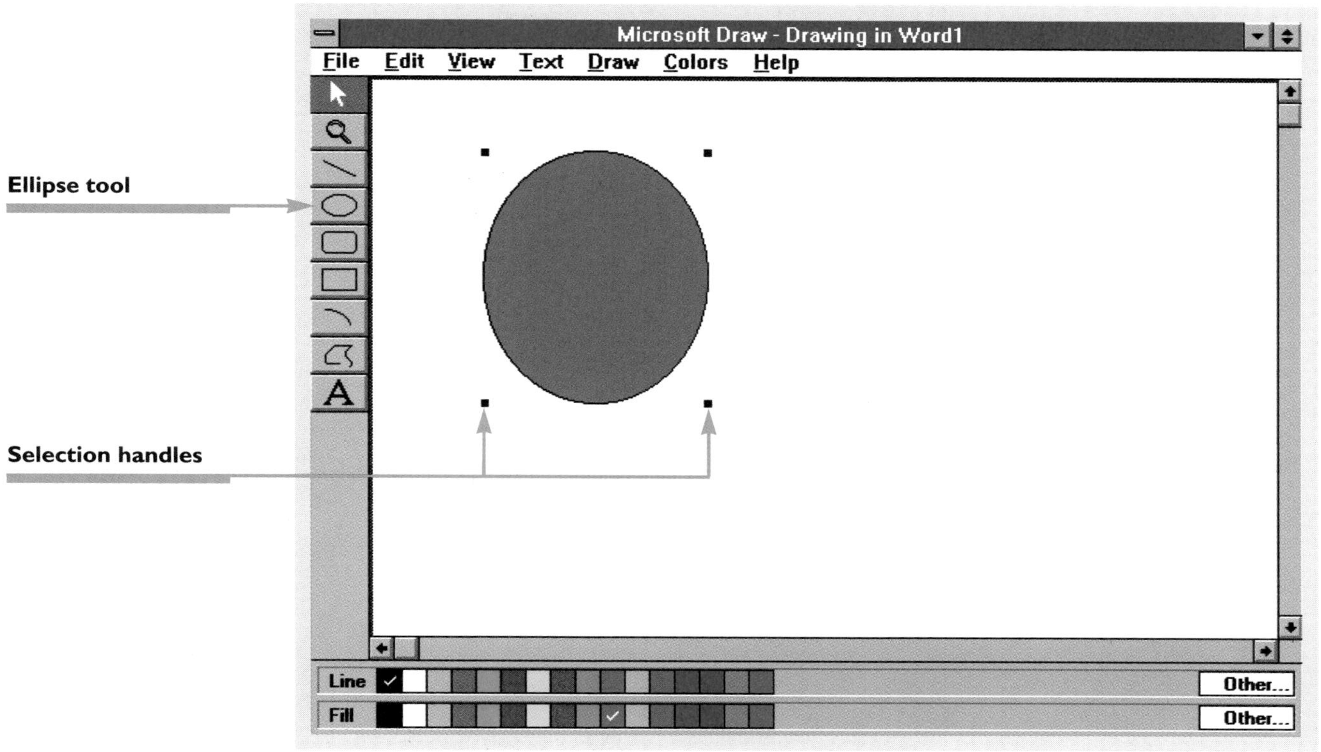

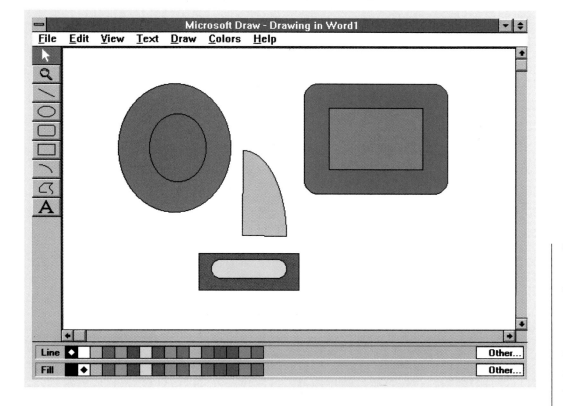

Ellipse tool

Selection handles

FIGURE 12-4: An abstract face created with the Ellipse, Rectangle, and Arc tools

QUICK **TIP**

The Select All command on the Edit menu selects all the objects on the canvas, allowing you to drag the whole set of parts as a single entity.■

Creating a kite illustration

In this lesson you'll use the Freeform and Rectangle tools to create a kite you can use in Outdoor Designs' reports and brochures. The Freeform tool lets you create polygons (many-sided objects) and freehand drawings. You'll use the Freeform tool to create the diamond shape of the kite and the tail of the kite, and you'll use the Rectangle tool to add bows.

STEPS

1   Click the **Freeform tool** 🔲
The Freeform tool highlights and the mouse pointer changes to crosshairs. The Freeform tool is different from the Ellipse and the other shape tools. You can use the Freeform tool to create polygons (such as triangles and diamonds) by moving the mouse to each vertex (corner) in the shape and clicking, then double-clicking the last corner. Or you can create a freehand drawing (such as a signature or a jagged line) by holding down the mouse button and moving the crosshairs, then double-clicking when you're finished.

Now try creating the diamond for the kite illustration with the Freeform tool, referring to Figure 12-5 for the proper shape. If it takes you a while to get the hang of it, don't worry. You can always select the diamond, delete it, and start over again.

2   Click near the top of the canvas with the **Freeform tool**, release the mouse button, then move the crosshairs down and to the left
A line extends from the Freeform tool to the point you clicked. This is the top left edge of the four-sided diamond kite.

3   Click to mark the left corner of the kite, then move the crosshairs down and to the right to the bottom of the kite
A line extends from the left corner of the kite down to the bottom of the kite.

4   Click to mark the bottom of the kite, move the crosshairs to the right edge and click, then move the crosshairs to the top of the kite and double-click where the first line begins
The diamond shape of the kite is complete, as shown in Figure 12-5. If your diamond doesn't look quite right, select it, delete it, then try again.

5   Click the **yellow color box** in the Fill palette
The diamond kite fills with yellow color. Now use the Freeform tool to draw a tail for the kite, referring to Figure 12-6 for the proper shape (you'll add the bows in step 7).

6   Click the **Freeform tool**, then click the bottom of the diamond, hold down the mouse button, draw a wavy line (like a kite tail in a breeze), then double-click the end of the line
A tail appears below the kite, as shown in Figure 12-6. Again, if you're not happy with the object you've created, select it, delete it, and try again.

7   Add several tiny kite bows to the tail with the **Rectangle tool**
You can either create one rectangle, copy it to the clipboard, then paste it several times, or you can create the bows individually.

8   Fill the bows with different colors using the **Fill palette**
When you're finished, your kite should look something like the one in Figure 12-6.

FIGURE 12-5: Creating the kite diamond with the Freeform tool

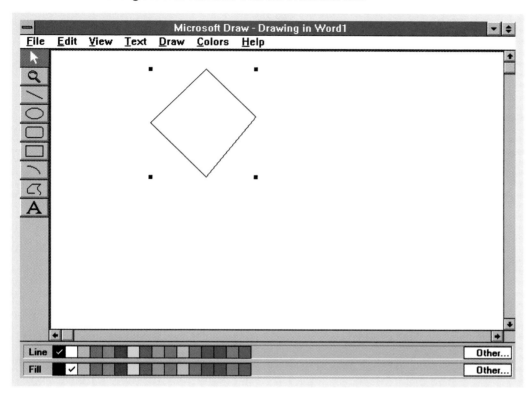

FIGURE 12-6: The kite illustration with color and a tail

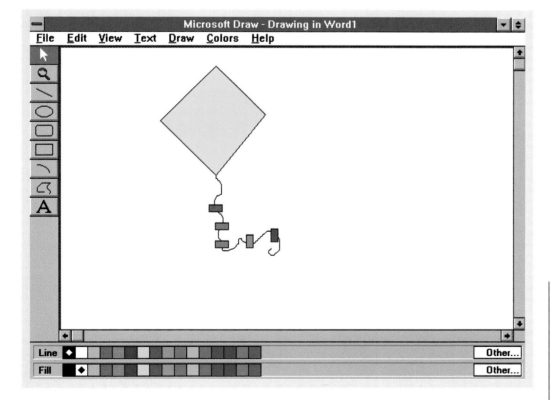

QUICK **TIP**

You can rotate drawn objects, such as the kite bows, with the Rotate/Flip command on the Draw menu.■

Adding text to the illustration

In this lesson you'll add some text to the kite illustration with the Text tool. The Text tool lets you place the cursor anywhere in the illustration and type characters to add information to the drawing. After you enter the text, you can select it and move it with the Arrow tool, and format it with the commands on the Text menu. Try putting the text "Outdoor Designs" in the kite now.

1 Click the **Text tool** 🅰 and click in the kite near the top (see Figure 12-7)
   The Text tool highlights and the mouse pointer changes to a blinking insertion pointer (similar to the insertion pointer in the Word Processor).

2 Type **Outdoor** and press **[Enter]**
   The text Outdoor is added to the illustration and is selected.

3 Click in the kite below the word Outdoor with the Text tool

4 Type **Designs** and press **[Enter]**
   The text Designs is added to the illustration, as shown in Figure 12-7. Now change the font of the two words to Times New Roman, change the style to boldface, and change the size to 14 points.

5 Hold down **[Shift]**, click **Outdoor** in the kite, click the **Text menu**, click the **Font command**, then click **Times New Roman** in the font menu
   The two words in the kite are selected, then changed to Times New Roman.

6 Click **Text**, then click the **Bold command**
   The two words are formatted for boldface style.

7 Click **Text**, click **Size**, then click **14**
   The size of the two words changes to 14 points.

8 Move the words with the **Arrow tool** (if necessary) to arrange them neatly in the center of the kite
   Congratulations! You've finished creating the kite. Yours should look similar to the one shown in Figure 12-8.

FIGURE 12-7: Entering text in the illustration with the Text tool

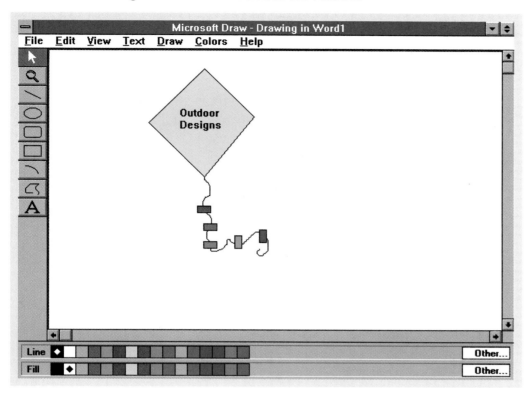

FIGURE 12-8: The final kite illustration after text formatting

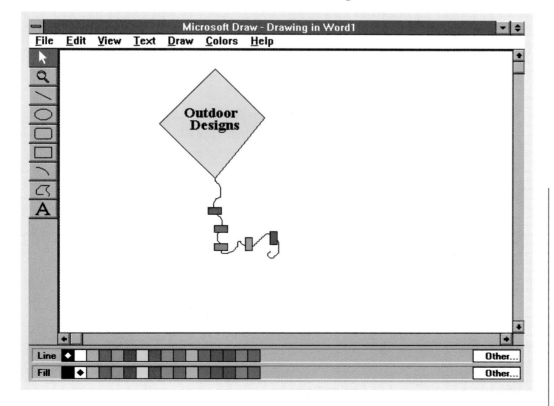

QUICK **TIP**

You can zoom in on your illustration as you work with the Zoom tool and the sizing commands on the View menu. Getting up close can make it easier to work with text elements or other objects.■

Saving and sizing the illustration

To save your Draw illustration you need to return to the Word Processor and save it in a file. A Draw illustration can be stored by itself in a file, or it can be stored along with text and other graphics in a word-processing document. When you have the illustration in the Word Processor you can also change its size and alignment. Return to the Word Processor now and save your illustration, then practice formatting it.

1   Click the **File menu,** then click the **Exit and Return to Word1 command**

Works displays a dialog box asking if you want to update the open document in the Word Processor. This gives you the opportunity to discard your illustration if you want to.

2   Click **Yes** to keep the illustration

The Draw accessory closes and the kite illustration displays in the Word Processor, as shown in Figure 12-9. Notice that a cursor the height of the illustration blinks to the left of the kite. You can use this cursor to select the kite and format it, if you wish. Now save the kite illustration to your Student Disk.

3   Put your Student Disk in drive A, click the **File menu**, then click the **Save As command**

The Save As dialog box appears.

4   Type **kite_art** in the File Name text box, click **a:** in the Drives drop-down list box, double-click **my_files** in the Directories list box, then click **OK**

The kite illustration is saved on your Student Disk under the name KITE_ART.WPS. Now practice selecting and aligning the illustration in the Word Processor.

5   Click the kite illustration to select it

A dotted line and eight selection handles appear around the illustration.

6   Click 🖼 on the toolbar to center-align the illustration in the document

The illustration moves to the center of the document. You can also use the Left- and Right-align buttons to change the alignment of an illustration. Now resize the kite with the selection handles.

7   Click the **lower-right selection handle,** drag it down and to the right, then release the mouse button

The selection box enlarges as you drag the selection handle. When you release the mouse button the kite enlarges, as shown in Figure 12-10. You can use the selection handles to resize an illustration, to make it fit as needed in your document.

8   Click the **Format menu,** click the **Picture/Object command,** then click the **Size tab**

The Size tab of the Picture/Object dialog box displays. This tab gives you precise control over the dimensions of your art, and displays the original width and height so you can restore the illustration to its original size if necessary.

9   Note the original size, then type the original width in the **Width text box,** press **[Tab]**, type the original height in the **Height text box,** then click **OK**

The illustration returns to its original size.

FIGURE 12-9: The kite illustration in the Word Processor

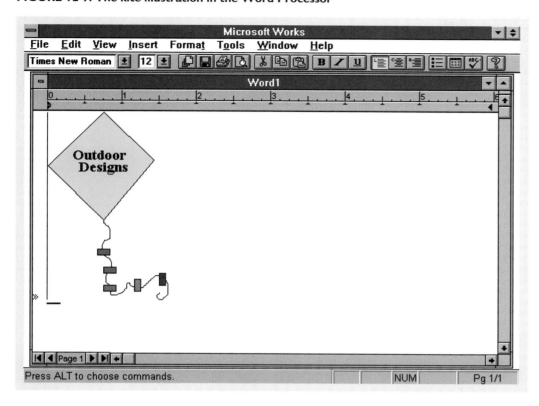

FIGURE 12-10: Sizing the kite illustration

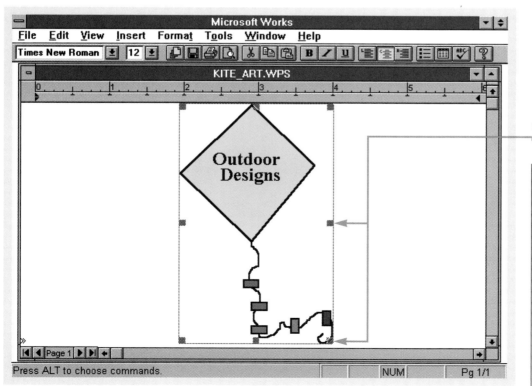

Selection handles

QUICK **TIP**

You can move an illustration from one location to another in a document with the drag-and-drop technique or by cutting and pasting. To delete an unwanted illustration from a document, select the artwork, then press **[Del]**.■

Printing the illustration

When you've finished creating the illustration and have placed it in your document, you can print it with the Print command. As usual, it's a good idea to examine your illustration in Print Preview before you print to identify any sizing or layout problems associated with your artwork. If you don't have a color printer, your printed kite will appear in black and white. Print your kite illustration now.

1   Click 🖻 on the toolbar
    The kite illustration displays in Print Preview as it will be printed.

2   Click the kite twice with the **zoom pointer**
    The kite appears in full size, as shown in Figure 12-11. The kite looks good.

3   Verify that your printer is ready, then click the **Print button** in the
    Print Preview window
    Works sends the document to the printer. After a few moments, the final kite
    illustration emerges.

4   Click 🖫 to save any changes you've made

5   Click the **File menu**, then click **Exit Works**
    The Works program closes.

FIGURE 12-11:
The kite illustration in
Print Preview

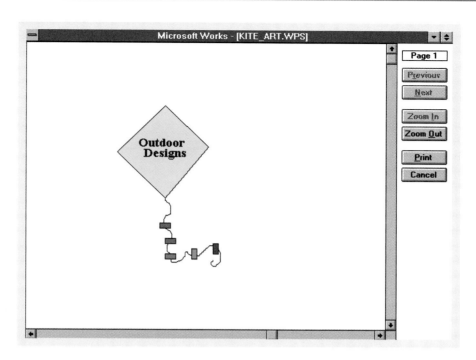

Editing ClipArt in Draw

Have you seen a piece of ClipArt in the ClipArt gallery that would be perfect with a few changes? You can make those changes by editing the ClipArt in Draw, then pasting it into your document. Here's the procedure: Start in the Word Processor. Choose the **ClipArt command** from the Insert menu and double-click the ClipArt you want to modify. Next, click the ClipArt then choose the **Cut command** from the Edit menu, then choose the **Drawing command** from the Insert menu. Maximize the Draw accessory, choose the **Paste command** from the Edit menu to paste in the ClipArt, then edit the artwork as you see fit. See Figure 12-12. When you're finished, exit the Draw program, click **Yes** to update the document, and the revised ClipArt will be pasted into the Word Processor. Nothing to it!

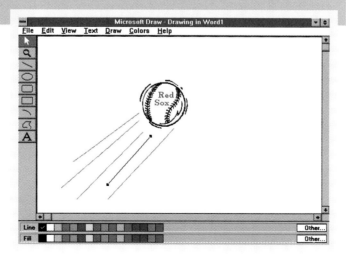

FIGURE 12-12: Editing the baseball ClipArt in the Draw accessory

QUICK TIP

You cannot print from the Draw accessory. You must print your illustration from the application where the artwork is located.■

CONCEPTSREVIEW

Label each of the elements of the Draw accessory, as shown in Figure 12-13.

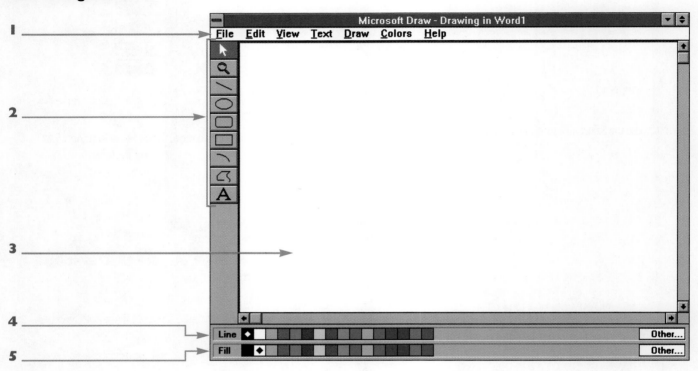

FIGURE 12-13

Match the drawing tools with their functions.

6   a. Creates a rectangle

7   b. Creates polygons and freeform lines

8   c. Creates an ellipse

9   d. Inserts text in an illustration

10   e. Selects and moves objects in an illustration

Select the best answer from the list of choices.

11 The Draw accessory is started from the:

   a. Program Manager

   b. Works Startup dialog box

   c. Word Processor or Database application

   d. ClipArt accessory

12 What is the document window called in the Draw accessory?

   a. The form

   b. The document

   c. The canvas

   d. The easel

13 Which of the following is *not* a drawing tool?

   a. The Ellipse tool

   b. The Rectangle tool

   c. The Arc tool

   d. The Fill palette

14 What is the function of the Arrow tool?

   a. It selects objects in the illustration and can be used to move objects.

   b. It creates a straight line.

   c. It enlarges part of the illustration.

   d. It creates an arrow in the illustration.

15 What does the Rectangle tool do when you hold down [Shift] while drawing?

    a. It creates a rectangle with rounded edges.

    b. It creates a square.

    c. It creates a polygon.

    d. Holding down [Shift] has no effect.

16 How would you move an object from one place to another on the canvas?

    a. Drag the object with the Arrow tool.

    b. Double-click the object with the Freeform tool.

    c. Choose the Select All command from the Edit menu.

    d. Select the object and press [Del].

17 How would you add color to the inside of a rectangle?

    a. Click the Edit Palette command on the Colors menu.

    b. Click the rectangle object, then click the color in the Fill palette.

    c. Click the rectangle object, then click the color in the Line palette.

    d. Double-click inside the object.

18 What shape will you create with the Freeform tool if you hold down the mouse button and move the crosshairs?

    a. A kite

    b. A rectangle

    c. An ellipse

    d. An uneven line

19 What tool would you use to add text to an illustration?

    a. 🔍

    b. ＼

    c. △

    d. A

20 What key would you hold down while clicking to select more than one illustration object at once?

    a. [Ctrl]

    b. [Alt]

    c. [Shift]

    d. [F8]

21 Which of the following procedures has no effect on Draw objects that have been inserted into the Word Processor?

    a. Alignment

    b. Resizing

    c. Deleting

    d. Character formatting

APPLICATIONS REVIEW

1 Open the database file UNIT_9.WDB (the Outdoor Designs customer database) from your Student Disk and save it in the MY_FILES directory as **TRUCK.WDB**.

    a. Put your Student Disk in drive A.

    b. Start Works and click the Open an Existing Document button.

    c. Open the file UNIT_9.WDB from the Student Disk and save it as TRUCK.WDB in the MY_FILES directory.

2 Position the cursor at location X5.42" Y1.25" and start the Draw accessory.

    a. Use the direction keys to move the cursor to location X5.42" Y1.25" (near the upper-right corner of the form).

    b. Click the Insert menu, then click the Drawing command to start the Draw accessory.

    c. Maximize the Draw accessory window.

    d. Identify the elements of the Draw accessory.

3 Draw a simple truck using the Rectangle, Ellipse, and other tools. Keep the drawing small so it will fit on the database form.

    a. Draw the body of the truck with the Rectangle tool.

    b. Draw the wheels of the truck with the Ellipse tool (hold down [Shift] for circles).

    c. Draw additional details—including a driver, mirrors, and antennas—as desired.

    d. Fill the truck body and wheels with color using the Fill palette.

4 Use the Text tool to write the name **Outdoor Designs** on the truck.

    a. Type the name **Outdoor Designs** on the body of the truck.

    b. Change the font of the text to Arial.

    c. Change the text style to italic.

5 Exit the Draw accessory and save the database form with the new illustration, then resize the illustration as necessary.

    a. Click the File menu, then click Exit and Return to TRUCK.WDB.

    b. Click the Save button on the toolbar.

    c. Resize the illustration with the selection handles as necessary to fit the truck on the form.

6 Print the first record in the database.

    a. Verify that your printer is ready to print.

    b. Click the File menu, then click Print.

    c. Click the Current record only option button, then click OK.

INDEPENDENT
CHALLENGES

The Draw accessory contains several commands you didn't use in this unit. The Draw menu includes the Pattern and Line Style commands, which let you vary the fill pattern and line types in the Fill and Line palettes. The Colors menu includes the Show Palette, Edit Palette, Get Palette, and Save Palette commands, which let you change the colors in the File and Line palettes. Practice working with these commands now to create additional shapes, lines, and colors. If you have any questions about the commands, consult the Draw on-line help.

You can use the Draw accessory to create simple shapes and graphics for use in flyers, brochures, and other documents. To gain experience with Draw, try creating the following outdoor designs:

a. A tree on a rocky bluff

b. A sailboat on a pond

c. Sun setting behind some clouds

d. A globe showing the outline of North and South America

e. An array of gaily colored flags

You may be surprised at how effective your simple designs can be. As you experiment, try using some of the options in the Draw menus. For example:

1 Select one of the rocks in the rocky bluff, enlarge the view to 200% or more, choose Edit Freeform, and see how you can adjust the details of a drawing.

2 In the Draw menu, practice using the Pattern and Line Style commands to fill areas or change the weight of the outline. Select a shape and use the Rotate/Flip option to change its orientation.

3 Explore the options on the Colors menu. Look at the various palettes available with the Get Palette option. Click Show Palette to display the available colors at the bottom of your screen. And explore the color mixtures available when you choose Other (to the right of the Line or Fill color display).

The Draw tools may seem a bit awkward to you at first. However, if you continue to practice, you'll find the work becomes much more satisfying. If you have questions about any of the Draw commands, consult the on-line help.

UNIT 13

OBJECTIVES

▶ Create the cover letter

▶ Insert an illustration

▶ Insert spreadsheet data

▶ Insert database fields

▶ Add a footer and print

Combining
WORKS APPLICATIONS

Throughout this book you have used the Works applications and accessories to create useful business documents for the Outdoor Designs company. In this unit you'll combine several of the documents into a six-month sales summary that the Outdoor Designs president will send to the customers and investors in the company database. ▶ First you'll create the cover letter in the Word Processor using the Outdoor Designs letterhead as a template. Next you'll insert the kite illustration you created in Unit 12, and the spreadsheet table and chart you created in Unit 8. Finally you'll insert fields from the customer database you created in Unit 9, and print a customized copy of the summary for each business on the mailing list. ▶

Creating the cover letter

In this lesson you'll open the letterhead file you created in Unit 1, save it to your Student Disk under the name JULYREP.WPS, and type the cover letter for the six-month sales summary. Create the cover letter now.

1   Start Works from the Program Manager. Open the file **UNIT_13A.WPS** on the Student Disk, and save it as **JULYREP.WPS** in the MY_FILES directory on the Student Disk
    Works starts and the Open dialog box displays. The letterhead template displays in the Word Processor, as shown in Figure 13-1. Now you'll type the cover letter below the letterhead.

2   Press **[Ctrl][End]** to move the cursor to the bottom of the document, press **[Enter]** to add a blank line, then type the following text, pressing **[Enter]** as indicated. (See Figure 13-2.)
    July 29, 1994 [Enter]
    [Enter][Enter]
    Dear valued customer, [Enter]
    [Enter]
    I am pleased to send you Outdoor Designs' financial summary for the first six months of calendar year 1994. The past two quarters have been an exciting time for our business. We have added several new products to our growing outdoor equipment line, including a high-country backpacking tent kit and several new kite kits. Our sales representatives have established new accounts in several important areas in the United States and our total sales volume rose 4% between the first and second quarters. We also experienced strong growth in every region except the Midwest, where we are currently restructuring our operations. Our combined sales figures for the first two quarters of 1994 are shown in Figures 1 and 2 on the next page. [Enter]
    [Enter]
    I'd like to thank everyone who has helped make the first half of 1994 such a success, including the dedicated employees at Outdoor Designs, our valued suppliers, our retail partners, and especially our investors, who have supported us since the beginning. We look forward to a strong summer and another record-breaking six months this year. [Enter]
    [Enter]
    Sincerely, [Enter]
    [Enter][Enter][Enter]
    Rebecca Singer [Enter]
    President [Enter]
    Outdoor Designs [Enter]

3   Click ![ABC] and check the spelling in the document

4   Click ![disk] to save your changes

FIGURE 13-1:
The Outdoor Designs letterhead template

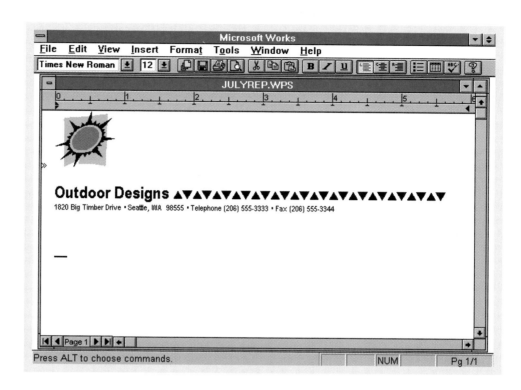

FIGURE 13-2: The six-month summary cover letter

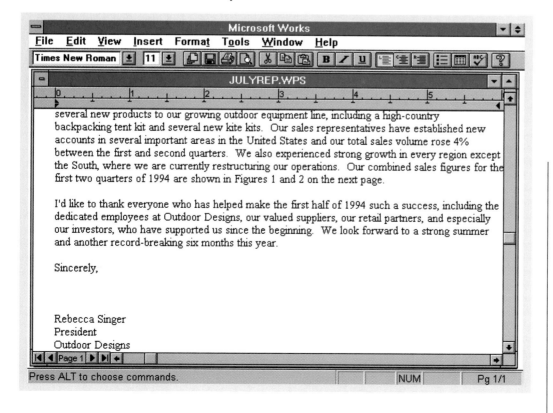

QUICK **TIP**

A typical business cover letter includes the name and the address of the recipient at the top. You'll add these later with database fields, so the same form letter can be sent to anyone in the Outdoor Designs database.■

Inserting an illustration

In this lesson you'll insert a kite illustration into the cover letter, then you'll use the Picture/Object command to position the art in the center of the page and wrap text around it. The kite illustration is the same drawing you created in Unit 12 with the Draw accessory (the file has been renamed UNIT_13B.WPS). Insert the illustration into the cover letter now.

1　Click 🖻, then open the illustration UNIT_13B.WPS on the Student Disk
The UNIT_13B.WPS document opens and the kite illustration displays.

2　Click the illustration, then click 🖺 on the toolbar
The illustration is copied to the clipboard.

3　Click the **File menu**, then click the **Close command**
The kite illustration document closes.

4　Press **[Ctrl][End]** to move the cursor to the bottom of the cover letter, then click 🖺
The kite illustration is pasted into the cover letter. Now you'll select the illustration and position it in the center of the page along the right margin.

5　Click the kite, click the **Format menu**, click the **Picture/Object command**, then click the **Text Wrap tab**
The Text Wrap tab of the Picture/Object dialog box displays, as shown in Figure 13-3. It lets you specify how text wraps around your illustration and where your illustration is positioned on the page.

6　Click the **Absolute button**
Absolute positioning is selected, meaning that your kite will be placed in a specified location on the page, and everything else will wrap around it.

7　Click the **Horizontal drop-down list box** and click **Right**, then click the **Vertical drop-down list box** and click **Center**, then click **OK**
The dialog box closes and Works displays a message recommending you view the document in page layout view.

8　Click **Yes**
The document displays in page layout view and the illustration aligns to the center of the right margin. (See Figure 13-4.) The text of the cover letter wraps around the illustration automatically. The kite illustration has been **positioned**, and will remain in the same place until you position it again or delete it.

9　Click 🖫 to save the artwork in the cover letter

FIGURE 13-3: The Text Wrap tab in the Picture/Object dialog box

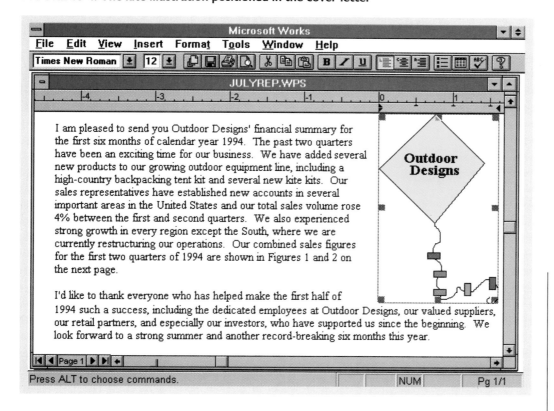

Absolute button

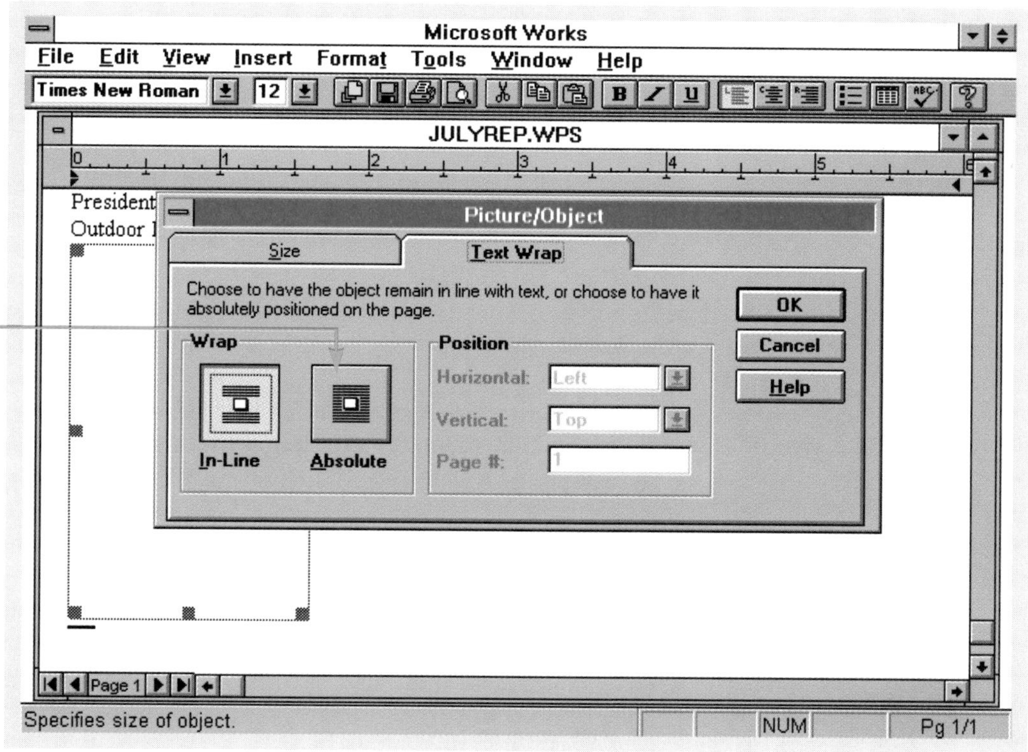

FIGURE 13-4: The kite illustration positioned in the cover letter

QUICK TIP

To edit the kite illustration, double-click it. This returns you to the Draw accessory, where the drawing tools are available. ■

Inserting spreadsheet data

In this lesson you'll insert the heart of the summary, the two figures showing the regional sales data for the first six months of 1994. This is the information you created with the Spreadsheet application and Chart accessory in Unit 7. You'll use the same copy-and-paste technique you used in the last lesson. Insert the spreadsheet data now.

1 Click ⬚, then open the spreadsheet UNIT_13C.WKS on the Student Disk
The file opens and the sales spreadsheet displays.

2 Select the cell range **A5 through C10**, then click 🗐
The sales spreadsheet is copied to the clipboard.

3 Click the **Window menu**, then click **JULYREP.WPS** (the first filename in the list at the bottom of the window)
The cover letter document window moves in front of the sales spreadsheet window. As you learned earlier in the book, Works can have several files open at once. You use the Window menu to switch from file to file.

4 Press **[Ctrl][End]**, press **[Ctrl][Enter]** to insert a page break, type **Figure 1: Outdoor Designs sales totals**, then press **[Enter]** twice
A page break is inserted at the bottom of the cover letter and a figure caption displays at the top of the new page.

5 Click 🗐 to paste in the spreadsheet table
The sales spreadsheet displays in the sales summary, as shown in Figure 13-5. Now add a chart to the report.

6 Press **[→]**, press **[Enter]** four times, type **Figure 2: Outdoor Designs sales by region**, then press **[Enter]** twice
The caption for the chart displays in the document. Now copy and paste the chart.

7 Click **Window** and click **UNIT_13C.WKS**, click **View** and click **Chart**, then double-click **Chart1**
The sales chart you created in Unit 7 displays in the Chart accessory window.

8 Click **Edit** and click **Copy**, click **File** and click **Close** twice (to close the chart window and the spreadsheet window), then click 🗐
The sales chart is pasted into the six-month summary, as shown in Figure 13-6.

9 Click 🖫 to save the spreadsheet data

FIGURE 13-5: The sales spreadsheet in the six-month summary

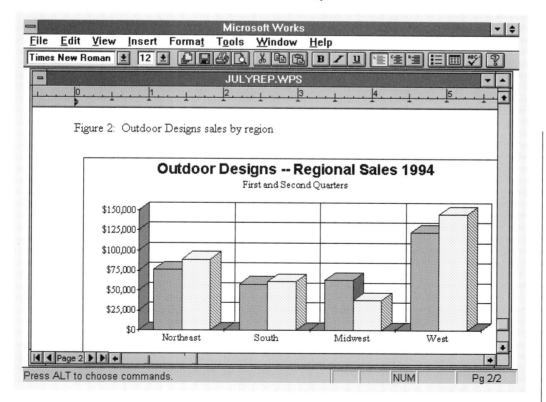

Microsoft Works

File Edit View Insert Format Tools Window Help

Times New Roman | 12 | B / U

JULYREP.WPS

Figure 1: Outdoor Designs sales totals

	1st Quarter	2nd Quarter
Northeast	$76,500	$89,000
South	$58,000	$61,300
Midwest	$62,800	$37,600
West	$122,400	$145,200
Totals	$319,700	$333,100

Page 2

Press ALT to choose commands.   NUM   Pg 2/2

FIGURE 13-6: The sales chart in the six-month summary

Microsoft Works

File Edit View Insert Format Tools Window Help

Times New Roman | 12 | B / U

JULYREP.WPS

Figure 2: Outdoor Designs sales by region

Outdoor Designs -- Regional Sales 1994

First and Second Quarters

$150,000
$125,000
$100,000
$75,000
$50,000
$25,000
$0

Northeast   South   Midwest   West

Page 2

Press ALT to choose commands.   NUM   Pg 2/2

TROUBLE?

Saving your sales summary to a floppy disk will take some time because the file contains artwork and application objects that are quite large. Saving to your hard disk would be much faster, but it might not be practical in your lab setting.■

Inserting database fields

The basic structure of the sales summary is complete. Now you need to insert database fields to make your document into a form letter. A **form letter** is a document that contains a standardized text body and a customized header for each recipient. The Works Word Processor lets you create form letters in which you insert fields from the database. This process is known as **mail merge**. You'll insert fields from the Outdoor Designs customer database now.

1 Press **[Ctrl][Home]**, then press **[↓]** nine times to move the cursor to the line above the greeting Dear valued customer

2 Press **[Enter]**, then click the **Insert menu** and click the **Database Field command**
   The Insert Field dialog box displays.

3 Click the **Database button**, then double-click **UNIT_13D.WDB** in the list box
   UNIT_13D.WDB is the Outdoor Designs customer database you created in Unit 10. If this file does not appear in the list box, click the **Use another file button** and locate it on your Student Disk. When you double-click the file, the database opens and its fields display in a list box.

4 Click the **Business field** in the database list box, then click the **Insert button**
   The Business field is inserted into the form letter and surrounded by chevrons (« »), as shown in Figure 13-7. The chevrons tell Works to insert field values from the database into the Word Processor when you print the form letter.

5 Click **Address** and click **Insert**, click **City** and click **Insert**, click **State** and click **Insert**, click **Zip** and click **Insert**, then click the **Close button**
   The Address, City, State, and Zip fields are entered into the letter and the dialog box closes. Now you'll arrange the fields so they look like a mailing address.

6 Edit the fields so the Business and Address fields are on their own lines, and the City, State, and Zip fields are together on one line

7 Type a comma **(,)** after the City field and add another space between the State and Zip fields, then edit the letter so there are two blank lines above the mailing address and two blank lines below it
   When you're finished, the fields should look like those in Figure 13-8. Congratulations! Your form letter is finished. In the next lesson you'll add a footer and print it.

8 Click 🖫 to save the database fields

FIGURE 13-7: The Insert Field dialog box

Insert button

Database fields

Database button

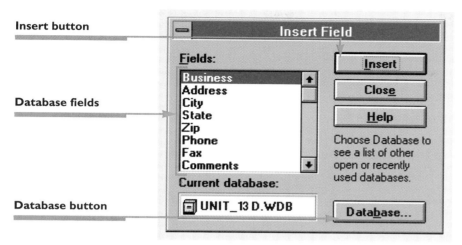

FIGURE 13-8: Database fields in the form letter

Database fields

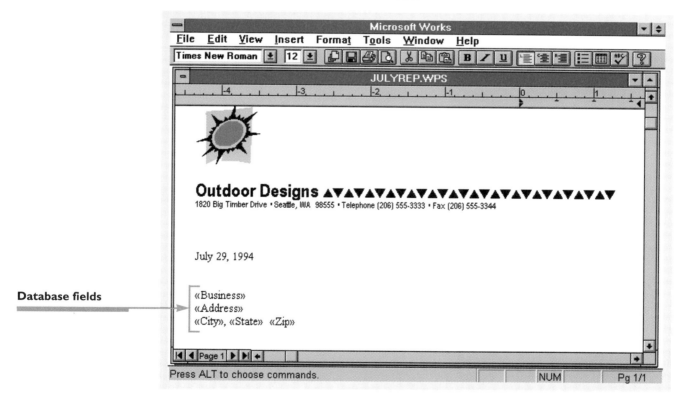

QUICK TIP

You can also use the Form Letter WorksWizard to create form letters.

Adding a footer and printing

In this lesson you will add a footer to the six-month sales summary, examine the document in Print Preview, and print copies for the customers in the database. The completed report demonstrates the integration strength of the Works software. With Works you are able to combine documents from several different sources and organize them to create a compelling report. Complete the project now.

1   Click the **View menu,** then click the **Headers and Footers command**
The Headers and Footers dialog box displays.

2   Press **[Tab]**, then type **&lSix-month Summary &cJuly 1994 &rPage &p** and click **OK**
A footer including the report title, date, and page number displays at the bottom of each page in the document. (See Table 3-3 for a description of the footer codes.) Now examine the report in Print Preview.

3   Click ▣ on the toolbar
A Choose Database dialog box displays, as shown in Figure 13-9. It lets you select the database you want to use for the mailing address fields in the document. Because you've already selected UNIT_13D.WDB, that database is highlighted. (Your list of databases may be different.)

4   Double-click **UNIT_13D.WDB** in the list box
A dialog box displays asking if you want to merge (include) all the records in the database. Because you're sending a six-month summary to every business in the database, you'll click OK. If you wanted to send the letter to only a few customers, you would click Cancel, then open the database and use the Create New Query command to select the specific records you wanted. (See Unit 9 for information about running a query.)

5   Click **OK** to merge all records
The dialog box closes and the first page of the document displays in Print Preview.

6   Click the **Zoom In button** twice
Notice that the database fields in the document have been replaced with the mailing information from the first record in the UNIT_13D.WDB database.

7   Click the **Next button** to review each address in the mailing list (there are four businesses)
Because each summary is two pages long, you'll find a total of eight pages. Use the scroll bars to view the rest of the document and verify that the text, artwork, figures, and footers are in the right places.

8   Verify that your printer is ready, then click the **Print button** to print the documents
Click **OK** in the Choose Database and Merge dialog boxes. After a few minutes, the completed six-month summary reports emerge from the printer. Congratulations! You've finished your final project and are ready to take the documents to the company president for her signature. She'll be impressed with all that you have learned in such a short time.

9   Click ▣ to save your changes, then exit Works

FIGURE 13-9: The Choose Database dialog box

Database containing
mailing addresses

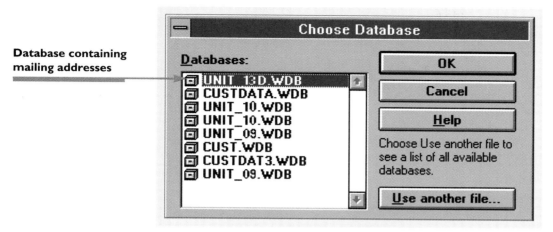

FIGURE 13-10: The six-month summary in Print Preview

Addresses from
database

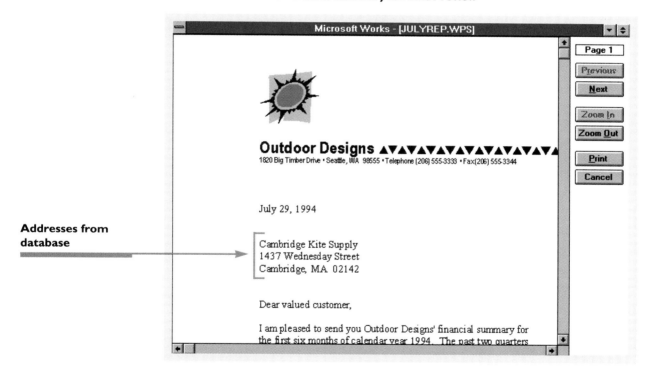

QUICK **TIP**

You can print matching envelopes for the form letters with the Envelopes and Labels command on the Tools menu. See Unit 9 for more information.■

CONCEPTSREVIEW

Select the best answer from the list of choices.

1 What keys do you press to move to the bottom of a Word Processor document?

a. [Ctrl][Home]

b. [Ctrl][End]

c. [Ctrl][PgDn]

d. [Shift][Enter]

2 What is the name of the container Works uses to temporarily store information that is copied from one document and pasted into another?

a. Windows clipboard

b. ClipArt gallery

c. File Manager

d. Floppy disk

3 Which toolbar button would you use to paste information into a document?

a.

b.

c.

d.

4 What element in the Picture/Object dialog box would you use to position an art object so that text can wrap around it?

a. Horizontal drop-down list box

b. Vertical drop-down list box

c. In-Line button

d. Absolute button

5 How would you edit an illustration that has been pasted into the Word Processor?

a. Choose the Drawing command from the Insert menu.

b. Double-click the illustration.

c. Change to Print Preview, then click the illustration with the zoom pointer.

d. Select the illustration, then press [F1].

6 What toolbar button would you click to open a Works application?

a.

b.

c.

d.

7 Which menu would you use to switch between active Works documents?

a. File

b. View

c. Tools

d. Window

8 What keys would you press to enter a page break in your document?

a. [Ctrl][Home]

b. [Ctrl][End]

c. [Ctrl][PgDn]

d. [Shift][Enter]

9 A document that contains a standardized text body and a customized header is called a:

a. Six-month summary

b. Form letter

c. Spreadsheet

d. Footer

10 Which command in the Word Processor would you use to add database fields to a document?

a. Database Field

b. Footer

c. Form letter

d. Spreadsheet / Table

11 A database field in a document is identified by:

a. Parentheses

b. Chevrons

c. Square brackets

d. Selection rectangles

12 What does the &p code do in a footer?

a. Print the filename

b. Print the page number

c. Center the text

d. Right-align the text

13 How would you verify the database addresses inserted into the documents you are printing?

a. Examine the database fields in Print Preview.

b. Double-click the addresses in the document.

c. Click the Print button on the toolbar.

d. Examine the records in the database.

14 What command on the File menu would you use to close a document window?

a. Create New File

b. Close

c. Save As

d. Exit Works

15 What command would you use to print matching envelopes for form letters?

a. Headers and Footers

b. Database Field

c. Envelopes and Labels

d. Page Setup

APPLICATIONSREVIEW

1 Open the six-month sales summary JULYREP.WPS you created in this unit.

a. Start Works, then put your Student Disk in drive A.

b. Open the file JULYREP.WPS in the MY_FILES directory on your Student Disk and save it as **JULYREP2.WPS** in the MY_FILES directory.

2 Position the kite illustration in the bottom center of the first page.

a. Click the kite art object in the document, then choose the Picture/Object command from the Format menu.

b. Click Center in the Horizontal drop-down list box, click Bottom in the Vertical drop-down list box, then click OK.

c. Use the scroll bars to verify that the illustration has been moved.

3 Change the text in the kite illustration to July 1994 (it currently reads Outdoor Designs).

a. Double-click the kite illustration to start the Draw accessory.

b. Click once to remove the selection handles, hold down [Shift] and click the words Outdoor and Designs, then press [Del] to delete them.

c. Click the Text tool, click in the center of the kite, type **July 1994**, then press [Enter].

d. Format the text as boldface 14-point Times New Roman.

e. Click the File menu, click Exit and Return to JULYREP2.WPS, then click Yes to return to the document.

4 Format the column totals in the sales spreadsheet (Figure 1 in your document) with boldface.

a. Double-click the sales spreadsheet on page 2 of the report.

b. Select the two column totals (cells B10 and C10), then click the Bold button on the toolbar.

c. Click to the right of the spreadsheet to return to the report.

5 Add the words **such as** and the Business field from the database after the words *retail partners* in the last paragraph of the cover letter.

a. Click after the words *retail partners* in the first sentence of the last paragraph, then type a space, the words **such as**, and another space.

b. Click the Insert menu, then click the Database Field command.

c. Click the Business field in the Insert Field dialog box, click the Insert button, then click the Close button.

6 Examine the mailing addresses in Print Preview and print the documents.

a. Click the Print Preview button on the toolbar.

b. Click the Zoom In button twice and verify the mailing address and Business field in the first summary report, then click the Next button to examine the remaining reports.

c. Click the Print button, then click OK twice to print the reports.

d. Save your changes, then exit Works.

INDEPENDENT
CHALLENGES

Selling the Great Outdoors! is the title of this year's sales training course at Outdoor Designs. All of the company's sales representatives will attend this week-long sales seminar in the fall. You are currently preparing a brochure to promote this course and explain the main points to be covered.

To complete this Independent Challenge:

1 Plan the brochure. You'll want to include tips on how to make your products more marketable, including advice about knowing the customer. For example, the sales reps will gain self-confidence by knowing the product, understanding the competition, and being aware of customer needs.

2 Open a new document in the Word Processor and save it as SELLING. Begin by creating a graphic for use on the front of the brochure. For example, you might want to open the Draw accessory, import the camping scene available in the ClipArt Gallery, then add a couple of trees by copying and pasting. Add the title Selling the Great Outdoors in the sky above the trees.

3 Bring the drawing into your document and write the text of the brochure.

4 Insert the following quote at some appropriate spot in the brochure: "Knowing something about your customer is just as important as knowing everything about your product."

5 Use the footnote WorksWizard to create a footnote for the quote: it is from Harvey Mackay, *Swim with the Sharks Without Being Eaten Alive*, Ivy Books: New York, 1988, p. 21. Choose Chicago Manual of Style.

6 To illustrate the popularity of outdoor activities, use the UNIT_06C file showing the total number of Amazing Adventure trips sold by Outdoor Designs in 1993. (Cut and paste headings and totals to create a new chart beneath the main data range). Add a column called Projected '94, and enter data showing an increase in all categories except Hang Gliding. Copy the data and paste it into the brochure.

7 Create a Combination chart showing the '93 totals in bar format, with the '94 projections as a line graph above them. Paste the chart into the brochure.

8 Use Print Preview to examine the layout and check the accuracy of your brochure. When you are satisfied with the results, print a copy of it.

In this unit you combined information from several different Works applications and accessories into a single report. You can also insert information from other Windows applications into your Works documents. For example, you can copy data from a Microsoft Excel spreadsheet and paste it into a Works spreadsheet, or you can copy text from a Microsoft Word document and paste it into the Works word-processing document. Because Works is a Windows application, it can exchange information with other Windows applications through the Windows clipboard and through a cut-and-paste technology known as Object Linking and Embedding (OLE). Ask your instructor about the Windows applications on your computer, and try copying information from one of them into a Works document. As you work with Windows applications in the future, you'll find you exchange information between them often.

Glossary

Absolute positioning   Placing an object in a specified location in a Works document. Used when you want to wrap text around an object.

Accessory   A software tool in Microsoft Works, such as the Draw accessory.

Active window   The window on the desktop you are currently working with. Other windows are considered background windows.

Alignment   The horizontal placement of numbers or text, relative to the page margins. For example, right, center, and left alignment.

Application   A software program, such as Microsoft Excel, or a module in a software program, such as the Works Database.

Area chart   A line chart in which each area is given a solid color or pattern to emphasize the relationships between the pieces of charted information.

Argument   A value, cell reference, or text used in a function. Arguments are separated by commas and enclosed in parentheses; for example, AVE(A1,10,5).

Arial   A TrueType font supplied with Microsoft Windows that can be used in Works documents.

Baud rate   The rate at which data is transferred over the phone lines by your modem.

Bold   A font style used to emphasize text in Works documents.

Cancel   A command button that discards the selections in a dialog box.

Canvas   The document window in the Draw accessory.

Cell   The intersection of a row and a column in a spreadsheet.

Cell range   A collection of adjacent cells.

Cell reference   The name of a cell in a spreadsheet; for example, A1.

Cell reference box   A box in the Works Spreadsheet that shows the currently highlighted cell.

Chart   A graphic representation of selected spreadsheet information. Types include bar, pie, area, and line charts.

Chart title   The name assigned to a chart.

Clicking   Pressing and releasing the mouse button.

ClipArt   Ready-to-use artwork accessed through the ClipArt accessory.

Clipboard   A temporary storage area in Windows for items that have been cut or copied and may be pasted.

Control menu box   A box in the upper-left corner of a window used to resize or close a window.

Copy   A command that copies the selected information from the document to the clipboard.

Cue Cards   An on-screen adviser in Works applications.

Currency format   A type of formatting that adds a dollar sign ($) and two decimal places to a number.

Cursor   A blinking vertical bar indicating the insertion point in an application.

Cut   A command that removes a selected object from a Works application and places it in the clipboard.

Database   An organized collection of information stored electronically in a file.

Default   A value or setting that is assumed by Works in an application. For example, the default extension for a spreadsheet file in Works is WKS.

Desktop publishing   A type of word processing that combines text, artwork, and other elements to create professional-looking documents.

Dialog box   A window that displays when more information is needed to execute a command.

Directory   A section of a disk used to store specific information, much like a folder in a file cabinet.

Document window   A window in the Word Processor containing the document's workspace.

Double-clicking   Pressing and releasing the left mouse button twice, quickly.

Dragging   Holding down the left mouse button and moving the mouse to a new location.

Draw accessory   A Works tool used to create original illustrations and artwork.

Drawing tools   The electronic tools used to create and edit an illustration in the Draw accessory.

Drives   A disk or area of a network used for storing files. Drives are organized by directories.

Electronic mail (e-mail) A computer-to-computer version of interoffice mail or the postal service.

Embedding an object Pasting an object from another application into a Works document. To edit an embedded object you would double-click it.

End-of-file-mark A horizontal bar indicating the end of a Word Processor document.

Field A category of information in a database. Each field in a Works database has a unique name.

File name A unique name assigned to a Works document on disk.

Fill palette A palette in the Draw accessory used to change the colors of the shapes in your illustration.

Find A command that searches for a word or phrase in a Works document.

Font A typeface used to display text in a Works application.

Footer codes Special codes in a footer (prefaced by an ampersand symbol) that format the text in a header or footer.

Footnote A marginal note or citation placed at the bottom of a page in a Works document.

Form The window in the Database application where information is entered and displayed.

Form letter A document that contains a standardized text body and a customized header for each recipient.

Formula An equation that calculates a new value from existing values. Works formulas can contain numbers, mathematical operators, cell references, field names, and functions.

Formula bar A bar in the Spreadsheet and Database applications where you enter or edit formulas.

Function A calculation used in a formula. Works includes 76 built-in functions.

Graphical user interface (GUI) An operating environment, such as Microsoft Windows, that uses meaningful pictures and symbols to replace hard-to-remember commands.

Gridlines Horizontal and vertical lines connecting to the x-axis and y-axis in a chart.

Help A command button that displays on-line help for the options in a dialog box.

Icon A picture or symbol that represents a command or identifies an object on the Windows desktop.

Insertion point The blinking cursor in a Works application or accessory; indicates where in a document text will be inserted.

Internet A global network of computers and telecommunication services.

Internet address A unique name used to identify a user on the Internet network; for example, mikehal@carson.u.washington.edu.

Italic A font style used to emphasize text in Works documents.

Justified text Text that is aligned to both the right and left margins.

Label Descriptive text used to identify data in a spreadsheet.

Launch Start a software program so you can use it.

Legend A key explaining the information represented by colors or patterns in a chart.

Line chart A graph of data that is mapped by a series of lines. Line charts show changes in data or categories of data over time and can be used to document trends.

Line palette A palette in the Draw accessory used to change the colors of the lines in your illustration.

Line pointer The shape of the mouse pointer when it is in the left margin in the Word Processor; used to select more than one line at a time.

Linking documents Connecting documents so that information can be passed between them automatically. The Paste Special command is used to link documents in Works.

List view A way of examining the records in a database. A database is formatting in rows (fields) and columns (records) when in list view.

Log out The process of disconnecting from a remote computer.

Mail merge A process in which mailing addresses are automatically inserted into form letters from a Works database.

Menu bar The area under the title bar on a window. The menu bar provides access to most of an application's commands.

Modem A communications device that enables a computer to transmit information over a standard telephone line.

Mouse The hand-held input device that you roll on your desk to position the mouse pointer on the Windows desktop.

Note-It accessory   A Works accessory that adds notes to your documents.

Numeric value   A number in a spreadsheet cell.

Object   An item in a Works document that was created by an application other than the current application; for example, a spreadsheet table, ClipArt image, or Draw illustration.

OK   A command button that confirms the selections in a dialog box.

On-line services   Telecommunication services such as CompuServe or GEnie.

Opening a file   Loading an existing application file with Works.

Operating system   A comprehensive control program such as MS-DOS that helps you run application programs and manage your computer.

Operator   A symbol used in formulas, such as + or -.

Page break   The point at which the flow of text in a document moves to the top of a new page.

Page layout   A document view in the Word Processor that displays artwork, columns, and footnotes as they will be printed.

Parameters   Settings required in a telecommunication session; for example, baud rate, data bits, and parity.

Password   A secret combination of letters and numbers used to gain admittance to an on-line service or remote computer.

Paste   A command that moves information from the clipboard to a Works application.

Pie chart   A circular chart that displays data as slices of a pie. A pie chart is useful for showing the relationship of parts to a whole.

Point   A unit of measure used for fonts and row height. One inch equals 72 points.

Pointing   Positioning the mouse pointer over an icon or object on the Windows desktop.

Print Preview   The command in a Works application that displays a document as it will be printed.

Printer port   A special connector on the back of a computer used for printing.

Program Manager   The main control program of Windows. All Windows applications are started from the Program Manager.

Query   A question that compares one or more fields in the database with one or more values.

Random Access Memory (RAM)   A temporary storage area in a computer that is erased each time the computer is turned off or whenever there is a fluctuation in power. When a program is launched, it is loaded into RAM so you can work with that program.

Range   A selected area of adjacent cells.

Record   All the information in a database pertaining to a business or other entity.

Replace   A command that searches for a word in a Works document and replaces it with another word.

Replicate   To copy a cell into one or more adjacent cells with the Fill Down or Fill Right command in the Spreadsheet application.

Report   A summary of database information specifically designed for printing.

Report definitions   The instructions that create a database report.

Row height   The vertical dimension of a cell.

Ruler   A measuring tool in a Works application below the title bar.

Run   To start or operate a program.

Scroll bars   Bars that appear on the right and bottom of a window on the desktop that give you access to information not currently in the window.

Selected   The state of an object in a Works application or accessory when it is highlighted.

Selection handles   The boxes that surround an object when it is selected in a Works application. You can use the selection handles to enlarge or shrink the size of an object by dragging them.

Serial number   A special number Works uses to store dates and times internally.

Serial port   A communications port on the back of a computer. Suitable for connecting a modem, mouse, or printer.

Shading   A pattern of dots or lines placed in a spreadsheet cell or database field to emphasize it.

Sizing buttons   Buttons in the upper right corner of a window that can be used to minimize or maximize a window.

Sort　To arrange contents of a database or selected range in a particular sequence.

Sorting　Ordering the information in a Works application alphabetically or numerically.

Spell Checker　A tool in a Works application that checks the spelling of a document.

Spreadsheet　An electronic ledger you use to organize rows and columns of information and create charts.

Startup dialog box　The dialog box in Works where you can open Works applications, templates, and WorksWizards.

Statistics　Descriptive calculations used in database reports, such as sum, average, or count.

Superscript　A font style that places text above the line in Works documents.

Synonym　A word that has a similar meaning to another. The Works Thesaurus lists synonyms.

System administrator　The person in charge of a network, remote computer, or on-line service.

Tabs　The name of the windows in a dialog box if it contains multiple-screens of options.

Task List　A dialog box that lets you switch between applications running on the Windows desktop. To display the Task List, hold down [Ctrl] and press [Esc].

Telecommunicating　Communicating with another computer over phone lines.

Template　A standard document that can be used for many tasks.

Thesaurus　A tool in the Word Processor that lists one or more synonyms for a word.

Times New Roman　A TrueType font supplied with Windows and available in Works applications.

Toggle indicators　Indicators near the lower-right corner of the screen for the Num-lock, Caps-lock, and Insert toggle keys.

Toolbar　The row of drop-down list boxes and command buttons beneath the menu bar in a Works application or accessory.

User name　A unique name used to identify the user of an on-line service while telecommunicating.

WCM　The default extension for a Works Communications file.

WDB　The default extension for a Works Database file.

Window　A framed area on the screen in a graphical user interface. Each Works application runs in a window.

Windows desktop　The entire screen area in Windows; an electronic version of a desk with workspace for different computing tasks.

WKS　The default extension for a Works Spreadsheet file.

Word Processor　A Works application that creates and manipulates text-based documents, such as a memo, newsletter, or term paper.

WordArt　A type of stylized text created by the Works WordArt accessory.

WorksWizard　A tool that creates the structure and formatting of a Works document automatically.

WPS　The default extension for a Works Word Processor file.

X-axis　The horizontal line in a chart.

X-axis label　A label describing the x-axis of a chart.

Y-axis　The vertical line in a chart.

Y-axis label　A label describing the y-axis of a chart.

Zoom pointer　The mouse pointer in Print Preview; used to magnify a document in Print Preview.

Index

SPECIAL CHARACTERS

: (colon), 138
... (ellipsis), W 13
& (ampersand), 52, 53
* (asterisk), 68, 69, 86, 87
^ (caret), 87, 161
« » (chevrons), 230-231
" (double quotation mark), 80
= (equals sign), 86, 102
- (minus sign), 87, 161
( ) (parentheses), 87, 161
+ (plus sign), 87, 161
/ (slash), 87, 161
\ (backslash), W 16

A

ABS function, 107
Absolute button, 226, 227
accessories, 3. *See also* applications; combining applications; *specific applications*
Accessories group, W 6
Accessories group icon, W 6
Accessories group window, W 6, W 7
Accessories group window title bar, W 6
active window, W 6
Add button, 176, 177
alignment
    fields, 147
    illustrations, 216
    spreadsheet cells, 90-91
    text, 10, 11, 44-45
Alignment command, 147
Alignment dialog box, 90
America On Line, 190, 191
ampersand (&), headers and footers, 52, 53
And conjunction, 166, 167
And option button, 166
applications, W 1. *See also specific applications*
    closing, W 8, W 21

combining. *See* combining applications
    running, W 8-9
    starting, 6-7
Applications group, W 6
Apply Query command, 165
area charts, 119
arguments
    in functions, 100, 101, 107
    functions as, 107
arrow keys, scrolling, W 7
Arrow tool, 210
arrows, scroll, W 7, 8
art. *See also* ClipArt; Draw accessory; WordArt
    inserting into documents, 226-227
    sizing, 73
asterisk (*)
    footnote reference mark, 68, 69
    mathematical operator, 86, 87, 161
AutoFormat command, 93
Autosum button, 102, 103
average statistic, database reports, 179
AVG function, 100, 101, 106-107

B

backslash (\), directory names, W 16
backup copy, databases, 141
bar charts, 119, 121
baud rate, 194, 195
Baud rate drop-down list box, 194
blink rate, cursor, W 12, W 13
Bold button, 10, 11
boldface style, 8, 10, 11, 42, 43, 64, 65
Border command, 148, 149
borders
    fields, 148, 149
    text, 62-63
Breaks and Spacing tab, 45
bulleted lists, 48
business cover letters, 224-225

C

calculations. *See also* formulas; functions
    statistical, database reports, 179
Calendar application, W 8
Call Waiting, telecommunication, 191
Cancel button, W 12, 50
canceling
    editing changes, 29, 50, 85, 245
    WorksWizards, 15
canvas, 208, 209
Cardfile application, W 8
caret (^), mathematical operator, 87, 161
Cascade command, W 18
Category list box, 66, 67
Category option buttons, 102, 103
cell ranges, 86
cell reference box, 78, 79
cell references, 87
cells, 78, 79
    alignment, 90-91
    dragging borders, 84, 85
    selecting, 84
    too narrow to display information, 91
Center-align button, 10, 11, 44, 216
Chart command, 131
Chart window, 121
Charting buttons, 121, 122, 123
charts, 117-131
    creating, 120-121
    error correction, 125
    fonts and colors, 126-127
    legends, 121, 125
    pasting into Word Processor, 130-131
    planning, 118-119
    subtitles and gridlines, 124-125
    3-D, 119, 122, 123
    types, 119, 122-123
check boxes, W 13, 9
chevrons (« »), inserting database fields, 230-231
Choose Database dialog box, 232, 233
clicking, W 4